LOOKING FOR THE RIVER

A SEARCH FOR IDENTITY

GEORGE SYLVIE

Cover image © Library of Congress

www.innovativeinkpublishing.com
Send all inquiries to:
4050 Westmark Drive
Dubuque, IA 52004-1840

Print ISBN: 979-8-3851-6384-7
eBook ISBN: 979-8-3851-6385-4

Published in the United States of America

Dedication

The author would like to dedicate this book to the memories of Fred LaCour Jr., Anna Mae LaCour, Mark Sylvie, Mark Vigar Sylvie, Lair LaCour, Laocadia LaCour, Brazil LaCour, Florian Gallion, Joseph Roque, and Anthony Llorens and in humble appreciation of the Frenchman communities of the United States, particularly those in Louisiana and Chicago. Without these individuals, I could never have developed a strong commitment to our heritage, upbringing, and Cane River spirit.

The author also would like to thank the following for their support and love: Annie Marie Chevalier, Donald Ray Sylvie, Earl Joseph LaCour, Amelia LaCour, Calvin LaCour, Matilda LaCour Llorens, Joseph Gordon Chevalier, Wilfred Dupree, Doris Rachal Dupree, Phyllis Blackwell Graham, Nancy Morris Staats, and Sylvia LaCour Williams. The nourishment, guidance, and help these folks provided over the years have been invaluable and instrumental in the making of this project.

Finally, my thanks go to my family—my wife Kathy Sylvie, my son Ryan Sylvie, and my daughter Emily Anna Sylvie. Their love has been constant and always encouraging. I love them with all my heart.

Table of Contents

Author Biography

George Sylvie was born in 1954 in Shreveport, Louisiana, the last son and fourth child of Mark and Anna Mae Sylvie. He attended Catholic schools until 1972, moving on to Louisiana State University in Shreveport. He went on to get a master's from the University of Missouri and a doctorate from The University of Texas at Austin, between which he worked at The Shreveport Journal. Before earning a doctorate in communication and management in 1987 from UT, he married his wife Kathy and they later raised two children in the Austin area. George retired after 26 years at UT, earning the title of associate professor emeritus in 2018.

Preface

The original idea for this book was to chronicle the struggles of my late cousin and collegiate and California prep basketball star Fred LaCour Jr. The 6'5" athlete was considered California's top basketball recruit and was drafted by the St. Louis Hawks of the NBA in 1960 after outstanding seasons with the University of San Francisco Dons, which he helped lead to deep runs in the NCAA tourney, including one year in the Final Four. He also was a Frenchman troubled by his identity, and at odds with the dominant view of society toward people of color. His NBA career was short-lived, and Fred, 38, died in 1972 before I could ever meet him. Because of sourcing issues and timing, the project

Former NBA player and cousin Fred LaCour Jr. poses with his mother Ethel LaCour (right) and aunt Mary Louise Rachal.

took a sharp turn and became a personal memoir, with many of the same struggles represented. I hope that I have done justice to the topic.

George Sylvie

1

Frenchmen

In childhood you learn by listening to and watching the people around you. So it was with a 6-year-old boy, the youngest of four in a family without a father. That kid—me, in case you haven't guessed—didn't pick up on matters quickly, mostly in bits and pieces. My knowledge was only what I heard the family discuss, which tended to focus on relatives, their families, and how they went about their lives. Such was the information circulating around my Chicago home in the early 1960s. Pete, my eldest brother, entering his 20s and establishing himself as my first hero, helped Mamoo—as we called our mom—to keep a handle on things, run errands, work part-time, and watch over my sister Ree, brother Duck, and me while keeping us in good spirits with jokes and tidbits he'd heard from the Cane River network.

A brief history: "Cane River" was our name for the Northwest Louisiana community of our Catholic Creole ancestors living around the Cane River. This loose concoction of landowners, sharecroppers, fieldhands and other farmworkers tilled the land surrounding the Cane River. The area was adjacent to the Louisiana French post of Natchitoches, whose founder and commandant "leased" to his favored slave mistress Marie Therèse Coin-Coin to businessman Claude Thomas Pierre Métoyer to manage Métoyer's house.

Modern-day Melrose Plantation, home to Marie Thérèse Coin-Coin, businesswoman, former slave, and primary ancestor of the Frenchman community.

She bore him 10 children; he eventually "bought" her, gave her freedom, some nearby land, and a yearly stipend, enabling her to raise tobacco. She and her children built another house. To help run her growing business, Marie Thérèse added slaves to the few extended family members she hired. Many employees earned their way out of slavery, amassed their own holdings, and oddly—to the modern sensibility—had their own slaves. This structure financed the growth of the Metoyers' assets (including more than 1,100 acres) and, in time, their ascension to predominate Cane River status, spreading subsequent Cane River society and, in large part, its economic system. By the late 1950s and mid-60s, life consisted mostly of cotton or pecan farming, horse riding, swimming in the Cane, marrying at an early age at nearby St. Augustine's Catholic Church, having large families, regularly going to church and occasionally dropping by the dance hall. The Sylvies one day became part of that society.

But if you grow up Creole, your life's slightly complicated. Disagreement dogs the name "creole"; many (Google users know who they are) take it to mean creoles are of "mixed" parentage—they had

St. Augustine Catholic Church as seen across from Cane River in Natchez, Louisiana.

at least two, distinct ethnicities or cultures playing significant roles in their background. In that case today, we might say they're "multicultural" or "bi-racial" or had some other form of hyphenated heritage. But "river" Creoles claimed either French or Spanish (but usually French) and African lines (although some downplay this aspect), which often confounded others (i.e., those of non-creole parentage) as to what exactly these Creoles were. "Where you from?" or "Who your people?" (in rural Louisiana-speak, of course) would not be an unusual question to hear. From a Creole perspective, you could further confound your questioner with multiple answers—Creole, white, black, all the above, or my all-time favorite (because of its rarity) "I'm part Indian." Or you could keep them guessing by ignoring the question. Six-year-old me hadn't reached that level of sophistication, so when I stuck with "creole", for follow up questions all I could parrot was, "I'm a Frenchman," the response Mamoo would give me. She would say it with her jaw jutting up in the air and a certain assurance, which I neither understood nor could quickly summon, but merely saying so seemed to add an air of finality for her.

(You're probably wondering from where the name "Mamoo" originated; I have no idea. Still, such nicknames probably come from where all nicknames come: Someone decided to make it up for a personal or contextual reason—perhaps it was personality, or common error, or a close derivative to an existing name. Or something wholly unrelated, such as earlier times when so many were named "Jean Baptiste" or "Marie"—to distinguish from another, similarly named person. Or it's because a person came from a certain area of the state. Or it was the result of parental whim—Daddy called my infant daughter Emily "Sassafron" simply because she reminded him of the name he'd

My mom Anna Mae Sylvie and dad Mark Sylvie, aka Mamoo and Boo, at our Allendale home in Shreveport.

heard somewhere before. Whatever the reason, it's become sort of a Creole semi-tradition.)

The Frenchmen—male and female—seemed to be of like mind on the issue of ethnicity or race. I never heard anyone say that they were all white or all black, but they still acted as if they were not surprised by the question being asked. Frenchmen always considered themselves a group apart from white or black people, to be highlighted and distinguished. Only occasionally, when a person was of darker complexion, did issues of race ever enter the conversation. Even so, your "Frenchmanhood" mattered more than anything else.

GETTING SCHOOLED

I never dealt with such matters until I started first grade for the first time (I only remember getting beat up as the public school playground monitor listlessly watched and how much I hated going there, even for half-days). But my light brown hue and curly hair did me no favors, as my skin wasn't quite ebony or fair enough and my curls were loopy and fine, too European-looking. No wonder I never really had any friends until I started going to a Catholic school for my second stab at first grade (the nuns said I was too young the first time through to absorb anything). Fortunately, most of my Catholic classmates were too uninterested to know follow-up questions or to be intimidated by my veteran first graded-ness intelligence. My exoticness (to them) quickly wore off when they discovered I could draw jets (which Pete had taught me), the unofficial logo of our secret first grade boys' "gang" and which everyone was required by our leader Wayne—with whom I was buds—to carry on a quarter sheet of paper).

Meanwhile, life was mostly good. My Chicago cousins (with whom we'd earlier moved in) were around my age, lived only three blocks away and we'd had a ball so far) also went to this school. Plus, we walked together to and from school—Frenchmen ruled! Or so it seemed. I learned how to play kickball; from our new black-and-white TV I watched baseball, cartoons and westerns; Santa Claus entered my awareness; and I made friends with kids in the neighborhood. More importantly, I met more and different Frenchmen—some distant relatives, some closer, some fresh from the river, some veteran Chicagoans, some shady, but all Catholic and of many more shades and hues than I could have imagined. They taught me their lineage, but what hit home were the many nicknames (my Dad had nicknamed me "Pookie"), the soft-yet-semi-twangy southern accents, the propensity to curse (or "cuss", as it was pronounced), the mangled French often used in nostalgic annoyance or pique, the on-again/off-again centrality of the church in most of their lives, and the unspoken dreams they had brought to Chicago. But the picture was always incomplete. Before our arrival, Daddy had left Mamoo for another woman—this would turn out to be somewhat temporary—so I could recall little of him then, except through my aunts and uncles and cousins. Obviously, much of my recollection wasn't good. For a time, we depended on relatives—Daddy's and Mamoo's—to help us on our feet: transportation, jobs, housing, solace, entertainment, a touch of "home", though I remembered none of it.

My energies—and Mamoo's focus—went toward school. She always was so proud of my academic achievements, stemming back to her first conference with Sister Joseph, my first-grade teacher at my first Catholic school, St. Matthew. Apparently, I was the studious wunderkind of the class; they "wish they had more like George," Mamoo quoted. I didn't care; all I wanted was to read, have fun, and avoid Sister Joseph's massive, darkly painted closet, where she kept supplies and whoever acted up in class. This was 1960-61, a six- or seven-year-old only knew reward and punishment and holy cards. I put "Frenchmanhood" largely on hold so I could earn enough holy cards by remembering as many of the martyred saints—I particularly recalled St. Stephen and his unfortunate end (apparently there were no living saints)—as I could. We never saw too many of us go in Sister's closet, but just as academic excellence became my scholastic hallmark, fear became a close dark horse contender. Grades became a double-edged sword in my Creole world: Make good grades, get the holy cards, and join the privileged class—all while avoiding the closet. If you made the grades most of the class made, you took your chances, depending on the day and the classroom task. I immediately began to identify with "the smart kids", something I continued throughout my younger life (not that I was smarter than anyone else; I put it down to having a good memory and liking to read). It seemed a simple enough thing to do, and it kept Mamoo (and teachers) happy. It seemed to be my place in a world that appeared to demand that you find your place if you wanted people to go easy on you, especially since "Frenchman" wasn't something I could fully grasp yet. I couldn't speak French; I wasn't allowed to curse, I didn't know the rules and ways of the church, and no one I knew (except maybe some of my cousins) was remotely the same skin color as me.

This is six-year-old me in front of our Walnut Street house in Chicago.

Outside of school, things were different. At home, as the youngest, I was low man on the totem pole. I did as I was told, which wasn't much except maybe to pick up a toy or two off the floor. We had a small brownstone basement flat within which I mostly followed Mamoo around or played my Disney 78s on Ree's record player or watched cartoons or the Cubs on TV. My siblings were all in their teens and had lives outside the house. During the day, Mamoo babysat for her brother Earl and his wife Amelia, so I got to know my younger cousin Dwayne well and did my best "big brother" impressions for him, illustrating the pretend games that I had learned and sharing stories I'd read or heard. Weekends were more interesting as it was almost a certainty that Cane River relatives would visit, take us for a ride in their cars, or invite us over. The women always retold the latest Cane River scandals, sipped coffee, shared cake samples, while updating Mamoo on the births, baptisms, weddings, and funerals from the river. The men preferred to joke, hang outside around their long, chrome-covered cars, and have a can of beer or bottled whiskey or wine nearby, usually wrapped in a brown paper bag that drew Mamoo's ire when they would reach for it in their pockets. You got the idea that they half-expected her wrath, even needed it before they could take a drink, almost with an attending air of satisfaction, as if a

Me and my Frenchmen cousins sitting on a car in Chicago. Pete's behind me in black.

ritual providing an ironic seal of approval had been duly performed. There was no role for me, except to watch and listen and take mental notes on what made Mamoo laugh or curse. The laughs usually dominated, and the curses were usually followed by putting her forehead in her hands and a loud utterance of "Lord have mercy!" I got the impression that my family came from a place of high highs and extremely low lows, and that its members often experienced life with tragic zest. In my mind, this ran counter to what school was teaching me—that you should put a lot of thought into something before you acted or at least try. I doubted that that was the case with many folks from Cane River.

LOVE THY NEIGHBOR

Back at school, I learned several lessons. First, never stare at vomit for too long if you didn't want to start your own pile of vomit. Second, the nuns were praying for me, and they liked their habit pleats crisp (Mamoo took a job ironing for them). Third, and probably most importantly, I more so noticed the other students, particularly girls. Call me an early bloomer or a wannabe Romeo, but they behaved differently than I did. Girls were fascinating: They seemed calmer, more thoughtful, quieter, and studious—this happens when teachers begin to segregate you, on the playground and whenever you leave the classroom ("Boys on the right, girls on the left! Shortest in front, an arm's length apart! Eyes to the front! Blah blah blah…").

Such linear pairings resulted, however, in my adoration of one girl, Carmine, an Italian beauty who had a nice smile, the cutest ponytail, wore a neat-looking cardigan, and was nearly always paired next to me in our second-grade line (OK, so sometimes my eyes wandered). I never heard her speak, but a smitten 7-year-old never requires such formalities. I just had a feeling that we were meant to be together. So, what else is a 7-year-old to do except the next logical step—one day after school I borrowed a move I had noted from TV westerns, and bought an expensive 25-cent faux-"diamond" ring from the candy store across the street from school. The next day, in my courtliest manner, I gave the ring to her on the playground; she seemed slightly surprised, smiling but speechless. My clueless brain took it for pleased acceptance. The next week, I borrowed a quarter from Pete and did the same thing, but this time it was a "ruby"-looking bauble. She inhaled, and I think she muttered something akin to "thanks". Surely, she was getting the message—whatever it was. The following Monday, while I waited for my cousins to gather to start the trek home, I saw this extremely tall girl stomping toward me at the corner of the playground fence. She seemed vaguely familiar (I'd seen her hanging with the eighth graders) but simultaneously exasperated. "Hey, you!" she blurted, pointing to me. "You stop giving my little sister rings, you hear me?" I shook my head, and she turned away. My eyes stung, and my throat felt as if she had slit it. I never asked Carmine for an explanation, and I never looked her way again. From that moment, she started to come off as sort of stupid whenever I saw her. One thing was certain: I knew rejection and, although I never learned the reason, I felt it was because she and I were different. Cane River people should always stick with Cane River people. It's less painful and more fun.

Or so I learned, at Ree's wedding to Sam. He was a tall, handsome, mustachioed Cane River guy who wore sport coats and fedoras, always hummed Lee Dorsey's "Ya-Ya," couldn't read, yet confidently swung his arms when he walked. Ree—a long-haired, pony-tail-with-bangs sporting, capri-wearing, sweetheart of a bobby soxer—had met him on a double date with her friend Freed (Cane Riverese for "Wilfred"), an upstairs neighbor and river guy who drove a Chicago city bus. Sam and Ree dated for a year or so and then married in the summer after my second-grade experience. That marked a big loss for me, as Ree was my de facto babysitter for much of her teen years. She took me to places—mostly to Elvis movies—in which Pete and Duck wouldn't dare set foot. One of the more interesting places was Midway Airport, where TV heartthrob Edd Byrnes—who played "Kookie", the parking attendant character on the early '60s TV series 77 Sunset Strip—was making a promotional appearance for some Chicago-area dinner theater production. There also were hundreds of girls there; beside me was Ree and, beside her, my cousin Michael. Everything was great until Byrnes hopped out of his airplane, calmly looked around, whipped out his comb, and started to run it through his enormous pompadour (this was his signature move, guaranteed to send girls swooning and other puzzling behaviors). Then this great rush of girls screamed and clawed their way toward him. I lost touch with Ree's hands, and my sight was covered, first by poodle and hoop skirts and then by Saddle Oxfords. Pure pandemonium. I panicked. I lost my Reety! I heard dozens of feet pounding on the pavement. Feet stepped atop me. I screamed, getting the most terrible, fearful sensation. No Ree! I didn't remember anything afterward except being home; Michael seemed unperturbed. When we got home, I'd never seen Mamoo so irritated.

So, whatever happens, I learned to stick with my people, such as at Ree's wedding. I was the ring bearer, which I was told was an important job. My beautiful cousin Angie—we had play-acted the crucial scenes from "Romeo and Juliet" (so maybe *she's* to blame for my school ring episode?), which she, being a year older, directed—was the wedding flower girl, and everyone in the wedding party also had ties to the river. The event was at the church adjoining my school, and the reception was in the school cafeteria, with a band and everything! Me and Angie danced a few times (I learned a little by watching "American Bandstand") and, as I had a third piece of cake, I imagined this had to be what it was like to have a girlfriend. Everybody seemed to have a great time, and some of the guys *really* partied on the floor, laughing with glazed looks in their eyes. And I looked very cool in my white tuxedo. Surely this portended great things for me, if I would only stick with my people.

But our volatile living situation meant we'd have more non-river folks in our lives. We lived in six different West Side places in our seven years North. Some moves had to do with money (Daddy sometimes was stingy with his welfare support), others involved neighborhood quality issues, some were a matter of staying within walking distance of relatives and jobs, and some probably involved the West Side's often turbulent, transitional nature—out comes one ethnic group, in goes two more. Plus, Ree and Pete were getting on with adult life and relationships. Our first stop, an apartment in a building among other apartment buildings, simply had too many domestic disputes and transitory people whose relationships often ended in violence and resulted in no connections. The next stop was better; we lived near a park and its conservatory, and we made friends with several folks—all African-American, including the McCovens family—Helen and her four kids—with whom we later would share another location.

We then rented a new place from a river lady named Mary, who had been in Chicago several years and had married a wealthy Mexican guy named Jésus (although we always called him "Pops") and introduced us to tamales. We rode places with them—Pops had a huge Chrysler—and I was particularly captivated with Shirley, their tall, adopted eighth grade daughter who introduced me to her dolls, the card game "War", and pretend games that I can only say were products of an extremely over-active mind. That family also owned our next place, exactly one block south, where I made friends with next-door brother-sister duo Francé and Sandy, as well as renewing ties with our upstairs friends the McCovens. We'd play softball, kickball, school steps, red-light/green-light, "mother may I" and tag. By this time, my friends were exclusively river kids and black kids—and that was fine. Their parents were all funny and good people, trying to raise a family while helping neighbors when needed. Mamoo grew particularly fond of The McCovens; she and Helen—a particularly beautiful woman—would frequently chat, laugh and commiserate about their no-good, missing husbands. Helen was always borrowing a cup of sugar or sending one of the kids to deliver something she wanted to share. From their relationship, I could tell Mamoo and Helen were just alike and Mamoo talked with her just as if Helen was river folks. Francé's and Sandy's parents were just as friendly. I still remember their mother Mona telling me, when I asked why her husband L.D. went by those initials, wryly giggling and blurting, "Sweetie, 'L.D.' means 'Lying Daddy'". I wasn't sure if she was joking, but somehow it made sense, as Mona seemed to know everything and usually corrected most of what came out of his mouth. I may have been just a little boy learning to get along with other people, but I felt a comfort with my new neighbors that I didn't get with others. Friendship was in generous supply. So was respect. Although we were the newbies on a block with a tavern on the corner, the neighbors welcomed us despite plainly seeing these Louisiana people were physically different. It was as if these, too, were my people, exuding the same good feelings I sensed from river folk.

This heartening attachment followed us a few blocks west and south from where another of Ree's beaus—bus driver and New Orleans native Aaron—uprooted and moved his family to the suburbs, and rented the smaller, top floor to us. That was fine, as just me, Duck and Mamoo were together by then; Ree was pregnant, and Pete was figuring out which girlfriend he was about to marry. The green, faux-tile-covered two-story rested just two blocks from our school St. Mel (named after an Irish nephew of St. Patrick (not surprisingly, the area had previously been an Irish stronghold featuring several Irish-named streets)). For the first time, we had a wonderful large yard, fitting for the football and baseball played nearly every weekend by my cousins (who were only three blocks away) and me. It was an ideal locale for several reasons: We lived less than a half-block away from a main, bustling north-south artery on the West Side that featured a handily close corner pharmacy, a nearby gas station, a neighborhood grocery store at the end of the alley, and a short, four-block walk to Goldblatt's, then one of the major department discount stores in Chicago and the Midwest. My new school pals and walking-to-school partners Cramer and Allan lived next door to each other directly across our street, facing our house on Jackson, itself a major thoroughfare. The community certainly provided a different backdrop—cars passing at all hours, stoplights every block or so, buses routinely stopping every block or so, and a major interstate just to the south. But I didn't notice those kinds of elements; my whole world revolved around Mamoo, my friends and cousins, and school.

A word about Mamoo. Born in 1922, the eighth of 11 farm children, Anna Mae LaCour was a smaller and feisty version of her mother, Amelie. She grew up "on the river," as she would often say, went to school through the sixth grade, had all kinds of friends and cousins, and became susceptible to *petit mal*, an illness she frequently had that she "grew out of" around the time she got married, at about age 18. A steady churchgoer and communicant, she often acted as "sheriff" or "mother superior" at family gatherings, policing and advising her siblings, young or old. She was a complex person: Fierce. Fearless. Persistent. Moralistic. Dismissive. Portly. Gregarious. Vocal. Wise. No-nonsense. Protective. Decisive. Loyal. Rough around the edges. A constant worrier. Friendly. Deferent to the clergy and authority.

Believer in prayer. And judgmental. My son, when he was a toddler, mimicked what he considered her one-size-fits-all utterance: *Ay ha!*, which could mean different things at different times—at once amazement, at others pity, deeply reluctant resignation, or sorrow. It's akin to the Spanish word *caramba*, except it conveys more than astonishment, anger, or dismay. When she used it on me and my siblings, it often meant disappointment or amazement in a particular skill or lack thereof. It could also signify "I told you so!" Often, we simply took it to mean, "Why me, Lord?" Of course, we loved her. She performed all the traits mentioned earlier, as well as the roles of mother, advisor, cook, laundry lady, seamstress, maid, papal assistant, weather predictor, family historian (not only genealogically, but meticulous storyteller) and chief networker, Bible interpreter, soap opera expert and country music lover. She dominated the family, the hen to us ducklings. Essentially the arbiter of all right and wrong, she never hesitated to teach, albeit more so like preach or "telling". I took most of my cues from her. I have no clue as to how things might have looked if Daddy had been around; but I didn't think about it much. Mamoo's cues about our final Chicago neighborhood were mostly positive, and that was enough. Except for one half-day visit from Daddy before I was age 8, I had no way of knowing the house was "broken", or that anyone was missing or that things were somehow amiss. But that was only a short while. I didn't know what a father did, much less how he should behave. His skin was twice as dark than the five of us at home, but his mustache reminded me of Richard

Mamoo standing in front of my car in Shreveport, waiting to go for a ride.

Boone, the star of the TV western Paladin. But our difference in skin color didn't register. I didn't see him *do* anything unusual or noteworthy. No big deal. Besides, my brothers were role models of a sort.

There were only two times that anyone confronted me—or had what amounted to a serious discussion—about my heritage or ethnic background. Once, when I walked home from school with my third-grade chum Manuel, he asked me what I was. Before I could answer he exclaimed, "You're not Mexican like me!" I replied that I was a Frenchman. He squinted his right eye at me and shook his head. "No man," he objected. "You're colored, aren't you?" There it was: the c-word—the one we used at the house to sometimes accurately describe most of our African-American neighborhood friends; and, in all honesty, it was a general term that I'd often heard associated with or accompanying descriptions of less-than-savory, "bad behavior" of some kind. Its usage implied "not like us". Miguel was my buddy, I wanted to be like him as much as possible. But he held no such notion. ""Uh-uh! Mm-mm," he nearly screamed, shaking his head sideways back and forth. "You *know* you're colored!" For once my vocabulary failed me. So, I pushed him hard from behind, to little effect since Manuel was slightly taller and stockier than me. But I *knew* he was wrong, and his words hurt for some reason. He just kept walking, repeating the hurtful words and laughing as if he'd discovered the Ark of the Covenant, the way kids laugh when they realize you've farted in class. His demeanor stung more than his words, because it came across as a bit of a celebration and because a small part of me thought that he was so certain, he might be right! I hated him from that day on and we didn't walk home together too many times thereafter. I didn't dwell on it, however. It wasn't something we often discussed at home. It was just the way things were. People were different in lots of ways and, as Mamoo would often point out, they didn't know much about each other, much less about Cane River folk. I began to see Manuel's little "discovery" was more a reflection of his ignorance or something to make him feel better about himself.

After the move to Jackson, I continued my academic mastery at a new school, beginning in fourth grade where I impressed Sister

Margaret by winning the spelling contest, scoring in the upper percentiles of the annual standardized tests, and becoming an altar boy. Again, I wasn't all that smart—just good at pleasing people. And I hit the lottery with altar boyhood, a high-status role for a Catholic boy—helping the priest perform the Mass—the Catholic term for our service—at various points. Before though, you had to run the gauntlet of learning and regurgitating the Latin spoken by the priest and recognizing when the Mass required the altar boy to pour wine, ring bells, light candles, carry the Bible, or otherwise assist the priest. My older cousin Tony altar-schooled his brothers and me in their downstairs basement several times, so we were aware of procedures, the terminology for the parts of the mass, what the priest's vestments were called, and how to help prepare the altar before things got underway. While the girls helped distribute class assignments and supplies, dusted off erasers, wiped clean the blackboards, and seem interested in every subject, "special boys" like me were chosen to perform other, more manly duties, such as taking attendance sheets to the principal's office, ringing the schoolyard recess bell, holding open and closing doors for water breaks, and acting pious during altar boy duty. This only added to my accolades as a holy card whiz (for learning the sacraments) and being a top-seller during the school's chocolate candy bars, donuts and cheap jewelry campaigns (it helped to have a large network of relatives and a big sis who worked in an office pool). Yes, life was sweet.

Until it wasn't again. In every competition, there's always someone who wants to knock off the top dog. Muhammad Ali had Joe Frazier. Willie Mays had to best Hank Aaron. Elvis battled Ricky Nelson for teen hearts. The Beatles beat back The Monkees on the Top 40. And I had Anthony, a clean-cut, soft-spoken kid with a coal-black faded haircut who liked to wear khakis, white socks, and loafers while relishing the role of monumental brown noser. When Sister Margaret looked for something, like a yardstick or an eraser or her trusty pointer, he always would jump up, eagerly-beaverly chirp, "I'll get it, Sister!", and rush to wherever the forlorn utensil rested. Or if she had to run down the hall for a second, he'd habitually volunteer for class monitor. If he'd had good athletic skill, he'd have been a "cool kid" candidate. Fortunately, his academic skills were average, so we tolerated him. One time he went too far. In a fit of competition on the playground monkey bars, he told me to, "Wait your turn, n-----." I'd only heard the word uttered by a male relative in reference to a black person who had wronged him somehow (it didn't seem to matter if the relative's skin was just as dark as the offender in question). I knew that Anthony's use of the term was mistaken—after all, I didn't think I was dark enough to be black and I hadn't done anything wrong, so I told him so. He repeated the slur, and that was pretty much all that happened. My Manuel experience had taught that once a foe made up his mind, you likely couldn't change it. Fortunately, I pushed him in his back, he slightly pushed back. Immediately, the recess bell rang for the first time, and we had to stop, stand in place, and freeze like two mute combative mannequins. Once the bell rang again, we lined up for class. I forgot the episode once class started, and Anthony made sure to never be alone again on the playground. Once you know you can beat a fool with your smarts *and* your fists, you don't let things rile you that much. I never reported the incident, but it irked me—not because he called me the name, but that he'd effective-ly escaped punishment (altar boys were expected to be paragons of the school, so I had a reputation to protect). I learned that restraint was a bittersweet mistress—words stung, I had no dominating verbal response, and the incident was short-circuited by circumstances.

The n-word still had a negative implication. It was derogatory and left a bad taste. To my ears, it was coded language for "a bad person who happened to be black". I didn't know its origin although I was sure it stemmed from the word, "Negro", and from past behav-iors during slavery. Oddly, you could hear it in black persons' refer-ence to other black persons. So, while I knew it couldn't exactly be off limits, I also knew that most black people wouldn't stand for the term being used by a non-black person. They viewed it as a sign of disrespect and degradation of their race: Thus, it became taboo for a non-black person to use it, although it was common knowledge that many non-blacks in Chicago often used it in anger or when blacks were not present. I first saw it used in books and movies—again, usually spoken by bad people or white southerners in reference to blacks in general or by black characters in close, intimate dialogue with other black characters. People with any decent amount of education did not use the term, I was told by educated folks; using the n-word showcased how stupid or uncultivated the user was. Still, I heard its usage often around people I knew—family, neighbor, or otherwise. Reminding anyone that it was "a bad word" often drew knowing glances, smiles, or muted giggles (if not pats on my head) from the user. I began to assume that such users were unschooled or raised in a less-than-desirable environment, or someone who grew up in the South, or a person not knowledgeable in some way. It didn't mean that these n-word-using people were all bad, or not deserving of well wishes or even love, but they had not learned proper behavior or had gone uncorrected. It was a lot of nuance for a fourth grader to digest, but such was 1960s Chicago.

Still, what was I to think of the black kid who stole my bicycle? Albeit something of an academic phenom, I was a late bloomer when it came to learning to bicycle ride. It was my favorite toy—a red, white, and black two-wheeler left by Santa in our first basement apartment when I was 7—and favored so much that I was afraid to some degree to ride it. I'd skinned my knee a couple times and damaged the paint when I rode it the following spring in and around an apartment complex courtyard with my cousins, who were more adventurous riders and thus had greater ease keeping their balance. It wasn't until my first spring (I'd just turned 11) at our latest apartment, with its wider sidewalks, that I tried riding again. Not soon thereafter this kid, about a year or two older, came up to me one day and started asking about the bike. He asked if he could ride and I mumbled something non-committal about not knowing, since the tires were low, and he might be too heavy. He said that was no problem, that he could help get some air and take it to the gas station (where air was free!) right around the corner, a block south. Before I could say anything, he commandeered the handles and quickly started walking and steering the bike that way. I didn't know whether to think he was being aggressive or just a smarter big kid. I followed him, although my stomach began to roil. In the five minutes it took, I noticed how much activity there was on the street and how disoriented I was beginning to feel. We arrived at the gas station, where he quickly took the air hose and applied it to each tire. I remember trying to get my hands on the handlebars, but before I could climb aboard, he was on the seat, heading back toward my street, confidently pedaling. I started to panic, slowly running after him, asking where he was going. When he didn't answer and reached the corner, I was running faster, saying, "Hey! Stop!" over and over, to no avail. A quarter down the block, I couldn't keep pace anymore and I started crying and yelling to any of the grownups passing by that "That boy is stealing my bike!" But no one stopped or even turned around to look, and my tears felt like boiling water on my cheeks—the worst thing that had ever happened was happening, and I was powerless. I ran back home, crying Mamoo's name in between sobs, runny snot accompanying the tears. One of my worst fears had come true: I was "done wrong" by a black person; I had become a victim. It was the worst feeling—reminiscent of the Edd Byrnes incident—not because the kid was black, but because, up until we had finished getting the air, I was beginning to trust him. Theft was nowhere near something that I expected. Up until then, the only person to ever breach my trust was Duck a year or so earlier when he told me he could use my sweater to make the moon appear; all I had to do was look up through the sleeve from the inside of the sweater while he held the other end of the sleeve up against the kitchen ceiling light. Of course, once I looked, he poured a pitcher of water down the sleeve. Typical older brother. I cried then, too, but this felt like the end of the world.

After I ran into the house and reported the bike story, Mamoo took off her apron, dropped what she was doing, grabbed me by the arm and headed outside. We headed down our street, toward the busy intersection, asking if anyone had seen a kid on a red, white, and black bicycle (Mamoo asked; I was still wiping tears and trying to hold back more). I don't remember how, but we got directed to a less-crowded, more residential side street, and continued to ask every resident we saw if they'd seen a boy on a bicycle, perhaps riding faster than normal. We met a lady, teaching some kids how to jump rope on the sidewalk. She could see how disturbed I was, fluids still emanating from my face, and asked what the problem was. Fortunately, they knew a kid who fit our description, and the lady said that she thought she knew where he lived. So Mamoo asked her if she would check whether this was indeed the boy and, if so, she should let us know. We gave her our address and left. Sure enough, not more than a couple hours later, the lady came to our house, bicycle and her kids in tow. She didn't want any reward, but I gave her my two special silver dollars—one from 1922, the other from the 1950s—as a token of appreciation. The bike was back, and all was well again. I had learned to be careful of strangers (but also to not be afraid to ask for help) and to not ride the bike without Mamoo or a sibling watching. Such an exhausting range of emotions—from antic- ipation, to bewilderment, to oppression, to bewilderment, to bereave- ment, to hope, to joy—in the span of a Saturday morning! Moreso, I'd been educated in race, fairness, prejudice, human nature, the swiftness and futility of feelings of value, and the wrongness of human assump- tion. It would be years before anyone besides me rode that bicycle. I slept well that night, but caution became a part of my life afterward, especially toward unknown black kids who went to the nearby public school. Their school dismissed around the same time as St. Mel, so we'd run into them heading home daily. The inevitable bullying by old- er kids meant these public school kids could be dangerous. One day I overheard Mamoo talking politics with someone, using political terms to describe who was better. From then on, I borrowed her term: Those kids were "Republicans".

GOOD TIMES

Still, probably more than any other influences on my under- standing of race and Creole culture, my cousins seemed every- where in my Chicago life. First cousins. Second cousins. Third cousins. Married cousins. Unmarried cousins. Cool cousins. Distant cousins. Adult cousins. Visiting cousins. Smart cousins. Dumbass cousins. Mentally challenged cousins. Loving cousins. Mentoring cousins. Military cousins. Never-to-be-seen cousins.

Of course, there was the afore-mentioned group with whom I generally played with throughout early grade school. Tony (leader of our altar boy practice) was a couple years older and knew stuff we didn't—like how most things worked. His brother Michael was probably my best friend: The same age as me, often in the same class, so we talked a bunch and found ourselves in agreement on most things. There were three other, younger brothers—Michael, Gayle (or Goo, as he also was known), and Arnold—and I loved spending time with all four. They were more entertaining than TV, always into something new, constantly arguing or talking about some actor or athlete, with never a dull moment. They introduced me to The Beatles! A bonus was Cousin Joe-Joe and his sister Angie (Juliet to my Romeo and my escort at Ree's marriage) who lived upstairs from them. The whole group was the center of my world.

And yet, I learned so much about the *real* world from other relatives. I understood how grocery shopping worked from Freed and his wife Doris; they'd take me on Friday evenings with them to the nearby Market Basket store and I'd help load the cart and watch them argue about prices and quantities. I also became the first babysitter to their daughter Jean and son Tony when the foursome moved in upstairs from us on Jackson. I didn't know anything about the job, but realized the best approach was to be entertaining (play with dolls, cars, and anything else they had) and know where the snacks and milk were. And to call Mamoo when I didn't know what to do.

My Uncle Earl and Aunt Amelia often took us—usually that meant me and Mamoo—with them when they traveled. My earliest memories of music, cars, and good times were thanks to Uncle Earl, who played the radio the whole drive home from Detroit to entertain us while he battled a snowstorm and cursed the oncoming drivers. The Top 40 fascinated me—the music, the rhyming, all the songs about love from a variety of singers. An earlier time we visited a Detroit suburb where I was introduced to the "Motown sound" at a relative's party. This time the music had a passion, melody, and emotion I hadn't experienced. Stevie Wonder and The Supremes could really rock! It seemed that people got friendlier with each other the more they partied (I knew what beer was but had no idea as to how happy it made people). Of course, they were constantly talking—about what I had no hint, but they never ceased to smile. Oh! And there were quite a few black people mixed in with the Frenchmen, the first time aside from school that I'd witnessed broad scale racial intermingling and the first I'd seen Cane River people in an overwhelmingly happy circumstance. The ease with which they circulated suggested this wasn't a rare phenomenon. Something joyous filled the air, although for the life of me I had no clue as to what. Michigan seemed a magical place, as I later that evening played my first rounds of Spin the Bottle with a similarly aged subset of my many Detroit cousins, as numerous as my Chicago play group; I didn't want the game to stop. Maybe it was the Michigan water? My lessons playing Romeo?

I noticed a pattern, however. Good times were great and all, but they didn't just arise out of nothing. There had to be a reason. A party? Yes, but something often had to precede the party—an event. It often took the form of weddings, of which there seemed plenty in the early 1960s. My parents' generation—those born after World War I but before World War II—began to get married around the 1940s, which meant their offspring born soon after were starting to mature in the early '60s and beginning to find mates. Many weddings resulted, and cousins with older brothers and sisters usually meant a wedding invitation was inevitable. Of course, it was the reception—not the wedding itself—that everyone anticipated. You knew there'd be cake, punch, music, dancing, and likely a couple of inebriated would-be boxers outside if you got bored or couldn't get anyone to dance with you. Every summer would mean wedding season, which didn't end until around October. The underlying lesson: If you waited long enough, and kept up with the TV dance shows, you'd be ready by April or May.

Unless, of course, you had relatives whose parents were still alive. This would certainly lead to funerals, which were like weddings—but without the booze and the dancing. Such events seemed to gravitate toward fall and winter in our Creole families (perhaps the departed had danced too much at a recent wedding?). Whatever fun you had, depended on the venue and the event crowd size. Whenever a Creole died, the family would usually ask the funeral home to hold a wake, sort of like a reception, but with the honoree deceased. Adults (sometimes with children in tow) would—in the case of an open casket—view the body and say a short prayer; this would not happen with a closed casket. Next, visitors would line up to offer sympathies and condolences (and kisses, if you were related) to the grieving family, which would be seated near the head of the room, adjacent to the casket. Once everyone had gathered and paid their respects, they would recite a rosary or Scripture-grounded prayer.

That's when the "adult fun" would start. No music: just greetings, hugs and conversations with rarely seen friends and family. Of course, much of this was in the adjoining foyer or room (so as not to violate the solemnity of late-comers or others still struck by grief) this included catching up on goings-on down at the river; discussing the deceased; compliments about attire (this was usually a dress-up affair); step-back, looks or jaw-droppings of fake shock at how much someone had grown or show svelte he or she looked; gossip about the latest unwed mother; or simply take a chance to grab a smoke or pull out a flask. Kids, on the other hand, would head for the outside where other kids were chatting about school, the latest No. 1 hit, or looking for the vending machines. The inescapable question of your relationship to the deceased would come up, along with additional comments about the body's appearance or inquiry as to whether you'd seen the body. Smaller kids would play tag or run around laughing and pulling each other's hair while older children often ventured on—or dared others to–a self-guided tour of the "other rooms" of the venue, hoping to see God knows what. While obviously social, these events doubled as moments of cultural solidarity (as in "nobody's going to mourn us except us"), reinforcing river and Catholic identity, as well as illustrating that even in death there is life.

Sometimes, instead of going to an event to have a little fun, the event came to you. In my case, the event often took the form of a person—usually a female relative, likely in her 20s, who had traveled from the river (or wherever) to Chicago to make a mark or some extra money or simply to get away from home. In more cases than not, it was a cousin who needed a place to stay while she worked. In other instances, she needed some "growing up," or couldn't get along with her parents or ran away from close supervision. In every event, after Ree's marriage and departure, it felt great to have what amounted to as "another big sister" to talk with and orient to the city. Sometimes their stays went well, other times they succumbed to boyfriend/lover issues and related arguments, to the point that they were unhappily returned home with "needs more work" admonishments from Mamoo. I wasn't privy to the details, but at times it seemed as if we ran a "boarding school for river young girls with potential" and every Chicago Creole could be drafted as an "instructor" at any time or summarily dismissed for conduct unbecoming a teacher. Again, this seemed to embody the extended notion of the river family, that we took care of our own as best we could, regardless of the risks.

Finally, simple brief visits to and from cousins I barely knew had varying impacts. Mamoo's sister Bernice brought her kids for a visit one Christmas from the river. I remember sharing my toys and our food while learning card tricks and comparing tales about schools and friends. Twice we had cousins serving in the military drop by on leaves. Their uniforms, duffel bags, shiny shoes, and southern accents made an impression, as did their humor about their jobs to that point. It was before Vietnam had become TV fare and they simply were young men looking for adventure but still talking of home while cherishing Mamoo's cooking. Occasionally we would take trips, either by train, bus or relative, to Louisiana—mostly for family reunions, make the rounds to Sylvie or LaCour homesteads, drop in on ill-taken elders or to pay respects at the Cane River cemetery at St. Augustine's Church. These adventures carried several tutorials.

While the Motown sound had made it to Shreveport and as far south as Natchitoches/Cane River, country music still was king down South. Ernest Tubb, Porter Waggoner, George Jones, and Hank Williams, with their bejeweled leisure suits, bandanas, cowboy hat and boots, strummed their guitars daily on local TV (only three channels, by the way), before and after the soap operas. The TV signal—still black and white—was iffy, depending on whether you lived on a hill or a clearing. That meant plenty of time to play outside, if you could stand the heat and all the bugs. As a result, I quickly understood the popularity of card games, iced sweet tea, and verbal give-and-take. The nearest playgrounds were schools and the roads were either dirt, gravel, or some gooey substance made of tar, oil and dirt. I rarely saw a fast-food place or a sidewalk. But I did see mosquitoes. Lots of mosquitoes. And rain in biblical proportions.

In addition to the environment, the language and behavior took me a while to acclimate. Whereas I felt I had options as to what I could do with my time, my Louisiana cousins seemed ordained toward a parenting style that came across as semi-authoritarian or militaristic. It was always, "Yes ma'am" or "No, ma'am". Parents were always addressed as "Mama" and "Daddy". You hailed neighbors with a "mister" or a "miss" before their first name. You didn't go to church; instead, you "went to Mass", and you stayed until the last hymn was finished. You went "up the road"; not "down the street" to borrow something. Children didn't get consulted on meals: Breakfast was eggs, sausages, biscuits and juice (teens could have coffee) or pancakes; lunch was sandwiches or leftovers from last night's dinner; dinner was always some rice (or mashed potatoes) and gravy with whatever meat—usually ham, beef tips, pork chops, or chicken—there was; forget burgers and fries or TV dinners. You made a good effort to eat what was in front of you, no arguing. You also bowed your head and recited the meal prayer; eyes closed. Again, there was no such thing as fast food. Forget about soft drinks with dinner (often called "supper"); you usually drank milk, water or, if you were lucky, iced sweet tea. A "treat"—usually Sunday evenings—meant a "trip into town" for an ice cream cone (no chocolate, please). If you were a lucky adolescent, there might be little dances and parties you could attend on weekends, or you could go swimming in the summer in the river or the local mudhole—fish, mudbugs or cockroaches were merely an inconvenience—but otherwise life slowed in semi-rural (or even modestly urban) Louisiana. The water seemed to have a metallic taste and only city cousins had indoor bathrooms. Staying around the river meant you had to know where "the pot" was.

When I wasn't playing, I liked to listen to the conversations Mamoo had with whatever other adult she could corral. Usually, the topic was relatives and usually centered on what I'll call The Top Ten, in reverse order of importance:

10. The fun things they would do together when they were younger. What would they change if they had a do-over? Who would they have courted if they'd known what they knew now?

9. The problems their children were going—or had put them—through. Ay-ha!

8. Which of our elderly had died recently and who attended the funeral; more importantly, who was a no-show? How'd the casket look?

7. Who was "getting along" among the families and who wasn't and what were people saying about them?

6. How good a pastor was the current priest in residence, how did he compare to the "last priest we got" and who was leading the movement to get a new guy?

5. How were our people's job situations, who was "making it" and who had the worst luck on the river? This also referred to how well were the major crops—cotton and pecans—coming along and the going rate per pound.

4. Who was having a baby and—of the illegitimate births—who were the daddies and how did her parents feel about the situation? Did they get married?

3. The terrible, sad state of Louisiana politics, how it affected river life, and how similar to Huey Long was this latest governor.

2. Was so-and-so still drinking? Who else was sick?

1. What are you doing with yourself these days and are you happy?

Of course, one or several of these conversations would end with one or both ladies shaking their heads in disgust, laughter, or both—such was the life of Cane River people. People always had the same old problems and solutions, and the river would keep on rolling. Nothing was ever permanently solved and all we had to count on, in the end, was "the Lord". The rest of the time they would discuss recipes, the stories (i.e., the soaps), or their troubles with their hair. Still, Mamoo had no idea how closely I listened to these discussions. I got tips on what was right or wrong, what typical bad decisions people made, and what people thought of life in general. I took away the Cane River people were like everyone else: flawed, loving, hopeful, sex-hungry, sometimes heavy drinkers, observant, fun-loving, and practical. No big surprises, except Creole men seemed to have a different way of communicating.

DAD BODIES

Because my parents were separated at the time, I spent much of my time with women, be they mother, aunt, sister, close friend or relative. Whatever holds that males (intentionally or accidentally) placed on my mind in Chicago occurred just as fleetingly as the wind—here one minute, gone the next, back again a couple hours later, only to quickly disappear until the weekend. Just a few stood out.

Anthony Llorens (whom I always called "Doc") was dad to my cousins Tony, Michael and the rest. It seemed as if whenever they moved to a new house, we weren't far behind. His wife Matilda was my first cousin, daughter to my Dad's Cane River-based sister; in fact, she was nicknamed "Daughter". As I've alluded before, we regularly visited them, usually to give me and the boys what parents today call a "playdate" or chances to get together. One last thing about Uncle Doc: He was a strong, devout Catholic; it was no accident cousin Tony could show us the altar server ropes—he had many Masses under his belt. Doc would later be in the first Chicago group to study to and become a deacon, like a substitute priest position that the Catholic Church created to shore up its dwindling corps of priests, to train young men for a couple of years, and to attract devout types who happened to have been stably married. Doc was perfect for the job—he worked as a supervisor all day at a wax factory, and then came home to chaos at home as calm and cool as you could be as a father of eight who idolized *him* despite Daughter being Mother Superior, the engine who made things run, run on time and kicked ass when they didn't. They were a great couple and always made me feel welcome; I could not figure why Doc always called me "George" instead of my nickname of "Pookie"—it must have been some deacon kind of move, to remind me of my given Christian name because no one else used it. But I occasionally saw Doc mete out punishment, which usually meant no play time or time out in the bedroom. He always did so in measured, even tones, taking his time and occasionally looking past the offender (so you could tell he was thinking about what he wanted to say).

One of the benefits was my automatic "plus 1" status when it came to things the family did; we would pile into their Pontiac Bonneville Safari station wagon and head somewhere exotic. I learned so much, for example, that downtown Chicago truly was "where the lights were bright," especially when we visited at night during the Christmas season to see the store displays. It was simply magical to 10-year-old eyes, as were all the other ex-

Anthony Lllorens, aka Uncle Doc, going over some notes in his Chicago home.

periences—visiting the first area McDonald's in nearby Des Plaines provided not only a "long" 45-minute ride in which to argue about our past Saturday's baseball game, which among us had the best batting average, the Cubs' latest loss, our favorite players, and who was the best up-and-coming altar boy. And then topping it by eating a fancy tasting burger! Or going to the nearest Forest Preserve—county-provided giant outdoor spaces for the public to enjoy nature, with various facilities, picnic stands, hiking and biking trails, and acres of green grass for baseball, football, or games for company outings, to one of which I accompanied my cousins. Good times, for sure.

While my Uncle Earl rivaled Doc for top Creole male status in my heart, he was a different type of role model. Mamoo's youngest, agilest, and handsomest sibling by 10 years, he left Cane River to seek his fortune in his 20s, got as far as San Francisco, then back to Louisiana, and finally put down roots in Chicago. I already mentioned the trips we took with him and his family, but that does not do Earl justice. He would always pick up his kids every day when they were small enough for Mamoo to handle and took the opportunity to stay a while and chat about whatever was going on or on his mind. So, he was a somewhat constant presence in my earlier school years, less so as his family grew. Like Mamoo, he could be direct, gruff, and sometimes agitated. But I just assumed he was trying to show me how to do things right. Also, like Mamoo, his language could be coarse—nothing major, just an infrequent goddamn or shit or hell, depending on his mood or if he felt you were being stupid. I discovered this when, as we made a rest stop on the return trip from Detroit, I hovered too long at a Michigan highway store's candy counter with my wallet carrying those two silver dollars I mentioned earlier. I had never held so much money in my life, and the candy options under the glass counter gave me a terrible case of procrastination. "Gimme that *goddamn* wallet," he said, grabbing the coins. "Now put that back in your pocket and let's go to the car." Since his tone was highly reminiscent of Mamoo, I did as told and got in the backseat, absorbing my first seminar in highway-induced adult stress. That was the end of it; nothing more transpired. Today, I laugh when I reminisce about it—it was classic Uncle Earl, furious at life for what a little money had done to his nephew's head. Now, not only can I perform a great impression of him (and all my LaCour uncles when they got angry or irritated, especially in saying "goddamn"), my veins pop through the skin in my neck just like his. Ask my kids.

Doc, Earl and others made up for my Dad's absence in many ways. My Uncle Calvin—I called him that because he was Tony's and

Michael's older uncle (Daughter's brother), so I repeated it—seemed to always be working in the alley garage on cars after work with his brothers Bootsy and Barry (two later Cane River arrivals). All three loved cars, smoked, and cursed like it was going out of style. Calvin and Bootsy lived separately with their families in half-flats upstairs from Doc and Daughter, who were buying the building. Calvin—when he was not working in the upholstery business or repairing cars— would drive us places with his family, as well. Especially memorable was a nighttime visit to Northwest Chicago with its Olson Park and Waterfalls, featuring Christmas displays including dozens of flowers and plants, colorful Christmas lights, three roaring-but-walkable waterfalls, and a giant Native American statue. Uncle Calvin, as was Doc, was a hands-off disciplinarian, leaving children's issues to his wife Lillian (whom we fondly called Auntee (emphasis on the TEE) and who mastered a unique technique called "the knees", a never-before-seen method of authority of grabbing smaller male juveniles who had confessed to mischief, pulling their heads toward her to between her knees, and taking a belt lightly to their bottoms). Boys and cousins on both floors unanimously respected Auntee, as her approach quickly and indiscriminately made you feel humbled and foolish. Neither did she care who watched the performance. What a woman!

I'd be remiss if I didn't mention my brothers. I didn't know much about their worlds except that they entered mine infrequently, as they, too, were growing up and going through their own evolutions. First, Pete—the oldest, probably the most sympathetic to Daddy, the tallest with an Elvis-height

Auntee, aka Lillian Kochinsky LaCour, sitting on the back porch of her Oak Park, Illinois, home.

pompadour and a pimply, fair complexion, and the sibling we usually looked to for help of any kind. He was a tremendous aide to Mamoo, as I mentioned earlier, working at various times for an electronics manufacturer, a candy business, and a box-making firm. As he often worked graveyard shifts, I saw him sparingly but remember hearing him in the living room, making Ree, Mamoo, and Duck laugh as they watched late-night TV, and I tried to sleep. These were side-splitting, belly-jogging laughs that I heard nary other time. Between his 19th and 23rd birthdays, Pete also presented a somewhat tragic figure. He was talented and smart, yet made friends with gang members and, for basically being in the wrong time and the wrong place (he ignorantly laughed when the gang was "settling a score"), he was arrested. He was adventurous, daring one night to walk across one of nearby Garfield Park's many frozen ponds on the way home. He often drank liquor and liked the ladies, to the point that one night he got too close to a snake charmer and her snake bit him in the eye, sending him (and us) to the hospital. Another time he fell behind in his Oldsmobile payments—he'd had it less than a year—and scrambled south to Shreveport to live with Daddy while the police (and creditor) heat died down; he wound up wrecking the car in Louisiana and Daddy sent him back to Chicago. Sometimes he wouldn't come home after work. Mamoo would always seem especially worried when he got into such fiascoes; phones were expensive and unattainable then, so she always got the news secondhand and was sent scrambling for a late-night ride. I remember my stomach churning at such times. His love of females got so great—read: sleepovers with the girlfriend—that Mamoo sent him packing (under the "bad influence" clause) to his girlfriend. It was a tremendously bittersweet time; the turmoil was gone, but so was Pete. Still, I worshipped his every move. He took me for rides in his car. He helped me with school projects. He introduced me to comic books—including Superman, Batman, The Fantastic Four, Mad Magazine, Casper the Friendly Ghost, Archie, Richie Rich, and many more. I copied his drawing style, and my art skills flourished. He had so many talents, except good judgment. Probably one of his worst decisions involved marrying Tina to effectively dodge the Vietnam draft; their marriage was one of great turmoil, and they had trouble accommodating each other's faults. Still, Pete was a sweetheart.

On an abnormally cool day in the summer of 1963, he and I watched the Cubs play a home game against the (Los Angeles) Dodgers on TV. Remarkably, the Cubs led 2-0 late against the Dodger ace Sandy Koufax as we continued to watch. But it got ugly in the last inning as the Dodgers came to bat. Two singles, a strikeout, a walk, another single, a groundout, *another* single, and the Wrigley Field crowd booed loudly. An intentional walk ensued, followed by *another* single, an error, *another* walk, and *another* single until the Dodgers had scored *six runs*, as Pete began to laugh loudly and uncontrollably at the Cubs' ineptitude throughout the horrible episode. I started crying more than I'd ever cried and he, being a sensitive soul, bet me $2 that the Cubs would come back in their half of the ninth. Being no fool and not that great a Cubs fan at that point in life, I took the Dodgers and, eventually, $2 to soothe my soul. What a great brother. Again, $2 played a pivotal role in my life.

Duck was a different matter altogether. He was the Ying to Pete's Yang. He had enjoyed nine years of being "the baby" in the family until I appeared. He was about 15 when we moved to Chicago, and I had no recollection of his pre-Chicago life. His teenage youth was spent growing to about an inch taller than Pete and going his own way—quite a change from his status as a slightly darker Elvis-lookalike and chick magnet who spent hours (ok, it only *seemed* that long) in the bathroom on his appearance. School often wasn't his friend; it was always someone else's fault, he would tell you, and you'd probably agree after you heard his side. He and I tolerated each other; he liked to cut his own path, so his and my lanes seldom crossed. He had his own group of friends and cousins that he spent time with (of course, he was nine years older than me), and I hardly saw them unless they had gathered at someone else's home on the weekend, by which time I was deep in my own social circle or TV to notice. We'd bicker over what to watch on afternoon TV—baseball or dance shows—so Mamoo had us take turns; miraculously, he would often forget when he'd taken his turn the previous day. We'd also fight over Mamoo's cake batter—again, she finally had to make it a "take turns" thing as a result. Whereas I basked in the glow of school, Duck developed a real disinterest in schooling by the time he entered high school (Pete was already working)—especially as he got older; toward the end, his getting up in the morning to go to school turned into a real battle between him and Mamoo. She won, of course, and I suspect part of the argument was that Pete had flunked out of high school (after three tries at 10th grade); but Duck found ways—especially girlfriends—that would help him through academic tough times. It helped that he loved basketball, which he played at school and in the Catholic Youth Organization (CYO) league. One night after a CYO game, Pete came home marveling at and praising Duck's basketball court performance; this was news to me. Mildly surprised that Duck could do *anything* well, I took an interest and went to his next game. I don't recall any outstanding play or point tally on his part, and his team lost, but for the first time I was fascinated by a sport-not-named-baseball and developed a lifelong affinity. This was no slow-moving game and there were lots of running, squeaky sneakers, flashy uniforms, and it was indoors, to boot. After that, I started to pay more attention to what he said and did. Funny how that works. I discovered basketball and a brother who played it well, who—although it took a while—I would come to love dearly.

At this point, no doubt you're wondering about the names and roles of many of the folks I've mentioned. First, you probably have lost track of which cousin was which, there are so many. If the many people on Creole Facebook interest pages are correct, it's not unusual to only know a Creole by his or her nickname, as my own cousins have told me (I'd be rich if I had a dollar for every time I heard, "I didn't know your real first name was 'George'!? I always only knew you by 'Pookie'"). And let me spell it out for you: Spelling nicknames is another problem altogether; spelling always varies by person trying to do the spelling. For example, Mamoo can be spelled in myriad ways: Mamoo, Mamou, Mamu—you get the drift. Regardless, you might find the following "cousin chart" handy.

COUSIN CHART		
PERSON	**REAL NAME**	**RELATIONSHIP(S)**
Doc	Anthony	Daughter's husband; father to Tony, Michael, Gayle, and Arnold; brother-in-law to Calvin
Daughter	Matilda	Doc's wife; mother to Tony, Michael, Gayle, and Arnold; sister to Calvin; sister-in-law to Auntee; my first cousin; Daddy's niece
Uncle Calvin	Calvin	Auntee's husband; father to Angie and Joe-Joe; brother to Daughter; my first cousin; Daddy's nephew
Auntee	Lillian	Uncle Calvin's wife; mother to Angie and Joe-Joe; sister-in-law to Daughter
Uncle Earl	Earl	Mamoo's brother; Amelia's husband; father to Dwayne; Daddy's brother-in-law; my uncle
Aunt Amelia	Amelia	Earl's wife; mother to Dwayne; Mamoo's sister-in-law
Tony	Anthony Jr.	Doc's and Daughter's oldest son; my second cousin
Michael	Michael	Doc's and Daughter's second-oldest son; my second cousin
Gayle, Goo	John	Doc's and Daughter's third-oldest son; my second cousin
Arnold	Arnold	Doc's and Daughter's fourth-oldest son; my second cousin
Angie	Angelique	Uncle Calvin's and Auntee's oldest daughter; my second cousin
Joe-Joe	Joseph	Uncle Calvin's and Auntee's oldest son; my second cousin
Dwayne	Dwayne	Uncle Earl's and Aunt Amelia's oldest son; my first cousin
Bootsy	Paul	Daughter's and Uncle Calvin's brother; my first cousin
Barry	Barry	Daughter's and Uncle Calvin's brother; my first cousin

Freed	Wilfred	Friend of the family; Doris' husband
Doris	Doris	Friend of the family; Freed's wife
Sam	Joseph	Ree's husband; my brother-in-law

Living in Chicago at the beginning of my conscious life no doubt was a good thing for me. I'm not sure that I would recommend growing up mixed race, much less Creole in a time of tension in a large city, although the continuing diverse, population replacement cycle that such places encourage didn't hurt. The fact that my skin color tended toward a lighter shade of brown probably was a point in my favor, resulting in fewer schoolyard confrontations and incidents. But neither did the "Frenchman" card make for an easy gig in a world that preferred to limit its inhabitants to two categories of being. In fact, I think it drove me further into what I'll call "Creolistic reality", in which I took refuge in the company of my cousins, aunts, uncles and whoever else arriving from the river. I felt secure in the knowledge that I was loved, secure, and assured of the safety net of river folk who could explain, laugh about, and help me to forget whatever cruelties and bad behavior I experienced at the hands of white or black people, or so I thought.

Regardless, through Pete and Duck, I continued my adventure in learning how to be a brother and little man. The lessons began with Uncle Earl, Doc and Calvin, to be sure: Giving of yourself was just something you did, even if you did have other, important things to do, marriages to tend, and children to rear. Also, you strived to set a good example for others, sharing what you had and, if you had little, sharing your time always was a good idea. So, I saw Pete and Duck do many brotherly things. They were protective of Ree (even after she married) when she needed it; they fought, but they always made up with laughter and camaraderie, even as they were trying to grow up, too, and it must have been harder on them to have Daddy missing. The man was basically a no-show in the six years we'd been together in Chicago. He rarely visited and—even then—they were short stays, all happiness, sweetness and light, as if nothing was out of place. He remained a blank canvas, another body from Cane River, but one that hadn't registered any feeling in me toward the man. Sure, I had heard some family stories about him, and I knew that before Chicago there was life in Shreveport, where we had family who were largely faceless and whom I had trouble recalling. His decision-making didn't seem as advanced as Pete's, as he continued his convenience store butcher's life with nary a call or impactful presence (except to ask for a cut in the monthly aid check he sent us). The whole situation felt weird and surreal, but that was fine for me as I enjoyed school and feasted on the kindness of relatives from Louisiana who had come to make a new life in my favorite city.

Which is why I was shocked when Mamoo told me one day that she and Daddy were getting back together and that the two of us were going back to Louisiana.

2

Of The River

She had just returned one spring from a trip to Louisiana to visit family when she sat me down in the kitchen and quietly said, "Mama (she often talked about herself in the third person) and Daddy got together and had a talk, and we decided we're gonna try and get back together in Shreveport. We think it'll be better for you if both of us are around." I couldn't believe my ears. It was one of those surreal moments when you have this foggy image of someone speaking to you, as if you're watching it all on TV instead of living through it at that moment.

The audacity! How could they decide something so important without consulting me? How could something be better for me if I didn't like it or want it? Didn't she know that Chicago was *home* and Louisiana was like some foreign country, with cockroaches, mosquitoes and sweltering heat everywhere? I *hated* Louisiana (this last part wasn't exactly true, but I used it for effect anyway)! I frowned, stomped and stormed off into my room and sulked, my 11-year-old sense of autonomy severely wounded and thoughts of having to leave my friends and family spinning around my mind like a giant whirlpool circling around in a toilet resembling the shape of Louisiana. Those feelings lasted a few minutes, only to disappear in the haze of "stuff"—the events, people, places and things that occupy a young boy's mind while he's waiting for something to happen. I wasn't my usual happy-go-lucky self, but I wasn't a sourpuss, either. I knew I had no choice in the matter, and somewhere secretly my Catholic self was quietly, happily pondering the notion of somehow having a house with two parents, like everybody else. The truth was that returning to Louisiana—to me—was just another thing, another adventure to anticipate, something to occasionally think about, stuff. When you're 11 and the youngest of four children, you start to realize that events in the real world move slowly. You figure out somehow that it takes a while for things—important things—to have a direct impact on you. As the lowest of the low, your main concerns are: What's for supper? What's on TV? What homework do I have for school tomorrow? Is that a pimple on my nose? Does my hair look OK?

Still, I'd be lying if I said it wasn't of concern. Pete and Ree were staying behind to continue to build their families; each had a young son to raise. Duck had been drafted and would deploy to the Army soon from Louisiana. So, after he'd begin his tour, it would just be me, Mamoo, and Daddy in Shreveport. Leaving Chicago was part excitement, but heavy parts sorrow. A new school, church, friends awaited, but I was missing out on heading to middle school with my Chicago cousins that following fall. Mamoo and I left behind our whole social network—all those cousins, *de facto* aunts and uncles and the nice people who'd been our security blanket until then. All the things I'd learned about Chicago, its environment, Lake Michigan, downtown, the parks, the Cubs, the bus system, the street numbering approach, the West Side, our big yard—a thing of the past. I didn't know it then, but I would come to learn and appreciate a new history, land, and financial system that nourished a people and culture that I simultaneously valued and belittled for no reason except they were there. My enlightenment continued as I traveled a mishmash of status, division, labor, faith and courage and how they would combine in daily life.

MIDDLE DISCIPLINED

My first school in Shreveport was a re-hash of Chicago. Mamoo enrolled me in the sixth grade at Our Lady of the Blessed Sacrament Academy—another Catholic school near downtown Shreveport for which we had the lamest uniforms (khaki pants and white, short-sleeved shirts for boys, navy jumpers for girls) with an accompanying church (Blessed Sacrament Church, of course, founded in 1923) and convent of nuns who wore black habits. I had no sense that I was in middle school, since the student body consisted of kids aged kindergarten through eighth grade. It never occurred to me that there was a reason that St. Mel had classes that went through only to the sixth grade. It also was somewhat of a surprise to discover that everyone was either black or creole—not a white kid in sight. This didn't seem to matter all that much since, in Louisiana, if you weren't white, then you were "colored", the favored term then. It didn't matter if you had any "white" blood; your black blood meant you couldn't be considered white. You could call yourself a Frenchman, but that seemed to only interest the black folks who had no French ancestors—that was the reason you were lighter-skinned than other black folks. I often got the question, "Who yo' people?", which often meant the questioner was aware of a few Frenchman families and wanted to be able to place you. That was just the way it was, bizarre as it sounds. So, Blessed Sacrament was going to be a fascinating place of advanced learning.

Or so I believed. My love of reading, however, helped set me apart from the other kids. My vocabulary, enhanced sense of math and social studies, and my experience as an altar boy delighted my teachers. I wasn't any smarter than my peers, just exposed to these topics a semester or two ahead of my Blessed Sacrament friends. Fortunately, they didn't hold it against me, since I could play baseball, catch a football, and had naturally curly hair. All right, maybe the hair wasn't a factor, but I was the new kid who befriended everyone and loved to play—with anyone, it didn't matter who. And thus came my first southern lesson.

Our arrival in Shreveport that summer in June meant I enjoyed the better part of two months making new playmates with my Frenchman relatives. Particularly high on the list was my Cousin Sylvia, two years my junior but talkative, and my entrée to her circle of neighborhood friends. Her mom—who we called Nanny (she was Duck's godmother and one of Daddy's sisters) had known Mamoo since they were "Tut" (Mamoo) and "Put" (their pet names for each other as kids) and they became best friends for-ever. Sylvia was one of the smartest girls I ever met; not only did she make superi-or grades in school, but she would explain the import-ant-but-informal stuff that you needed to know there (e.g., fourth grade teacher Sister Sebastian was "an old fuddy duddy" not to be en-gaged lest you wanted her to pull you along by your ear) and elsewhere—which kids

Best friends: At left, Nanny (aka Put aka LaCadia Sylvie LaCour) and Mamoo (aka Tut).

were whiny, what department stores were the best for records and games, which of the cafeteria ladies was the nicest, what TV shows everybody in school watched, and what girl could play baseball like a boy (this was her next door neighbor Gianna, who was to become a lifelong friend). This latest morsel was especially important since we played baseball in the street every time I visited (I secretly thought her dad, Uncle Braz had wanted her to be a boy since together they would watch the Yankees on TV all the time); so Syl knew all the best pro players, impressing this Cubs fan. So, I had culture shock one day the first week at school when our principal Sister Louis (the white cornett, above her face and under her veil, made her look tall as an NBA player to a 13-year-old) interrupted our friends' game of catch to come up to me and ask, "Young man what are you doing?"

"Playing ball, Sister. With my friends and cousin."

"Don't you know," she said, her face turning grim, "that boys don't play with girls? You should be in the boys' yard." For emphasis, she pointed her long, pale, Irish fingers toward that way.

I wasn't smart enough to ask why not and was too church-indoctrinated to do anything but leave, but the entire episode felt like a huge admonishment. It was as if Carmine had come all the way down to Louisiana from Chicago just to tell me she didn't like the ring I gave her. I looked at Syl and Gianna, shrugged my shoulders, put my head down, and ran to the other yard, as if I had just struck out to make the third out in the bottom of the ninth inning. I couldn't quite put my finger on it, but this felt different, as if I was caught doing something everyone knew was wrong, something that felt unlawful or immoral—not like me at all, but I had no basis from which to argue because I never found out why it was wrong to play with girls. It never seemed wrong before. It was as if the boys' playground was for irregular people who couldn't quite cut it here. I'd had nuns as teachers before, but we'd always been simpatico. I'd never been disciplined by one. Something was off, an air of superstition lingered.

But there was nothing superstitious about class work, which went well. And the guys all seemed cool, but we were a small group, outnumbered by girls and constantly surveilled for "shenanigans" by our Irish overlords. That usually meant no joking, talking, chewing gum, ogling the girls, or behaving stupidly—whatever that meant. By my tone, you can tell whose side I was on. Part of that derived from our small number, part from Sister Louis' scolding, and part because you could tell that not much was expected from us, who usually got the brunt of the daily dressing-downs. The mean sidewalks of Blessed Sacrament implied your pockets would be checked for contraband unless you'd left your attitude and manhood on the playground, I'm exaggerating, but sometimes I felt sorry for my brothers-in-suffering as I never saw quite so frequent a usage of rulers on palms or backsides. This was especially true when, often as not, the punishment was on public display. Of course, we got our giggles when someone was screwing around or being silly; the culprit would sheepishly smile. Sure, the ruler or ear-pulling hurt, but somehow the emotional scarring seemed way out of proportion to the offense. Seeing a classmate defiantly stand—silently seething when taking physical punishment or accepting a verbal lashing often accompanied by steamy tears—signaled something amiss; a perceived injustice, perhaps, but sometimes a hint of something more pathological or severe going on elsewhere. It wasn't quite Attica or Alcatraz or the plantation, but I was impressed enough to stay out of trouble most of the time. I never considered the Irish militia might not be used to the hot and humid Louisiana heat, wearing all those black garments and not having any Atlantic breezes to help. Perhaps my strong alignment stemmed from the fact that there were more Frenchmen among my classmates than I'd ever seen outside of a family reunion. Of the 11 boys in our cohort, three were Frenchmen and two more could have passed for Frenchmen, their skin almost a mixture of creamy corn and a latte. Not only was my understanding of the color spectrum beginning to expand, but I also noticed Louisiana's many scholastic differences.

For example, sports—correction, sport. Mostly we played some variation of football, with a little dash of basketball, marbles, softball, and whatever version of "catch" or "tag" we could invent. In many cases, some of us sixth graders played with the older grades—mainly because you needed 11 members to play "real football" and sixth graders served admirably as pass-receiving decoys. Off the playground, it was the same; in history, instead of the role of Mrs. O'Leary's cow in the Chicago fire, we studied the difference between a county and a parish (none). In geography, we substituted the Mississippi (long and muddy) for the Great Lakes (huge and blue-green). In math, we bought two peaches and three pears from the hypothetical grocer, instead of five apples. In social studies, we learned why cotton was so important instead of why the South lost the Civil War. In literature, we read about Evangeline in place of The Song of Hiawatha and replaced JFK's inaugural address with The Sermon on the Mount. Free enterprise and "laissez faire" economics were lionized at the expense of unions and The New Deal. Not every curriculum difference was so severe, of course. Grammar, spelling and punctuation were equally boring at Blessed Sacrament.

Because of its missionary church directive to minister to ignored African-American and Mexican populations, Blessed Sacrament had a homogenous student body that came from the same lower-middle class as I had in Chicago. My friends' parents usually were—at the higher end—either principals or teachers at Shreveport's many black public schools, or they felt lucky to have regular "working" class jobs such as janitors, cooks, waiters, gardeners, and maids. The exceptions were a handful of doctors, dentists, lawyers, and self-taught skilled workers such as electricians, plumbers, or morticians. This also meant Blessed Sacrament's tuition tended to be low and the fundraising frequent. Whereas St. Mel directed us to sell donuts, jewelry and chocolate candy bars, as well as to collect for The March of Dimes. Blessed Sacrament favored numerous raffles—think turkeys, hams, cars, the odd appliance, and, of course, chocolate candy bars, with the yearly Lenten collection of pennies "for the missions". This often culminated in October at the annual church two-day bazaar, where we were induced to spend (or lose) whatever our parents could spare on balloons, ice cream, brownies, meat pies, or—if you really had a gambling bug—racetrack roulette or bingo. The event doubled as a great way to meet a state legislator up for re-election or a connected candidate for city council. Hormonally growing young lads and lassies also used it as a chance to sneak kisses in the unpatrolled recesses and gaps of the school campus. Still, you had to be blind to not know that the sisters prayed for not only your soul, but for monetary happiness.

DADDY AND THE WIDER WORLD

My three years at Blessed Sacrament went by unremarkably enough. Things at home got better. I started talking more and more to Daddy, who worked a 12-hour day six days a week and half a day on Sunday at a nearby Italian-owned corner grocery store, the latest and last stop in his career as a butcher—a skill he picked up watching and helping Grandpa Vigar (pronounced

"Vee GAW") on their sharecropper plot on Cane River; Boo (Daddy's nickname, though I never used it) could split a chicken into four with three forceful hacks of his meat cleaver. The first man I ever knew to wear a moustache, he would start his slow walk from the apartment at 8 a.m., make the four blocks to Catanese Grocery, come home at noon to eat lunch—another change I had to learn was that dinner was cooked and eaten earlier around noon, so that the afternoon sun couldn't combine with the heat from the stove to make your un-air-conditioned home unbearable— take a short nap, walk back to Catanese for 2 p.m., and work until 8 p.m., at which time he'd head home, eat leftovers from lunch, watch TV, and head to bed. Occasionally we'd get some gossip from the store out

Daddy, in his younger days

of him, or he'd go on about "dem damn Republicans" or "goddamn white people".

At the time, however, Daddy had traded in his womanizing for gambling and whiskey, which he sometimes combined when he played the store's pinball machine, some nights for hours. I remember some nights when Mamoo and I would wait for him, sit on the porch steps of our apartment, and watch him come down the street to see if he walked without staggering. It was a game, of sorts, at first. I worried later, more about gambling and what it did in terms of lifestyle and domestic peace. He and Mamoo often would argue about something or another, but it usually involved money or Daddy's bad pre-reunion habits. He was not a churchgoer, not used to keeping a clean house or feeding more than one person, and he dominated the

TV when he was home (he loved football and westerns). He could be funny when he wanted, especially in discussing relatives and Cane River life (he had the best stories about others' drinking habits and about who had the best baseball arm or had been kicked by a mule).

His joy for living paralleled Pete's, especially when it came to interacting with people. Every woman (usually his customers at the butcher counter) was "sweet" or "baby" or "darlin'" or "doll" or "sugar" or "puddin'" or "Li'l Mama"—this would cause the biggest eyerolls from Mamoo and their honey-dripping responses—and every man was "Bro (fill in the blank)" or "Bubba" or "Sarge" or "Junior" or their actual nickname. They knew him as "Butch", short for "butcher". He was a consummate bullshitter, not so much in a lying, conning or exaggerating way, but as in light conversation about everyday things—some real, some not, and ranging from the usual manly drivel ("Hey, Bro Bob! You keepin' up with them womenfolk?") to the welfare check ("Puddin' you doin' all right? How's that man treatin' you?") to fake skepticism ("Bubba, what'd you do with that chicken I gave you?") to the pure far-fetched ("Tom! Let me hold five dollars 'til Sunday!"). And the customers willingly engaged, much as they might do with their favorite bartender or barber. I admired this skill and drew upon it later in my days as a reporter. Nothing like bullshitting to build rapport with people you often see; not everybody likes to chat about the weather. Daddy was in the people-pleasing business, priding himself on his return customers and knowing what was on their minds. On his breaks, he would sit outside the store on top of the generator housing, warm his bronze toffee arms by rubbing them, throw out some bullshit, and then people-watch with the stockers and the clerks, always with his legs crossed, a cigarette dangling out the corner of his mouth and his beret on backward. He may have had his problems, but he cut a dashing figure.

Part of his swagger came from his butchering skills and his seventh-grade education (which Mamoo boasted was "like a high school" in rural Louisiana back in the '30s). Daddy would always chat baseball with me because I listened to any game I could find on the radio. He was a loyal Dodgers fan, thanks to Jackie Robinson, whom he admired, and Bob Gibson, who could "throw that ball". He and Mamoo often discussed LBJ's agenda and whoever was "gonna do something for the po' people" as Louisiana governor, with her lamenting JFK's short-lived run and he warning that any future Huey Long disciple wouldn't live long enough to get anything done. I didn't pay attention to much of the politics, as I had my own political territory to navigate at Blessed Sacrament as the "new smart kid in class". But Daddy gave off the guru aura in an arena that I hadn't experienced much in Chicago. In Shreveport, though, Daddy would get righteously indignant and so shakingly upset after making a political point that he'd go out on the apartment porch and start mumble-cursing Republicans, his boss, Uncle Braz (who'd stop by the store weekly after work for a couple beers and an argument clinic), or whoever dared argue the point that day at the meat counter. He was a take-no-prisoner debater, who instead of giving in would show amazement at his opponent's stupidity or ignorance. My take-away was that political beliefs had not just import but life-and-death consequences in Louisiana, where people of color still had a difficult path ahead. Occasionally Daddy would use "black people" as part of his supportive arguments and Mamoo, ever ready to play the foil, would roll her eyes at his indignance, and remind him that she wasn't black. I never knew if she was saying she and Daddy were different, or whether he needed to remember our Cane River heritage, or arguing substance or declaring victory. She never said.

Still, Daddy made it clear that adults had responsibilities, even if he didn't always live up to his. I didn't dare put it to him like that, since I needed all the guidance I could get. He must have sensed as much, or at least thought I needed some semblance of "the talk", because occasionally he would abruptly ask whether I was "getting any vittles", or "chitlins" or "hog maws" (usually while Duck happened to be around, awaiting deployment), despite Mamoo's admonishment, "Aw Boo! Stop asking him that!!" By her tone, I pretty much got most of the drift and swung my head sideways. Although I thought my ring-giving days were over, I interpreted his inquiry as some southern term for "girlfriend", and I just shook off his questioning with a weak giggle as boys usually would discuss such matters only amongst themselves, away from their parents, where they could get the real scoop on what really worked with girls. Besides, after hearing for years Mamoo's hand-wringing about unwanted pregnancies on Cane River and beyond, I wanted no part of anything remotely smelling like trouble. To boot, I didn't know how that sort of stuff worked, and all I wanted to know about was kissing, to be honest. I think Daddy—using hip material he'd either heard used by the young black males frequenting the store (for Thunderbird, Jim Beam, Gallo or worse, Boone's Farm) on their way to a party, or from the several meat delivery men he'd see every month—thought he was compensating for lost time with me. I'm unsure, really, but the use of street lingo showed me how much he'd been assimilated into—or adapted to—black culture while we were in Chicago. I don't know if he was just trying to be a good father, but he sent a clear cultural clue about pending manhood.

Other Daddy lessons came from watching him relate to others. Because of his job, his intermingling with his younger co-workers was, as you might expect, breezy, light-hearted, joking, and mentoring. These young black men were not only equals, but drinking and gambling buddies, and you could tell they thought Boo was special, dispensing wisdom, insight, and experience, and fearing no question. I didn't see him visit much with relatives, usually letting Mamoo do much of the conversing, interspersed with an occasional jibe, remark or joke. This was usually if the relative had dropped by for an unannounced visit (a Cane River tradition, it seemed), and Daddy either was watching (and hating) the Dallas Cowboys on TV or sitting on the porch with a cigarette. He never interrupted whatever he was doing to accommodate anybody, treating everyone the same—as if he was in the middle of something. If he was watching the Cowboys play (and cheat, he often would insist), he wasn't going to give relatives or their comments priority, no offense intended, as Sunday was his only day off. "Boo!" Mamoo would yell, then repeat the visitor's remarks. I'm not sure he valued his people all that much, since he never went with Mamoo and me when we would visit them. He was totally different whenever he addressed white people (as were most blacks and Cane River people in Shreveport), throwing in a "yes ma'am" or a "no, sir". He addressed the store owner with a "mister" and his first name; members of the owner's family were similarly addressed with "miss" or "mister"; they addressed him with "Mark" or even, as years went by, "Boo". I never asked about which salutation to use when, as I was too young to be in anything but the "sir" and "ma'am" phase with every-one, but I knew—from the way he disparaged many white people when he was home—that his approach wasn't out of mutual re-spect. Mamoo, when she later started working as a maid, used the same salutations.

Daddy and Mamoo at home in later years in Shreveport.

It probably wouldn't surprise you to know that Shreveport teemed with such social inequities, especially commercial enter-prises. In a city that was 64 percent white, entering and exiting a structure always meant whites went first. Hotels for blacks were hard to find, with even the famous soul singer Sam Cooke and Martin Luther King having to stay in all-black hotels in a less-than-desir-able and notorious red-light district that was a short stroll from our apartment. Movie theaters had separate sections for blacks, who also automatically were expected to move to the back seats of the bus and to take the rear exit when their stop arrived. Some of the finer restaurants still had not been seating blacks in the mid-1960s; no-body tried to integrate such places as they feared trouble (or a whole lot of staring) might brew. The same situation extended to city parks and certain white neighborhoods after dark. Most schools were seg-regated—even most of the pro-integration Catholic schools—and certain health professions and institutions didn't treat blacks (they had to patronize black doctors) or they had whites-only sections; churches followed suit. The city's pre-eminent public health facility usually only served black people or poor whites from East Texas. There were no black elected officials, only a handful of black policemen, and very few black lawyers. The 1960 census listed the predominant black female job as maid (52 percent), with another 26 percent in service-style occupations; for men it was "laborer" (26 percent), another 24 percent were operatives of some kind. Slightly fewer than 5 percent of black men were in professional or managerial jobs, compared to almost 8 percent for women. Shreveport had its ways, but didn't stop the black populace from building their own institutions and businesses and creating their own social structures (some described in Chapter 3). Post-World War II was a good era for the city's black businesses, but you wouldn't find many Frenchmen-created establishments outside the Creole-themed restaurants run by non-Creoles. Frenchmen were a minority within a minority and bank loans to non-whites were hard to obtain in the 1960s; few government programs existed for such a purpose and word of mouth was key to knowing who knew how to finagle such resources. Thus, the stage was set for church-related influences.

But it wasn't easy. As told in various Holy Ghost Fathers' publications, it wasn't until 1944 that the local bishop approved and largely funded the building of another small, mission-centered church for 150 people ("dedicated to the spiritual and moral advancement of the colored people" in the southern part of Shreveport), effectively dividing the city's black Catholics into two districts as the city's population began to move away from the city center. The 1944 site was the officials' second choice, as the pastors of the new church and Blessed Sacrament feared that white opposition would be too great at the first option. They named the facility St. Daniel's, after the prior bishop, and renovated an old chicken coop to house their first services; a more permanent locale was started during World War II and finished—through collaboration of parishioners, nuns, local priests, church-friendly local businesses, an attorney with statewide clout—because of mostly donated labor. The first services were held July 4, 1946, to the delight of the 28 founding families (96 total people, swelling to 170 in 10 years and adding a pastor's residence, community room, and street paving in the meantime). It just so happened that I was baptized at St. Daniel's, as we lived nearby. I remember going to Mass there only once, however, as part of my weekend sleepover at Uncle George's house; it was wall-to-wall Creole as I'd never seen it. The church closed in the mid-70s, but not before reaching its peak of 240 parishioners and fostering more solidarity in the Frenchman community that made up most of its members, unlike Blessed Sacrament, where black members made up a substantial plurality. Both churches cohesively organized, creating groups for every function and purpose, from fundraising to grounds and building maintenance to everything in-between, as well as recruiting for, financially supporting, staffing, and consistently rescuing the Blessed Sacrament school and its corresponding high school, Notre Dame.

But the church provided so many unseen advantages. First plusses, and they were a carryover from Chicago, came through the actual Mass and my altar boy experience. While my classmates prepared for their confirmation ceremonies—a process of memorized Q-and-A on church doctrine, prepping for questions from the bishop as the congregation and throngs of relatives watched and listened, and choosing a sponsor—I'd been fortunate to skip it since I'd already been confirmed at St. Mel. Instead, I assisted the bishop in the ceremony. I can't tell you how many brownie points this provided in the eyes of the adults and my classmates. The bishop was the superstar of the local church, and to be in his "entourage" as such was hot stuff. From there, it was a quick journey to being allowed to read aloud the "epistles", or the seven religious letters from apostles to the general members of the church— again, "hot stuff" if you were among the chosen. I'm bragging, but you can't imagine the confidence boost this gives a 12-year-old, not to mention adulation from adults who could read but not read as if they *understood* the nuance and the intent behind the words. Unbeknownst to me, it also gained me a lifetime of church-related duties, jobs, and "privileges" that would crimp my later attempts at—ahem—"style".

Such honors took various forms and what I first thought of as "perks". My first real job, for example, was being an assistant church gardener/landscaper/flunky. Mr. Gallion, an ancient, 77-year-old, limping bespectacled Frenchman with a dark complexion and matching mood, was my superior as he had done the job for many years after retiring from the gas company. I hated the job but learned a lot—including that I hated the job, especially fighting the wasps in the hedges. Mr. Gallion was a perfectionist, who showed me that a good job is a job done well—there's no other way to describe something that demands precision, an eye for outdoor spacing, alignment of something so mundane as grass, and weeding, among other skills. I liked the money but getting up at 7 a.m. on Saturdays was a pain. And Mr. Gallion always seemed to be there, watching and critiquing until I finished whatever I was doing to his liking. Fortunately, he was so deaf that he couldn't hear me practicing my curse words under my breath; the lawnmower's rat- a-tat-tat roar helped (it also explained his deafness). Of course, I picked up on other clues from the Blessed Sacrament Old Man Brigade: A gentleman always dressed *up* for Sunday Mass if adults were to take him seriously. So, a tie, shiny black shoes, neatly cropped hair, a decent watch and leather belt were the order of non-altar-boy days. Luckily, this was during double-knit's heyday. You also were peer-pressured to volunteer for any task minus a man to do it—passing the collection basket, running to the rectory to fetch the bottle of wine, or adjusting the public address system, ushering, and an occasional carrying of a casket—one of the coolest jobs ever. It didn't occur to me then, but this mishmash of grunt roles effectively constituted networking, and would lead to better opportunities in high school and later in my professional career. It didn't matter that many of the church men worked in (or retired from) subservient, back-breaking trades during the week. On weekends, they were role models, in charge, and trusted to lead. They never outwardly spoke about life in Shreveport, but you knew they knew enough about it to give good advice on how to navigate the working world.

To refresh your memory, my social circle—despite its dominance by the church—also extended about 90 minutes south of Shreveport to Cane River. Of course, all my Chicago relatives hailed from "the river", as we call it; the same was true of those in Shreveport, since many had relatives in Chicago as well. I always left with strong impressions. First, of course, was that Frenchmen—despite their economic and entrepreneurial strides in and around the river—still were subject to governance by the white ruling class in Natchitoches, the parish/county seat. In the local newspapers in the 1960s, "Creole" was a nearby town, a type of cooking, or the most common adjective to describe shrimp or cooking. "Frenchman" received a similar fate—usually referring to French natives or visitors. At best, "Creole" would be the hyphenate of "Acadian" to describe South Louisiana natives of French Canada. If you want the knock-down, drag-out version of the origins of this ignorance of Frenchman culture, read *The Forgotten People* by historian Gary B. Mills. Suffice it to say that Frenchmen—free, part-white Creoles—comprise a little-recognized third (not white, not black) status of people in the Isle Brevelle area around Cane River in North Central Louisiana. If you were like most whites in 1960s Louisiana, you thought that all people with African blood shared a loyalty or camaraderie; and you'd be wrong. This attitude wasn't out of disrespect for blacks, nor was it borne of hatred toward whites; instead, Frenchmen insist it's because they have their own, unique French history. Still, they had no political power to speak of when we returned to Louisiana.

That didn't stop the various river families from progressively forming their own cultural island there. Through an adherence to the land-based agricultural life, Catholic Church doctrine and structure, respect for elders, and a fondness for cultural storytelling, Frenchmen succeeded in many respects. I gathered that wealth wasn't always one of them, as Daddy's and Mamoo's rural nieces and nephews in the Isle didn't have fancy houses or cars. They had dogs and cats, but they still largely raised what they ate, as I learned while watching the butchering of the odd chicken, rooster, pig, squirrel, rabbit, goat, or duck. Usually there was a well, a chicken coop, a butane gas tank, and an outhouse. A muddy driveway led to a makeshift garage surrounding a house that contained a black and white TV, a fireplace, and a bathroom with no running water, and, of course, the inevitable chamber pot. A shotgun was kept near the door for use in case foxes and coyotes tried to raid the coop. It was normal to go on the front porch and wave at the passing, honking cars barreling down a curvy, two-lane state highway. Often there was a comment about who that driver was or who was with them in the car and if the latest news about them was good or bad. Or you went down the bank of the river and skipped stones or fished. If you were feeling lucky you tossed the football or baseball to your cousins while you all stood in the highway. If you were feeling extra lucky, you'd munch on the various "snacky" parts of today's kill and top it off with pecan pie.

In "town", as they referred to Natchitoches, most residents had more modern homes and nearby commercial establishments, restaurants, and gas stations, but everyone still knew everyone else and on what street they resided. There were defined neighborhoods—some for college-student renters, some family homes, an apartment complex or two, old-timey, ornate plantation-style monstrosities, and many streets that eventually fed into the two major highways crisscrossing the city. Outsiders quickly attracted attention, as I did when a white city cop wearing a Stetson in a patrol car slowly pulled up to me as I rode—alone, about a block ahead of my cousins—one of their bikes around the neighborhood, "You from around here?" he asked through the window from his driver's seat; too afraid to speak, I shook my head sideways. "You visitin' somebody?" Odd questions for a 13-year-old on a bike, but apparently a safe response was that my relatives lived on East Second Street, around the block. "OK," he countered, "just stay around the neighborhood, you hear?" With that, he slowly drove on his way. Was he just nosy, just preventing an abduction, profiling, or just keeping tabs on unknown juvie suspects? I'm guessing all the above, but it was my first police encounter of any kind, except for The Andy Griffith Show. My Aunt Flossie, Mamoo's youngest sister, was kind of shocked and indignant, saying her kids hadn't experienced any such interrogations. "Uh huh," Mamoo chimed to me. "You see he thought you were the wrong people." I couldn't fathom what kind of people I was *supposed* to be, given that everyone in Natchitoches was either white, black, or Frenchman. Besides the supposed lesson of there being safety in numbers, the encounter suggested that I needed to stick with my own people.

Weirdly, this same feeling started settling into my brain whenever we made the trek to either place or I could detect the community-ness coming to a head. Being or acting Frenchman was in everyone you meet—they're obviously different, but just like you. It's the way you'd greet each other: A soft kiss on the cheek, a warm-but-swaying hug, a "Hey *cher*!", or "Lord have mercy, looky you!", or a grab of the hand that you hadn't felt in years, or remembering he's *always* "Uncle Earl" to you. A feeling of coming home even if you're miles away—there is no right or wrong way of fitting in; everyone knows you belong. It's in much of the conversation you hear, carrying either a French inflection or a positive affectionate attitude toward arguing as a method of moving along a discussion, almost to the point of joy (does that make sense?). It's in the mmmms, moans, gurgles, gulps, and ahhhhs everyone makes when food's about to be eaten. It's in the way the women walked, as if they were enjoying it, using it to think of something good or happy. It's in the way the men freely poured their whiskey or bourbon. In church, it was in how they napped during a sermon, walked up to get communion, how quickly they darted to the car after the priest said, "The Mass has ended; go in peace."—privately. This physical onslaught of sorts made you feel confident, secure, yet wary that you were not like other people; "different" meant you were on defense and offense when discussing your familial origins. You must *teach*, but without coming across as moralizing or maligning your listener. This meant that you must sense when others start to lump you into groups of which you don't belong, jump in with a gentle correction, and allow them to continue their thoughts; you must not become the topic itself.

Conversely, this meant you must develop a worldview that acknowledged all the above, but especially the sense of uniqueness that each Frenchman feels while simultaneously trying to fit into the whole of society. You start questioning yourself: How do I carry myself when I'm with a particular crowd? Do I act black? How much black is enough? Am I getting carried away with it? How do I shake hands? Do I give "the nod" or wave my hand when I come across a fellow Frenchman? How do I judge this person I'm about to meet? Is a handshake or a hug appropriate? Do I ease into Ebonics in this crowd, or do I hold onto those "Gs" in my conversation? How much do I have to explain to this person about Creoles? Are they hip enough to get the drift, or do I have to drop a 15-minute lesson on this guy? What if they want to be "black" in this instance: Will I come across as "uncool" or "too white"? When can I just be myself? *What is* my true, public self? Am I overthinking this stuff?

None of this affected my relationships with my classmates at Blessed Sacrament or with other playmates; we were just kids being kids, at least in my mind. I never had thoughts of which was the proper way to behave, except around girls perhaps, since they seemed so much more mature than we guys. I often had to rely on a go-between, such as Cousin Sylvia or some other relative who would explain situations when I looked lost. There was, for example, the time I and my Cloutierville-area cousins walked to the store and, on the way back, we got caught in one of the roughest, most violent-sounding downpours I'd ever experienced. The sky was so dark, the wind so high, and the lightning so close that the resulting thunder literally shook the abandoned shack where we had taken shelter, rattling its tin roof. Being a city boy, I'd never been so close to nature, so I was visibly shaken and afraid we wouldn't make it back to my Uncle Newt's house, about a mile down the gravel road, now mostly mud. My cousins had a good time at my expense, pointing at me and repeating the dreaded words, "He's scared!!", followed by belly laughs that only rural people can make. Fortunately, Cousin Shela saw that I was shaking and put her arms around me, gently urging her brothers to stop laughing, and assuring me that we were going to be all right and that nothing worse was going to occur. I learned that Creole kids were tougher than I had imagined and that perhaps I might need to increase my coffee-and-biscuits intake to their levels. The Frenchman alliance took care of its own, whether it meant older cousins intervening to allow sixth-grader like me into a football game dominated by eighth graders or taking it upon themselves to inquire as to potential matchmaking with a close girlfriend, or inviting you to the manly philosophizing group congregating on the little bridge over the ditch across the street at night on a Friday sleepover. These mediator moments smoothed the road to my full investment into Frenchman fellowship, Louisiana middle school style. I could have used it more often, it turned out.

SELF-LOATHING IN THE STREETS

When you are the youngest of four kids by nine years, you tend to grow up without the protection of older siblings, simply because they're elsewhere, enjoying their own friends, families, and lives. Nobody teaches you to box, or to woo girls, or to navigate a transportation system, or to simply talk to adults. Such lessons often occur through experience and the inelegant maneuverings of dealing with people and being a Frenchman, subsequently affecting your already-low sense of adolescent self-esteem. Case in point: my last three years of grade school.

I was never one to hang out with random kids in the neighborhood, thanks to my slimly founded fears in Chicago of "Republican" school kids, who came across as a gang of pirates more dangerous than Al Capone and his confederates. My fears continued in Shreveport along the three-and-a-half block walk to Blessed Sacrament from our first house, a three-room cockroach-infested apartment on a busy intersection. Because Allendale was the worst-looking neighborhood (dead or too many cars in front yards, unchained dogs, unkempt grounds, houses and apartments in varying stages of shabbiness)—with Mamoo sharing the daily little blurbs in the newspaper about its latest shooting, stabbing, or police arrests—I was always on alert for trouble, even though it hardly showed its face; the worst I'd ever seen were our neighbors yelling and cursing across the street in a late-night argument to which the police were called. I was in a new neighborhood, easily recognized as a Catholic because of my khaki-and-white-sleeved-shirt uniform and my Creole good looks. I felt like I had a target on my back because of this, and because I recognized no one on the way to school, and likely because there was a tavern and a convenience store about midway. Of course, my fears relaxed in a matter of days as I became more familiar with the route and had deduced that the winos who I encountered along the way were harmless, especially since I rarely carried money. Things seemed to be settling down and I concentrated on school.

But the road to school often was loaded with a big obstacle. For my seventh-grade year, we had moved to a new house the prior summer; it was still only three rooms (as many shotgun houses were then), but the three of us made do with slightly more space—with our bedrooms swelling as living and TV rooms and a small but functional kitchen. Perhaps the best aspect wasn't the added space so much as it was the neighborhood, which was an upgrade with a residential feel and no real busy streets such as those encountered near the first apartment. Plus, the owners lived right behind us and were Frenchmen—Mr. Gallion and his Mrs. (both elderly but amiable and a free ride to Blessed Sacrament Church for Mass). We shared the yard, which was a nice bonus and served as a social meeting place for our families. Back to school: Like any community, however, there were bald spots—a 24-7 ancient oil rig across from the Gallions' home, a decrepit, shabby corner surrounding the nearby bus stop and doubling as an abandoned car lot, and a really rundown area encompassing two solid blocks of rundown housing, abysmal tar-covered streets and overrun with more than a few scruffy drifters seeking their next wine bottles. This stretch also sat between my neighborhood and Blessed Sacrament, meaning I had to daily navigate it while hoping the dreaded "Republican" kids would let me pass through unscathed.

The afternoons were fine, with no problems since we happened to dismiss earlier than the other neighboring schools, which meant I'd only see the homeless and the inebriated on the way home. But no such luck in the mornings, especially down the northernmost street of this ghetto within our ghetto. One morning, I met an oncoming kid who looked particularly unkempt, disheveled and grubby in the middle of the street (there were no sidewalks); I flashed a weak smile and meekly said, "Hi" to him, but he wasn't having any of my civil banter. It was almost as if I was wearing a sign that said, "Spit on me" or "70-pound weakling" in big red letters; whatever the reason,

I'm guessing I stood out that morning. He loudly inhaled and spat at me, placing a hefty projectile of saliva and mucus into the shoulder of my fake-mohair sweater. I was happy to have helped a fellow human being clear the irritants from his throat, but I didn't want a matching pair. I looked at the slimy phlegm, then at his laughing face, and ran like hell—not bothering to glance back—for the rest of the half-block to Blessed Sacrament, jumping the boundary fence as a couple of first graders stared, watching me run to the restroom to clean up my sweater. So, the next morning I took an alternate route and kept a look out for that kid for the remainder of my time at Blessed Sacrament. Although I was terrified, I simply saw it as the price of the neighborhood and the curse of the Catholic school student—to always have to traverse the road home with an eye to the dangerous riffraff. This was more than confirmed, as I learned to run fast and straight, to keep my head down as if I was mute, and to not look anyone I didn't know in the eye. I would see the offending juvenile once or twice when I had to go to a nearby corner grocery store; he'd sit idly on the outside steps, no doubt looking to cause trouble with his friends. Luckily, after I bought my items, I learned to quickly grab the paper bag and set speed records once out the door. But any time I would read about the police arresting "a Negro juvenile" in our vicinity I would hope against hope it was him and breathe a little easier. Cops were my allies thereafter, although I forever remembered Daddy's singular complaint about any TV law enforcement officer—from U.S. Marshal Matt Dillon to rancher Lucas McCain: They always arrived too late to save the poor victim from the indignity caused by the bad guys. The good guys never prevented the first offense; if they had, there wouldn't be a reason for them to be on TV. And so, my three Blessed Sacrament years almost felt like an exercise in hide-and-seek between me and "them"—from the winos who wanted to borrow my spare change, to the vagrants who'd just awakened to a hangover and needed directions to the nearest liquor store to even the ragamuffins who roamed their streets looking for someone to buy them some cigarettes or even candy. I never took the bait and perpetually stayed on high alert, almost as if my shoes were about to be stolen right off my feet. I knew I was a coward, but one who was going to live to see another day if he could help it.

My experience with girls was no less fraught. The only ones I ever saw were at Blessed Sacrament, obviously, and my early run-in with the principal sort of put a damper on any hopes I had of becoming anything close to a Don Juan. Truthfully, most of the guys in my three-year cohort were pretty much in the same boat—dead in the water, to carry the maritime metaphor to its logical conclusion; we were dorky as hell, although we were outnumbered by a three-to-one ratio. The closest I heard of any one of us having any success came second-hand and probably was highly embellished by male retelling. This is what I would usually hear: A boy (sneakily followed by a two- or three-boy support group) would sneak down the stairs from the boys' playground via the north entrance, which ran right past the main church entrance, and then saunter to the water fountain, pretending to need a drink. The fountain was in neutral ground, just outside the cafeteria entrance. If luck were on the male side, one of the more attractive female classmates would also happen to be going to the fountain (usually after she and her "entourage" had finished using the nearby ladies' room). The convergence of the two groups would eventually lead to some silly back-and-forth banter, the pulling of someone's sweater (or pigtails), or an occasional splashing near the water fountain—just enough to cause someone to retaliate. Of course, this all happened in hopes that a lunch or playground proctor or an adult passerby wouldn't suddenly appear. Successful forays lead the separate parties to run back to their respective playground before anyone else noticed—giggling, of course. Also, the incident would re-occur every couple of days and get blown into "Boy X likes Girl Y" gossip, which—if Cupid were watching—might lead to a peck on the lips or cheeks of Girl Y at the church bazaar or between the Sunday Masses. I never got this far with anyone, mainly because it took too much luck, and I couldn't work up the nerve to pretend to be thirsty or the social skills to roundup a supportive water fountain posse. Also, it was more fun (and less hazardous) to stay on the playground and play ball. On a positive note, the girls didn't seem to discriminate between Frenchmen or anyone else, and vice versa. And it's fair to say that the guys wouldn't have known what discrimination meant.

No doubt that at the heart of these timid-yet-tension-filled attempts at coupling and the lack of any discriminatory behavior was Catholic doctrine and the "free love" movement of the 1960s. Not that we were "free lovers" or even knew what that was—even at our eighth grade St. Valentine's Day dance hardly anyone danced or, at least, they saved any of their moves for the slower tunes, with the chaperones' eyes glued to anything suspicious. But I've mentioned the seemingly constant possibility of teen pregnancy that hung over adult conversations that I overheard. Any parent with a teen or a pre-teen at home knew they had to remain ever vigilant, less their household be the next hot topic. My own fear of falling to this menace (as well as not knowing how to even approach a girl) took form as I started to more frequently visit Nanny's house, and Cousin Sylvia invited me to join her and her friends' outdoor play. I started becoming more and more enamored of Gianna, so much so that I finally drummed up the nerve to "go out" (kid slang for "be my girlfriend"; besides, where could we go?)—but not before many phone calls with Sylvia (from the Gallions' phone next door, no less, for privacy and because we didn't have a phone yet) to see if Gianna was willing. It turned out she was, but there were some traditional formalities to go through, of course: such as holding hands in front of other kids in the neighborhood (so word could spread), writing her name inside my loose-leaf notebook, and the first kiss. I was all-in for my first real kiss, of course. Until I wasn't.

After we kissed that June Saturday night as I walked her home, my conscience started to worry, worry, and worry some more: What if she got pregnant? Later the following week, my worry was in over-drive: Would my parents find out she was pregnant from their gossipy relatives and friends? Would I be banned from Blessed Sacrament? Would it mean more pimples? So, I broke down and told Duck I needed a guy-to-guy meeting with him one night; I was too scared and embarrassed to ask Mamoo or Daddy, and Duck was available as he was just finishing up his Army hitch and visiting us before heading back to Chicago. After we sat down, he asked what was on my mind. I told him my worry. After much hooting, cackling, and slapping of his knees, he calmed down and assured me that she couldn't possibly get pregnant from only a kiss on the lips. I hadn't had "the talk" yet with Daddy, so how was I to know? I felt like an idiot; my brother could really be an asshole sometimes, but the humiliation was worth it because at least he had taken biology. Thanks Duck!

I didn't realize it as such, but I was beginning to sense that I didn't already know all the world was trying to teach me. My occasional cowardice, plus what I'll call my "lack of suave-ability" or worldliness, my shyness and ignorance on how to speak with girls who weren't my cousins, the hard-scrabble frontier of the working world, and the looming presence of high school all combined to make me extremely reticent to try new things. My hesitation came to a head one spring night in eighth grade. My grades and studiousness attracted the attention of a benevolent crowd of supporters—Frenchmen and non-Frenchmen alike. They were all good people, ranging from my cousin Kerry—a coffee-bean-dark Frenchman with fine, curly hair and a gold tooth—and Gloria Merchant, kindergarten teacher at Blessed Sacrament, and, unbeknownst to me, an advisor to Mamoo regarding my future. I overheard Kerry, an older cousin with his own family and an influencer among St. Daniel's parishioners, telling Mamoo that "they" said "they" wanted me at Jesuit High, a prestigious Catholic school in Shreveport. I don't know how Kerry, who rubbed elbows with Shreveport aristocracy at his part-time bartending job at one of the city's finest restaurants, got wind of that kind of information, but he was known among insider Frenchmen—if there was such a thing—to have access to political types. Although it sounded promising, I just blew it off as just so much Frenchmen gossip because I knew nothing about this school.

But it so happened that Mrs. Merchant's son, Leon, a Blessed Sacrament graduate two years my senior and an altar boy mentor of mine, was then a sophomore at Jesuit. She knew a lot about the school and the entrance process. She told Mamoo after church one

Sunday, "We want George to go to Jesuit. He needs to be there." I had no idea why this lady with a raspy voice took an interest in me, but she was always nice to me at Blessed Sacrament, Leon had integrated Jesuit, and he liked it. Every Sunday she would waddle over—she had the worst bunions in the church—to nudge Mamoo and ask if I had applied yet; in addition, after Christmas and every time she'd see me thereafter, she started telling me about the entrance test looming. "You better hurry up and apply," she insisted.

This set the scene for one of Mrs. Merchant's stabs at recruitment. Jesuit annually puts on a student-run Shakespear play. At the time, Jesuit had this whiz of a student actor—James McClure—so good that his portrayal of Richard III got rave reviews in one of the local dailies. My mom bought a ticket for me from Mrs. Merchant, who probably thought this stab at high-brow entertainment would certainly do the trick at converting me into the Jesuit stratosphere. So, the night of the performance, Mamoo directed me to dress in my best casual prep look and gave me money to take the bus to the play; all I needed was to take the Allendale bus downtown and transfer to the Line Avenue bus, which would drop me two blocks south of the school. Her directions were clear enough, except I had no idea what to expect from Shreveport's archaic bus system. I was to wait for my connecting bus on Shreveport's busiest street—Texas Avenue. I was afraid—of what I don't know—and I got an uneasy feeling in my stomach as I waited. And waited. And waited. And waited. Soon, all the prospective riders waiting at the stop were gone, I was alone, the sun was starting to set, and the knot in my stomach got tighter as the clock ticked and my connecting bus still hadn't come. I took matters into my own hands, walked back to my neighborhood bus spot and rode home, telling myself I had no choice but to return as it appeared there'd be no connecting bus. And feeling relieved. Upon arriving home, I told Mamoo the bad news and watched her head explode.

"You did *what*?" was all I heard before she grabbed me by the shirt collar and we headed out the door, back to the bus stop. "Well, I'll be goddamned," she shook her head, explaining to me that just because a bus hadn't come yet didn't mean it wouldn't ever come.

"Now you get your ass back on that goddamn bus and you go to that play. Now I mean I want you to go, you hear?" She said, not caring about an answer nor about the audience she had attracted. With that she handed me the bus fare and walked alone back to the house.

Her words still ringing in my ears, I pouted as I headed as far to the back of bus as I could without being noticed. I had never seen her so mad—and about a play, no less! Despite oncoming sunset and the lateness of the hour, I still had the familiar feeling of being deathly afraid of being alone in the adult world without knowing whether the damn connecting Line Avenue (what a stupid name) bus would ever really show up or whether I would survive the night. Oh, and did she have to create a scene like that? What the hell had happened to my sweet mama? And why is someone with a sixth-grade education suddenly so interested in all things Shakespeare? Was it because I couldn't perform the task? Was she worried that I was that stupid or did she worry that I was that helpless. I would have cried right there on the bus had it not been possible that I would look like even more of the loser that I appeared. She'll be sorry when I get mugged, I thought.

Of course, nothing happened. The connecting bus drove up as soon as I crossed the street to catch it, and I rode it to what was a hospital (at least I was close to an ER in case I got hurt), got off the bus, took a deep breath, and quickly marched the three blocks to the play's location, briskly walking in with my ticket as if I had planned to arrive fashionably late. For the first few minutes into Act I, my neck was still tight and my hands freezing cold. I tried to sort my emotions and make sense of why the events of the prior hour had occurred as they had. I scanned the room and, realizing I was among like-minded, high-brow intellectuals—who didn't know what it took to get me there—I breathed in and started to follow the dialogue. I didn't know a soul in the audience, and no one gawked at me (as I had expected to happen) but that was a good thing at the time. After the play's finale, I checked the change in my pocket, staying close to the traffic so I could see my way down the sidewalk back to the bus stop. Curiously, my mugging fears faded as I navigated the downtown streets to my connecting location, tried not to attract attention and caught the returning bus home. Exiting the bus, I hit the ground running back to the house, climbing over the Gallions' driveway gate through to our rear entrance. It was almost 10 p.m. and found my parents watching TV. Mamoo asked whether I enjoyed the play.

"It was all right," I said, "There were a lotta people there," I continued, nonchalant as I got ready for bed, feigning fatigue and acting as normally as I could. Just like any other night on the white side of town.

"Did you have any trouble getting the bus?"

"No," I responded, continuing to undress, then nonchalantly added, "I made it all right."

Daddy never took his eyes off the TV. Life felt different, but the same, too—that surreal feeling was coming back for a moment. Real life had interrupted my notions of normal and I wasn't sure how to feel. Regardless, I had a hunch that this night's events wouldn't be my last Jesuit-related test. Not only was I going to see just how far I could push my passivity and cowardly attitude toward the unknown, but also, I would have to re-examine my interactions with the outside world if I was ever going to have smooth sailing in my life. Growing up was getting more complicated and book learning alone wasn't going to cut it.

DISCOVERING THE RULES

I had a lot on my mind.

First, girls—specifically black girls such as Gianna, all of whom seemed intriguing as hell and, yet, not as simple as I had assumed. Gianna was a pretty tomboy who liked to play sports, but she was fine to 13-year-old eyes Being in the same classroom every day for three years and my continued visits to Cousin Sylvia's house also showed me how multifaceted she could be; I observed her in outings with her parents—she was the Big Sis of the family and the First Child who was expected to "know better" and be a role model for her siblings. She had above-average intelligence, but it had to have been difficult for her to meet what she thought were the expectations of her parents—both schoolteachers. They were nice enough, but how close can a 13-year-old get to know two diametrically different adults who seemed successful, larger than life and were honest-to-God professionals. Her mom was cream-colored, tall, beautiful, freckled, gregarious, happy-go-lucky, and constantly talkative with her brood of four children. Her dad was a shorter, darker, chiseled, manly man, a football referee in his spare time, and quiet. Her parents seemed to always be teaching their kids, whether grammar, manners, science, common sense, or how to do chores. This was a house of discipline, it seemed—that and two Cadillacs, which (along with the giant, white capital letter that would light up at night near the outside, front entrance of their black, modern home) no other house in the neighborhood could match. Talk about feeling out of your element, but I was still fascinated with the idea of my first girlfriend. Little did I foresee that my lack of knowledge about things that you could or should do at that age if one was "going with" someone. Girls were totally foreign to me; I just knew that I liked them—which would probably be the sum of gender intelligence you'd find if you took a knife and investigated the brain of someone like me. I was a Class A doofus, meaning that all I knew was—again—stuff I'd picked up from pop culture: protect the women folk from cads and bad guys, give them candy and jewelry, occasionally send them sickeningly sweet cards, open doors for them, hold their hands, and give them your handkerchief when needed. Oh—and sports would have to occasionally come second from now on.

But I also had to battle my concerns about what I saw was a general trend in Shreveport—the inherent mixing of black and Frenchman culture and my increasing involvement in it. Since Shreveport—meaning the ruling white class—officially recognized only whites and "coloreds" as the only two racial categories, it had no trouble of lumping Frenchmen into the same group with blacks; after all, Frenchmen had some African blood, didn't they? But remember, from early in the prior chapter, that Cane River Frenchmen resisted such over-simplified categorizing. So, what was up with this seemingly interracial mixing with black folks in terms of dating and marriage? Many Frenchmen I had grown up listening to would whisper or spell the term "black" or "Negro" when discussing who was the latest to accept such arrangements. Often, one conversant would ask if the "offending" father in an "illegitimate" child's birth was black. What's more, such questions would come from a person with daughters- or sons-in-laws or grandchildren who were black themselves. It sounded as if Frenchmen couldn't make up their minds as to what they wanted in a family, or as if they wanted to have their cake and eat it, too, so to speak. Was I being disloyal to the culture by going with a black girl? Or was I simply following a time-honored tradition of saying one thing and doing the opposite? Would the first sign of opposing cultural norms be the first signal that I should "jump ship" and find a nice little Frenchman sweetie? Didn't Frenchmen believe in loving the person first for who they were? I never mentioned any of this to Gianna, but I was sure that if I were having such questions, might she, too, have the same doubts about Frenchmen? After all, weren't looks only "skin deep"? This might be classified as overthinking a situation, or a topic way too heavy for a first courtship, but it was one of the things I liked to do to a fault, as I learned later. I can't imagine what people would do nowadays in the times of Ancestry.com and DNA testing, where your DNA distribution is broken down by region and country and can change every day with new scientific discoveries. Either way, this was a lot of worrying to be putting on a fledgling relationship and thank goodness I didn't have too much reflection in my approach to relationships at the time—or to anything else, for that matter. But I couldn't avoid the issue altogether. Cases in point:

On my second Christmas season in Shreveport, Blessed Sacrament co-sponsored this huge event. The plan was to join the other, older Catholic schoolchildren in the city for a singing Christmas extravaganza—a Festival of Lessons and Carols, the local newspapers called it—on a Sunday close to the holiday break. Joe Wise, a white guy who apparently was some kind of Catholic Church musicological genius, lead us in two or three sessions that had us practicing some traditional songs and some hip, upbeat Appalachian, Native American and Harry Belafonte-style calypso music—very uplifting and buoyant, compared to the dirge-like renditions most church choirs deliver. The day of the event, some 700 or so of us schoolchildren piled into the downtown Convention Center. But despite most of us arriving individually by cars, they grouped us in the center by school; they might as well have shouted, "Whites over here, you Negroes over there." The arrangements somewhat sucked part of the Christmas joys out of the event, although we still tried to impress the parents and sang enthusiastically.

Usually, nothing exciting or attractive was going to be in Allendale back then. Living in one of the city's largest black neighborhoods meant if you wanted to see new things, something more than people living life or just getting by, then you had to have transportation—which we didn't. One exception: SPAR—Shreveport Parks and Recreation—Stadium, in the most decrepit part of a neighborhood torn in half by nearby Interstate 20 by the time I saw the Cincinnati Reds play the Cleveland Indians in an exhibition game one Saturday in April. It was a glorious, sunny Saturday where some 9,000 folks would ignore the world's problems for three hours to congregate and celebrate a rite of spring. We didn't have the greatest seats in the world—that would be Wrigley Field in Chicago—but I did have one of the safest, thanks to segregation. Under the category of "Be Careful What You Wish For," the city still didn't like letting black people sit with other folks, so we sat mostly toward what was then the outfield. The white people in the grandstand weren't so lucky, as everyone stood for the traditional seventh inning stretch, a concrete slab broke, sending several folks about 15 feet to the ground. A somber, hushed tone descended over SPAR, stopping the game. Ambulances came in and took away a few people, who earned a standing ovation that fans usually reserve for injured players. The drama ended, the game continued, and the Reds went on to win, 8-5: Pete Rose went 2-for-5, Tony Perez homered.

One of my first vivid movie theatre visits came watching a John Wayne double feature with The Sons of Katie Elder and The Man Who Shot Liberty Valance, two not-so-current films at the time, enabling a low admission price. First, we felt this awesome air conditioning—this was, after all, Shreveport in summer—and, again, awesome seating arrangements for black people. My cousins and I entered the side entrance to the Don Theater downtown, ascended a steep set of carpeted stairs, and entered the rear of a section I would later know as "the balcony". We had the run of the place, which meant we chattered after every character was shot, changed seats when we got antsy, and loudly expressed emotions; such behavior annoyed the few white people who sat below—not that we cared; our seats made the screen seem closer and the movie was in color, which we'd hardly ever seen on a screen before. Initially I thought something about Technicolor (or was it the air conditioning?) seemed to be freeing. On further analysis, the cause probably was the anonymity of the dark theater and the feeling of invincibility and safety that the balcony provided. Regardless, we all continued to watch the movie, entertained especially by the political twists and turns endured by Jimmy Stewart's cowardly attorney character, who wound up an unlikely hero.

I've briefly commented about the bus system, but it, too, upheld my belief that white people had it all backward. Prior to Shreveport, I'd never seen a bus turn a corner before or run on an actual, residential neighborhood street. Although we always seemed to find our way to the rear, the seats up front nearly always only held only 1 or 2 whites; the rest of the riders almost always were black or partially black people riding home—many wearing white or khaki uniforms—after six or eight hours of cleaning or maintaining white people's suburban-style homes. Downtown, where they would transfer to the buses that took them home, you'd see these buses with exotic-sounding names—Broadmoor, Youree Drive, Line Avenue, Southern Hills, Queensborough—but only blacks would exit them, probably thankful that the vehicles existed, regardless of the formal or informal indignities they might have to undergo. A seat is a seat, no matter where you must sit; you still have a job.

Unless Uncle Braz or Uncle George drove by or carried us somewhere, the only places I shopped were the five-and-dime stores that served the many commuters mentioned above. Mamoo had a twice weekly maid job that paid her maybe $20 or $30 a week. She'd catch the Allendale bus headed downtown and then another bus to the Broadmoor neighborhood about seven miles southward, so the days she worked I arrived home before she did or, in summer, spent the day watching TV at home or reading library books. As my reward for not burning down the apartment, she'd buy me a package of baseball cards from Woolworth or Kress department stores for a nickel a pack; that was the extent of my "shopping" since I had no job until I was 13. But thanks to running errands with my uncles and cousins, I discovered giant "discount" stores where no bus I knew dared tread. Often, they were in something called "strip malls", adjacent to other, smaller businesses or merchants. The attraction, of course, was their store was so large that they could sell more specific items at a lower price than most competitors. It was like finding Santa had placed a price tag on everything in the store, especially things that most people would buy—health and beauty products, lawn and garden tools, clothing goods, various small electric appliances, and the ever-popular toys. Much of merchandise was slightly inferior, but hey, saving money is saving money. People go where they must go to do it.

But life came from every possible direction those first three Shreveport years, it seemed, especially one August Saturday afternoon in the summer after sixth grade. Returning home from the corner store, I was down the street about half a block from the front porch when I saw Uncle Braz drive up to our apartment. He slowly exited his car, and Mamoo met him at the corner of the porch that met the driveway. I could see she was listening to him intently, when she suddenly dropped to her knees, let out an anguished cry and started to scream at the top of her lungs. All I could hear was, "No, no, no, Braz!" and she ran into the apartment, weeping and wailing. Sensing something horrible, I ran the rest of the way home, still listening to her pleas and cries for God's help. As I caught up with Uncle Braz, he told me the unthinkable: My brother Pete had drowned earlier that day in a boating accident in a suburban Chicago lake, despite the best life-saving efforts of our cousins Charles (Braz's eldest son) and Bootsy (Cousin Daughter's car-repairing brother). I never saw such a pained look on Uncle Braz, a Caucasian-skinned, short, bespectacled man with big ears and curly black hair. The next few days were a somber blur, with many visitors, casseroles, buckets of crying, hugging, praying, and encouragement of varied kinds. It was yet another surreal scene: Many comforting loved ones who I was excited to see and visit, crammed between my waves of nausea at why they were visiting, mixed with wondering what this meant, and my last thoughts of Pete—his funny, joke-laced letters since we'd returned to Shreveport, our Chicago departure when he'd held his 18-month-old son Mark up by one hand to the train window for us, still working out in my mind the details of his death, and looking forward to soon starting seventh grade. And, of course, wondering when things would return to normal, and realizing that I needed normality, to be able to carry on with what my life had encompassed to that point—my classmates, my studies, my routines. But it felt as if life was going in slow-motion, like all the relatives wanted things to drag on leisurely so they could watch the suffering, down to the excruciatingly sad funeral Mass, during which I had to read the epistle, and after which was the only time that I ever saw Daddy tear up.

Examining these events now, in hindsight, I can see that many of those involved saw the inevitable need to move on at some point, while seemingly wanting to watch things unfurl to their miserable conclusions. No matter the hypocrisy of the Frenchman call for color unity, or the contrived structuring of the Christmas carol-Kumbaya gathering, the artificial assembly in the sun to watch a sport, the fancy coolness of the darkly bunched film showing, the compelled and daily transportation placement of working class folks, the pursuit of plummeting product pricing of the enormous stores, or even the tragedy of losing a loved one—the result was the same: People were obliged to pursue what was happening, regardless of need, background or desire. Afterward, they had to move on, to persist, even if they didn't know what it was that they were pursuing. In search of something, even in death was there no rest, no end to the search for the life ahead. And so it was that I, too, resumed my own search.

3

Schooled Into Identity

That search took me, naturally, to high school, Jesuit. If passing the admission test showed anything, this school was more serious about academics than any school I'd attended. If I had to move on—to persist—this place made the most sense, not just because I could continue learning about Catholicism there, but also because two of my Blessed Sacrament classmates also had successfully applied. According to Blessed Sacrament adults in the know, the folks running Jesuit *wanted* me there; who wouldn't want to be part of a group that desired him or her? And, if I'm being honest, I thought the Jesuit High uniform (grey slacks, necktie, a button-down shirt, and a blue blazer) was way cooler than anything I'd seen in Catholic school attire. Such garb signaled that I was a young man to be taken seriously, pursuing something seriously important, even if I didn't know what it was. Plus, we had won the state AA football championship the prior fall, and we had the coolest mascot—Snoopy—ever. Jesuit was hot shit, pardon my French.

The institution had tremendous upside, being a liberal arts college preparatory school with priests from the Jesuit order guiding the curriculum. I could repeat the usual, impressive cultural and historical achievements of the Jesuits that people normally mention, but that wouldn't do them justice. These were supposedly no-non-

71

sense guys who expected students to have a measured, thoughtful approach to the wonderful opportunity available to them. In other words, if you thought nuns were a handful, wait until a Jesuit corralled you in a class—using scientific or classical philosophical methods—and asked you a question; the pressure *made* you wish a nun was pulling your ear instead. It wasn't that your manhood was being examined, but your past and ego—you were recruited, after all, from the cream of your prior classes—made it seem as much. If it was your first year, then too bad: Welcome to Jesuit—forget your mama's apron strings.

Of course, it sounds much worse than it was, but that's what you were made to believe or had heard or—because you were so neurotic about the school's supposedly unrealistically high academic standards—you had swallowed. Such buy-in was easily achieved, thanks to the weightiness of the uniform, the extra degrees each Jesuit listed after his name, the simple red-brick exterior of the school, the photos of previous grads (in full regalia) on the hallway walls, the fact that you were no longer "George" but now "Mr. Sylvie", and the fact that you had to compete to be admitted. You expected you'd work harder than before, and you would learn to *like* it.

A recent photo of Jesuit, after its name was changed to Loyola Prep.

Returning to reality, this mythological buildup helped most of the teachers cover many of their deficiencies. There were instructors past their prime, or with severe cases of poor personal hygiene, or who were just a bit too enthused about their topics (think English teachers in love with hippy poetry or history teachers who too often digressed into football metaphors), or just too new to know any better. Some oddballs became personal favorites, to the point of constant imitation. In short, high school was high school, no matter what you wore or how much you liked learning.

Make no mistake: I enjoyed Jesuit. But I don't want to underplay the search that I mentioned at the start. Although Jesuit was a new experience, I brought some familiar mindsets to the experience. I was a Frenchman, this time in sea of white faces who brought more varied and stronger aptitudes in certain academic and athletic fields and who likely only saw me as the well-known "other" person—that guy who you'd heard rumors about but who was really a mystery to your own experience. To look at him is to ask, "What is he? Who let *him* in? What's up with that haircut?" I, on the other hand, was reminded of some advantaged kids—stainless steel wristwatch bands, Beatles boots, a lot of hair-primping, the search for immediate facial recognition of another guy in the group upon arrival, unafraid of asking questions or laughing at the answers—a certain air of familiarity with the setting. Rather than intently listening in class, I sometimes took in the entire backdrop, reverting to extensive self-comparison: How do I look? Was I a witness or a participant? Was my tie on straight!? I wonder how often I should shine my shoes!? I was already depressed by a sneaky feeling of not quite measuring up to all that rich, milky skin, despite being in the prestigious 1-A class group. Although everyone could see me, finding myself in this group wasn't going to be easy. Where was Sister Louis when I needed her?

Looks aside, the first few days of freshman year—in addition to being orientation-oriented—was a whirlwind of learning the fundamentals of locations of classrooms and the gymnasium, priests' residence, administrative offices, and the cafeteria. Plus, all the minor things—info on clubs and groups, gym gear, counseling resources, bus schedules, parking rules, book distribution, and behavioral expectations. All these explicitly laid-and-ordered bits of data lulled me into thinking that, although it wasn't Blessed Sacrament, everything seemed to make sense and was going to be just another normal school. Besides, if I didn't understand something or was confused, I could always ask or call Jerome and Blair, my Blessed Sacrament compadres, right? How difficult could it be?

I may have been in the top tier at Blessed Sacrament, but in truth, I was stupid when it came to new experiences—be they bullies, parties, games, girls, visiting relatives, you name it. I was a follower, not a leader. If I ever did become good at something, it was only after watching someone else do it. I did excel at answering questions, be they oral or on paper—which suited my abilities fine until my freshman year. I was not good at studying, since everything in my first eight years of schooling came easy. My memory of what I would read or observe was good, but when it came to difficult or denser material that needed analyzing, I had little to no practice; I usually only read only what I liked or easily digestible information. That didn't cut it at Jesuit, where everything seemed simultaneously easy and hard.

Not that some courses *weren't* easy—civics was a breeze (thanks to my newspaper reading and my skepticism of communism), as were French (thank you to Cane River and to my natural interest there) and U.S. history (Coach Hardy made it fun). I always was decent at logic, so Algebra made just so much sense. My biggest troubles came in what I believed were shoo-in, sure-fire-A courses, namely English and religion. English started poorly, as our first book to study was Rudyard Kipling's Captains Courageous, which I couldn't identify with, thanks to all the nautical terms and having a spoiled rich kid as the protagonist; I'm not sure I even finished it, the writing was so dull and plodding—which you would expect from a novel written 80 years prior. Judging from my classmates' comments after class, I wasn't alone in that assessment. Theology class was a different story: the priest-instructor seemed somewhat lacking authority (long, wordy answers) and scattered—he always spoke with a smile (as if he knew something damning that I hadn't noticed) and in lectures he seemed to be trying too hard to be "relevant" and "hip", coming across as somewhat insincere. I couldn't make heads or tails about what we were supposed to "know" exactly. One week we'd be talking about Scripture and loving our fellow man, and the next we'd be discussing key scenes in current films (think The Graduate) and listening to Simon & Garfunkel songs (think Mrs. Robinson) for thoughts on modern morality. My grades were all over the place—sort of like my mind—and ranged widely, from Bs to Ds. In both classes, however, my classmates seemed just fine, grade-wise, which alarmed me because it didn't feel as if I was trying to fail. I knew I wasn't dumb, either. After mid-term grades were released, my C- grades made me realize that I needed to try something different; I wasn't learning what was wanted on the exams. So, I identified two or three friendlier, better students and watched them closely in class for a few days. The only difference I could determine was that they weren't just listening to the instructors; they were taking notes—furiously—and not simply watching the teacher. Their notes couldn't have been simply main ideas—that's what I wrote down, and I knew that wasn't good enough. I deduced that they wrote main ideas, but with additional, certain details, material that I'd ignored as instructional blather or largesse by a teacher who liked to hear him/herself talk. And the more you started adding to the main ideas, the faster you became at it, meaning the more detailed your notes became; sure, your notes would be slightly messy—but only you had to be able to read it.

Making this distinction was a revelation—something I'd never witnessed any other students doing before. I'd never been told by a teacher to "write this down". This new method equated to learning to listen, and putting what you heard in your notes, so you'd have much more information to go over when it was time to review. Such a simple concept—how'd I ever miss it? This was the first of many discoveries I'd make that first year. So, I wasn't the victim of bad teaching. Despite my beliefs and prior habits, learning was supposed to be an active activity. It wasn't that people were just naturally smart, regardless of how much they read. And my Jesuit classmates weren't necessarily smarter than me, just more practiced at how to study. Unfortunately, a question then began to gnaw at me: Why hadn't I been taught this earlier? Was this what separated "us" from "them", the missing link? Was it a conspiracy or just a stroke of luck? Was it a "white person" thing, or simply something they learned at their previous schools by chance? What else didn't I know? Either way, there was no going back, not if I wanted to survive among all these white guys.

Such conspiratorial, paranoid feelings were new to me, but I feared that my self-identity as a so-called "smart kid" was under assault from the inferior grades in English and religion classes. Other things happened to fuel my suspicion. Blair and I decided to try out for the freshman basketball team; being part black, we naturally thought we'd blow these white boys off the court with our amazing roundball skills; wrong. Our peers had fundamental hoop talents far beyond what we expected, dribbling, passing, and shooting with astounding dexterity and finesse—they obviously had a lot of prior knowhow and practice. So, Blair, who was over six feet and who dominated our buds at Blessed Sacrament, and I—who fancied myself the next Oscar Robinson or Jerry West, based on nothing but the fact that I watched a lot of basketball on weekends and my brother Duck played in high school—doubled down, using all the jumping and shooting abilities we could muster. A few days later we were told we weren't "in district", outside Jesuit's geographic recruiting pool for freshmen, so we couldn't play in competition, although we were welcomed to continue in organized practice. Knowing the segregated history of high school districting in Shreveport and Louisiana in general, we declined. It felt that the coach was glad to break this news to us. Even if it was true, it seemed unfair that all our classmates in the gym happened to be district-eligible but we weren't. So, we stopped practicing, armed with another nagging question: Why had a school recruited students who weren't eligible to compete in the first place? Typical Shreveport deal, or so it seemed, despite assurances that the rule only applied to freshman sports.

If I'm honest, however, I have been told—as an adult, anyway— that I'm a textbook example of someone diagnosed with Attention

Deficit Disorder (ADD), a person who sometimes has trouble focusing, particularly when it comes to listening. Of course, in the '60s, I'd heard of ADD—it wasn't recognized by psychiatrists until the 1980s—and thought I had typical listening skills. But looking back, I could see that I lacked focus in certain situations. I would stare at a teacher's moving buttocks—male or female—when he/she turned his/her back toward the class and wrote on the blackboard. OK, maybe that's too weird an example; I do remember being the one in class who almost always had to have some portion of instructions restated so I could be fully informed. Or I'd forget a step or two in how to solve a mathematical problem, such as when and where two trains—traveling in opposite directions, leaving their respective stations at different times—would meet. Or I'd start drawing faces, airplanes, horses, Old English letter fonts, or whatever else would strike my fancy during a boring lecture. Occasionally, I'd lose a few class notes or forget to closely read instructions. So maybe my deficiencies weren't created by others; maybe they were just my fault. But don't tell that to a 13-year-old boy who's the apple of his church congregation's eye or who fancied himself the next Einstein.

But I strongly wanted to be accepted and liked, such as the time our civics teacher Coach Robards—in a spark of Christmas spirit— said he would give extra points on the end-of-semester chapter test the next class if we'd bring a Christmas ornament to our next meeting to decorate the small artificial tree he'd brought to the classroom. Of course, he knew some would forget to do so—likely because he was a pioneer detector of ADD—but I worshiped Coach because he was funny, interesting, and he didn't act like the dumb-ass jock like most of our coaches carried themselves. So, I entered brown-nose mode and brought a full box of 12, red ball ornaments that Mamoo let me take from our Christmas decorations stash. Before school for that next meeting, word spread that "Sylvie has a whole box of ornaments! Why don't you ask him?" Ever the entrepreneur, I gave away all the ornaments except one (OK, I charged a nickel for each). Coach was never the wiser, and a good Christmas was had by all—if you took the test in green or red ink, of course. That was a highlight of my first Jesuit semester, rivaled only by the run on the library. Everyone in our library orientation class persuaded almost the entire school to make a trip to library during lunch period one day to check out the most asinine book title he could find because—the excuse we would give to any disapproving adult—we supposedly felt sorry (not really) for Mrs. Bridges, the librarian; she had innocently made a comment one day in class about how quiet the library was most of the time. We wanted her to experience the "other side" of her job, and it was fun watching her continually blow a wisp of her hair out of her face and frequently dab her brow as she busily tried to handle an extremely long check-out line that day; I never had so much fun being devilish. All books were returned the next day, as Principal Father Schilling reprimanded us in a special speech over the morning intercom announcements. But such bonding was a great experience.

Except when it wasn't. The first year I encountered what I expected—the usual, bigoted jerks I had learned and assumed were going to be part of Jesuit life. Most classmates kept their own counsel about race and identity; many classmates went out of their way to make me feel welcome. After all, instead of being an inward-directed search for our places in the world, high school became a game of "Who was going to stop us from having a few laughs in this God-forsaken place?" and everyone participated—at least to a limited extent; we knew we were teen-age boys, and that "tradition" required as much. I never stopped to question such thinking, although identity was forever an interest. But it never ceased to shock me when I ran into racism, which—when I gave it some thought—I automatically classified the perpetrator as ignorant or lacking class in some respects. The words stung, of course, but I quickly rationalized about from where they came in order to not blow my top. For example, there was the East Texas redneck "local yokel" I'll call him, who drove in 30 miles daily from Piney Woods hickdom and who seemed to feel it his birthright that first year to drop the n-word whenever it pleased him—at least until it stopped being funny to his audiences or whenever I would counter with "honky" or "asshole", to which his vocabulary could never produce a novel comeback. His twangy accent and cowboy boots already signaled "ignoramus" to most of us who had real pals in the class, didn't want to be labeled racist, and learned to ignore the bait. Other times, there would be a smartass or two who would use the n-word in casual conversation as a cheap joke, not directed toward me but to the group at large. I didn't have to say or do anything, in such cases; it was understood to be in poor taste and usually followed by a headlock or twisted arm. But I always felt a small piece was aimed at me, thus erasing whatever goodwill I had previously associated with that person. After all, what is an all-boys school without physical comedy? In short, I would tell myself these incidents were my classmates' attempts at jokes, albeit in poor taste, and those in the group would then sort of go through a Three Stooges-style physical pushing and pulling of the offender that let everyone know there would be playful retaliation. I'm sometimes ashamed when I recall such weak-kneed, "go along to get along" responses on my part, but I knew that my classmates knew that I had a sense of humor (after all, I heard jokes from Frenchmen all my life about black people; sadly, this was nothing, new). Besides, I knew the "but I'm a Frenchman" retort would take too long to explain in the moment. It would have helped if Jerome, Blair and I could have compared notes as to how to handle the derision, but that was impossible mainly because we were in separate classes—I in 1A and they in 1B, and they never shared whether they had found a successful strategy. Plus—I can't speak for Jerome and Blair—but I assumed that seeing the three of us together that first year would just give the idiots in the peanut gallery a chance to try to taint the others' brains, so to speak, our three different shades of brown notwithstanding. It helped that my class had confronted racism headlong in a discussion toward the end of a civics class about the spring class party/trip; Coach Robards left, letting us have the room to ourselves. Class President David, a Mexican-American kid who had a black Beatles haircut but was darker than I was and whose official qualification was that he was quarterback of the freshman football team, told the class of a dilemma for the class end-of-the-year blowout: The rural lakeside camp they'd been trying to reserve didn't allow blacks. After the obligatory,

"Sorry you can't go, George" jokes, David asked us what we wanted to do. I didn't even know we were going to have a trip, so I silently listened to a brief discussion, after which we decided by voice vote to try another campsite. This made me know and feel like a part of the group, and I became a little more loyal and somewhat more tolerable about any derogatory remarks I'd hear, aimed at me or not. Besides, because of all our short attention spans I knew the "but I'm a Frenchman" retort would take too long to explain in any moment. Whether this was divine premonition on the part—essentially the split placement of Jerome, Blair, and me made us all akin to "class mascots" who the Jesuit fathers knew would need protection—or whether it was simply a plot to divide our Blessed Sacrament blackness and make two or three new, separate, yet integrated groups, I'll never know. But I and the members of my particular class seemed to have achieved racial détente.

Of course, I realize now that the truce exacted a price. Essentially, I was being peer pressured into saying I was black—which, even if it was Louisiana custom, was only partially correct, per the definition of a Frenchman. And I had no say in the matter, it seemed. At the time, that price didn't seem that high, as it meant everybody "knew" who they were, or at least knew his "place", and, as a result, there was no confusion, and life in the classroom was allowed to continue. I wasn't happy with such a settlement, as I knew the terms weren't entirely accurate and I felt as if I was somewhat betraying my ancestry by not insisting on our historical distinctions between ourselves and the black and white populations; being essentially told you couldn't be who you thought you were because it made things easier for others didn't exactly strike me as fair. Such an arrangement was commonplace, as we had several students who endured such partial labeling—take your pick: Cuban, hicks, Mexican, Chinese, nerds, overweight guys, doctors' sons, no one was safe. In speech class, we even put on a play with each ethnic role played by a guy of the correct persuasion and labeled appropriately "Joe (Ethnicity)", but as I tried to illustrate toward the end of the previous chapter, the will to persist and endure usually followed some struggle and conflict. This persistence is easier when you are 14 and trying to survive the turbulent waters of a unique environment and are battling ADD. There was always the next class to attend, the next opportunity for a laugh or a joke at a teacher's expense, or the prospect of making a new friend or joining a clique. Serious matters, such as self-identity, usually received momentary shrift, and I was more than happy to garner acceptance instead of daily running the race gauntlet.

In matters of identity, the most important characteristics on everyone's list were that you were a regular guy, with no effeminate mannerisms, could talk a good girl game, and you understood girls' place as opposite those of guys. Achieving such identity came easier through the existence of St. Vincent's Academy (St. Vincent), our all-female, Catholic, privately run, "sister school", provider of half our cheerleaders, attended by many a sister, cousin, or girl next door, mostly taught by nuns, and thus the most natural supplier of girlfriends and/or weekend dates for Jesuit students. If sports or playing sports were not your "bag"—a '60s terms for the thing you knew, could easily discuss, or had the most experience with—then "girls" were the default go-to, especially if you were trying to impress your classmates and steer them into thinking you were a guy's guy. There were many other formal connections between our institutions, of course, such as clubs, charitable groups, and fundraising, but socializing ranked uppermost. The only St. Vincent student I knew was Gianna, who later moved out of state the next year. Still, identity talk around the Jesuit grounds centered on how you were "getting along" with girls, usually the St. Vincent kind. If you excelled at such activity, your classmates expected you on Mondays to "spill the details" between classes—an educational duty if you had veteran dating status, or a tutorial benefit of Jesuit if you were a novice. Of course, such information could never be verified, and I imagined much of it included colorful lies; but the stories fascinated me because of my limited experience with girls and the fact that it shed light on my classmates' sense of morality—or lack thereof. "So, *this* is how they act," I thought at the time. Either way, as you might imagine, such stories objectified girls, who were seen as "nice", "skilled", or "easy" while at St. Vincent—according to my source—teen-age boys were graded as either "nice" or "jerks". At Jesuit, the desired goal varied by student; if you weren't a regular guy, you were expected to congregate only with the other "irregulars" and to stay out of the way of everyone else, to avoid potential embarrassment or, worse, bullying.

Honestly, achieving an identity at Jesuit was a difficult, complex task made more involved by the many opportunities the school provided us in the way of athletics, student government, clubs, and the like. I was constantly surprised to find a classmate, or another student had more than one interest. Seniors set the example for such behavior; not only were their experiences listed beside their yearbook photo, but you often would read about their activities (and those of the underclassmen) in the bimonthly newspaper, The Flyer. I also was jealous as most of these activities occurred after school or on weeknights, when I was home saddled with homework or by lack of transportation (I was slave to the bus schedule all four years). By the time we were seniors, several classmates had jobs or carpooled with other seniors. I, on the other hand, never had such opportunities—either through ignorance or not being in certain circles; I simply never knew about most of those organizations until I read the paper or the yearbook. So, I also felt a little mad, feeling as if a secret club society somewhere roamed the school hallways. My anxiety lessened by the time of graduation, as I noticed more chances to gain an identity.

Such opportunities, however, could be physically taxing and lead to ridicule. The Jesuit fathers' no-nonsense discipline could hurt for the simplest offenses—such as the time Brother Blouin, our short, perfectly pompadoured-but-stone-faced "prefect of discipline" (another term for "dictator") that year, caught a few of us on our lunch break throwing chinaberries into a classroom window from a side entrance one day in early fall 1968. We thought doing so would be hilarious, as a lecture was ongoing in the classroom. Brother Blouin disagreed, sending us on our knees on the hardwood floor entrance into his office—for 30 excruciating minutes. My kneecaps didn't recover for two days. And there was the time several of us had to do penance for excessive talking during a boring English lecture; this time we atoned by having to repeatedly subtract 3 from 10,000 (try it!), until we got to zero. Of course, the math didn't hurt as much as the writing and the sheer boredom of repetition. Finally, there was the lunch period in which we all went up to the lunch counter and lied about wanting another serving of something—I recall it as spaghetti or cornbread or both—as a joke on Mrs. C, the cafeteria director who thought the item must have been especially good if it was in such high demand, only to be notified that the plates were coming back to the dishwasher full of the item. Of course, she reported us to Brother Blouin, who assigned us a stay after school helping the janitor clean the classrooms—I didn't mind it so much, because I got to spend time with white-haired school custodian "Chris", who—unbeknownst to the entire student body—was Daddy's brother (nicknamed "Tuff", short for the last syllable in Christophe, and

pronounced "tough") and my uncle, who also didn't think the prank was funny (it was his job to clean up the resulting mess). But he had an especially good time laughing at my fruitless attempts to master the high-speed floor polisher on the first floor of the school; it was like trying to ride a bucking stallion with your arms, which were like spaghetti when I finished my turn and released the handles. Sometimes we weren't too bright in 1A, and the faculty and staff seemed to take great delight in

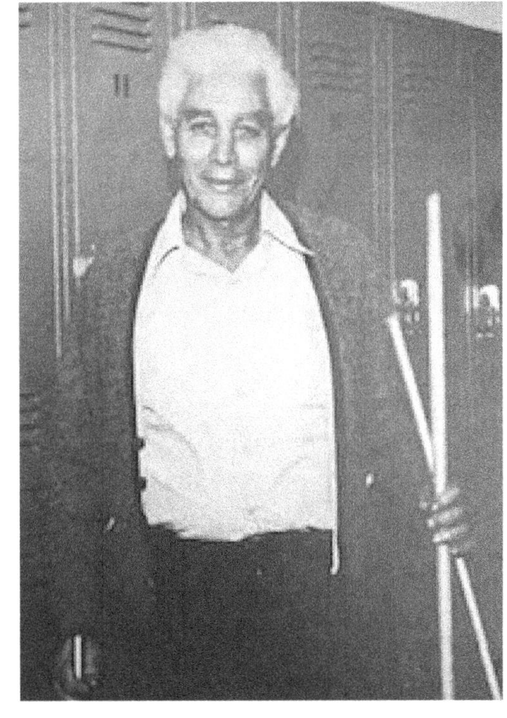

My uncle Christophe Sylvie, aka Tuff, with his Jesuit tools of the trade.

the administration of such practical lessons on the newest corps of Shreveport's best and brightest. Such instruction, however, came in fits and starts as I drifted in and out of the lifelong "liberal arts" revealed by the school's faculty.

THE MAKING OF A YOUNG FRENCHMAN?

Before I dive into the Jesuit curricular lineup, let me say that there's no doubt that I "learned something" from each course, as the readings, exams, and classroom discussions made certain that you had ample opportunity to learn something despite not pushing yourself. Sure, my classmates did their best to block any learning by their joke-laden questions ("Did you get killed?" one future ear, nose, and throat specialist asked our substitute freshman English teacher as he regaled us with anecdotes of his action in World War II), their repeated outbursts ("Drac sucks!" a student yelled from the rear of the classroom when Fr. Welsh—he of cold black hair, extremely pale skin, straight-laced demeanor, all-black priestly bearing, steel-framed glasses, and longer-than-normal incisors—turned his back to write something on the board during junior year-religion), or their pranks (as when a future brick and refractory salesman-turned-actor ranted in senior English about the faults of Henrik Ibsen's A Doll's House in a high-pitched, helium-balloon-induced Alvin The Chipmunk voice). There didn't ever seem to be a dull moment, but several instructors did their darnedest to make us think. Some even taught.

For example, Fr. Keller gave us an appreciation for Hinduism, Buddhism, Islam, Confucianism, and Christianity in our world religions course. No, that doesn't do him justice—he made us understand that the world wasn't as crazy as we thought, that people everywhere wanted answers beyond life, and that everyone throughout history struggled with their worst impulses and even worse rulers. On top of that (and little did I realize it at the time), in our freshman religion course he tried to give us more insight into girls and steer us away from the "regular guy" character or personality that he knew we were beginning to embrace. By introducing us to the concept of "the other", which basically says we think of other people in dual terms, inherently different or alien from ourselves (people like us, and people not like us), he was trying to provide the beginning of a more enlightened—and less selfish—view of girls. Plus, Coach Hardy showed us you could tolerate juvenile speech if your voice was among those heard—his assignment of "cool magazine photos" asking us to help make a wall collage, will always remind me that through our interests everyone is part of a diverse patchwork of people striving for similar things and causes. And by encouraging questions, he showed there was no such thing as a stupid question when it came to the world's push toward civilization. Moreover, Mrs. Kreis, my French teacher for two years, as did Fr. Keller, opened my eyes to a whole different—yet similar world—in France. Not only did the language sound melodious, but somewhat familiar; I could feel the Frenchman inside saying, "Mais oui! C'est plutôt ça (This is more like it!)", as if some kind of freedom had been discovered. She opened the door to a new-but-friendly world that felt like a homecoming of sorts; I had never felt such ease in course material, plus I sensed that the act of being a Frenchman had an entire, long-established, separate culture and people squarely behind it; I wasn't alone, and I was eager to know more about it.

In slowly opening my eyes to wider, ever-different worlds, the school quietly nourished what little curiosity I had. I say "quietly" because it's only in thinking back to that time that some harmless influences come to mind. First, and most obvious, were the two serious friendships that I developed during my studies. Mike, our eventual Mr. Basketball, became a close associate one day in the weight room as we talked about our lives, siblings, and our mutual interests other than basketball, such as Beatles music. And then there was Joe, who must have been the shortest, dorkiest-looking guy to ever wear suspenders, whose love of basketball could only be matched by his lack of athleticism and his big heart, being the only classmate to ever invite me to his house. Those two showed me that some guys had a serious side and were truly interested in getting to know me, that potential connections with others were possible. Another unseen influence, however, was the potential for true friendship and interracial understanding also was limited to vicinity—friendship sprouted when you had space to nurture it. Joe was a regular classmate and lunch-time basketball buddy, while Mike and I simultaneously were on the team for more than a year; they were the only classmates to which I ever began to explain Frenchmen. But the physical structure of the campus was small, consisting of the gym and the main classroom building, surrounded by a large, off-limits grassy front yard and lots of concrete—meaning you couldn't have privacy for in-depth discussion that didn't eventually become a joke fest or a gripe session. And too many lugnut classmates would start gay rumors, just for laughs, if they saw you spending too much time with only one friend; I know because I heard it all the time in reference to the nerds who perpetually hung together. Finally, and somewhat obviously, you had to have a certain capability to make friends, which meant you had to be somewhat self-assured and self-confident—looking back, I doubt that description fit many of the guys. This was compounded by the school's insistence in putting us in thinly veiled academic-ability cohorts that I mentioned earlier.

Despite that structure, however, there was a more normal-but-strange occurrence: Ridicule, in the form of joking, seemed an inescapable fact of daily Jesuit High life as to be pervasive. If a guy accidentally farted in class, that would become the day's running joke. If a teacher unintentionally made you the joke of the class—"Don't be a damn fool," Fr. Horstmann, our balding, slightly cross-eyed biology teacher was fond of saying to wrongheaded behavior—everyone knew it. The hallway exchanges between classes, when we'd all head to our lockers for books, could be brutal and had the potential for tears if the offended guy didn't remember to shoot back with the "single-finger salute," as we called it. This was in addition to the usual class-related slights—getting picked last for a side in physical education (PE), falling asleep (and being awakened by the instructor), walking down the halls with toilet paper stuck to your shoe, having a "kick me" sign on your back, running away from the dissectible car-cass-of-the-week in biology, and the like. Some of you may find such behavior repulsive and highly uncivilized, but, well…boys.

We considered you lucky if you had a "guardian angel," in effect, an upperclassman—often a relative or the big brother of a friend—who would intervene on your behalf in a potentially troublesome situation. That was a great thing about being on the basketball team for a year—I met older guys who considered me a teammate; and everyone knows you look out for your teammates. Sometimes a guy would just take pity on you—such as when Roy, a senior and the quarterback of the football team my sophomore year, took me under his wing during PE, and threatened to hurt someone who challenged my presence on the court; from then on, we were basketball buds. Of course, the football players—particularly the starters—were the school's demigods and usually got their way in most matters. Having the starting QB vouch for me provided a limited special status, my so-called "brush with greatness". My identity was starting to show signs of growth, or, at least, promise. And my feelings for some white guys began to steer toward the positive.

Still, it posed a dilemma: Was all this good feeling undermining my "Frenchmanhood" or my blackness? Without any black teachers, Jesuit made it hard to find like-skinned role models. Kenny—who lived down the street from me and who was also a backup center on the basketball team—and Leon, Mrs. Merchant's son—were the only black upperclassman beacons I knew after freshman year. There were potential others, but they drifted in and out of Jesuit; plus, Jerome and Blair transferred to other schools by junior and senior year, re-spectively. Kenny seemed somewhat reluctantly friendly—he barely spoke to me at school (I was, after all, a year his junior, and he'd gone to a Methodist private school before coming to Jesuit)—and it seemed Leon, a senior, had too many friends to really make time for me. At times, Kenny was so distant, he wouldn't say anything when we passed in the hallways. So, I was never close enough to re-ally pick their brains about "white guys". As a result, by junior year, I was essentially a lone wolf, and I worried about others thinking I was "acting white" because I seemed to be getting along well. I might have been more reflective if we had been encouraged to form a black student club or something similar, but that never happened. In my defense, too, there was little interest in blackness from my teachers, with one exception.

Algebra II was a hard class; no one is born understanding the difference between the sine of x and decongestant spray. And no one understood this more than Mr. Johnson, who'd been named assistant principal and discipline prefect. He was tough, but fair, and understood the teenage boy's mindset. But he did not suffer fools. I forget the prompting remark, but somebody in the glass jokingly mentioned the word "nigger" during one of his lessons. After a few uneasy chortles from the class, Johnson just stared at us, his face ashen as he ran his fingers through his crewcut, his hairy arms turning off the overhead projector, and then folded his football-player-sized biceps across his chest so that they seemed the size of pumpkins. I can't recall the exact words, but he questioned the offender as to whether he thought the remark was funny. "Yeah! We use it all the time," the idiot said nervously. Then the idiot added insult to injury by adding, "Even George thinks it's funny, don't you George?"

"Is that right, George?" Johnson asked, all eyes on me.

"It can be, sometimes," I said, also nervously, realizing as soon as I said it that the gasp I heard came from all black Shreveporters—past and present.

"Well, I don't, and neither should y'all," Johnson said, going on to explain the word's history and serious implications for speaker and listener alike. Then he added that we should all feel shame for laughing. The room turned dead silent as Johnson let the disgust in his body do the talking, waiting about five seconds before returning to restart the projector. Here was a man laying down the law. You could tell he was truly disappointed, which was what really drove the message home. That's the only class we ever left without speaking to one another. It impressed on me the importance of standing up for myself, but also that learning about race was something for everyone, regardless of color.

But the boost from Mr. Johnson wasn't the only help I received. Before I started classes at Jesuit, Mamoo—while attending a parent orientation meeting with Mrs. Merchant—had a conversation with Principal Schilling, a stout, rotund, no-nonsense man on a mission to diversify the student body. She realized that I wasn't as self-confident as most boys my age, and told him that, unlike the practice of many Catholic schools, she didn't want me to experience any bothers about money; Daddy had been a real SOB about promptly paying tuition at Blessed Sacrament, resulting in several personal reminders by the nuns (and even withholding report cards). She didn't want that extra stress to be my burden, to which Schilling promised to abide. Although I knew I was a reduced-scholarship recipient and had several after-school Jesuit jobs, school officials never broached the subject of money to me. Not that I didn't think about it—how could I not as I rode the 7:15 a.m. bus to school every day while my classmates parked their parents' cars in the student parking lot?— but that was a crucial piece of infrastructure in my mind, as I had always been money-hounded by nuns from Day 1 at St. Matthew and St. Mel in Chicago.

Fortunately, I had other types of support from family and friends back at the Blessed Sacrament community. My playmates still came largely from the Frenchmen in town, for which I was grateful, although many were students at Notre Dame—the Catholic diocese's high school intentionally built (with the help of a prominent local Irish family who donated the land) for black Catholic boys and girls in Shreveport. Of course, Jesuit, St. Vincent, and the public schools all competed for some of these students, but most went to Notre Dame, which meant they still were heavily indoctrinated with Catholic theology and nun-instituted teaching. This had its impact, making me slightly self-conscious at times when we'd socialize—I was out of the loop when it came to the popular songs or dance moves, or trends specific to black teens, but I was never ostracized or made to feel as if I was "acting white"; in fact, they didn't show the least interest in life at Jesuit or any signs of jealousy. While it was apparent to me that our respective curricula differed markedly—Jesuit had more specialized or more advanced classes in some areas—teens still were teens: Dating was your prime interest. I spent my final two Jesuit years dating a Notre Dame coed, Valerie, who filled me in on what I was missing: who were the bad and the good teachers, who was dating whom and causing what kind of drama, what were the social activities that I should attend, and so on. The only Jesuit-related line of inquiry I received from my friends or relatives went something like this:

"So, are you still going to the Jesuit school?"

"Yep!"

"You like it?"

"Yep!" or, if I was in a mood, "Yeah, it's all right."

"You want to go with us to the roller rink?"

"Yeah, sure!"

At least that's how I remember. It might have been that they were afraid to look or sound dumb in their questioning, or that their experience with white Shreveport was, at best, limited. But my biggest takeaway from the community at that time was learning the true nature of work—and working hard—every Saturday morning. I'd get up at 6:30 a.m., hurriedly dress, get my lunch that Mamoo would make, and listen for McCoy Roque's stick-shift Chevy truck. McCoy—a sepia-colored, bespectacled and mustachioed Frenchman who was a full-time city signage employee and Blessed Sacrament usher known as Joe when not among friends—noticed the excellent work (for high school kid) I'd done on the church grounds under Mr. Gallion's guidance. Needing an assistant, he asked me if I was interested; the job paid $2.50 an hour (compared to the then-minimum wage of $1.60) and that's all I needed to hear. It was a dirty job—we literally shoveled and densely packed dirt into wooden molds varying by dimension but nearly impossible to lift when full. Twenty to maybe 30 molds later, we'd pour 2,000-degree Fahrenheit melted aluminum into the top hole in the molds to make ornamental iron—fencing, gates, pontoons, lattice garden trellis—products; nothing was off-limits, think valances, castings, finials, even ashtrays. As soon as the aluminum cooled and hardened, we'd open the molds—knocking dirt everywhere—scrub clean the finished product, and transport it to the company's welders who welded and polished the product into work-of-art form for the customer. Our morning wasn't over until we returned the pile of dirt to its prior, beginning state. Not only did the job pay well, but it also taught me about safety, efficient use of my hands, arms, legs, and back that went into mold-lifting, and work habits that I didn't previously have—particularly the pursuit of consistency and a pleasing aesthetic in a product's look and feel. It was also sweaty, dirty, back-breaking work that taught me to appreciate the smell of smoldering dirt, but more importantly, that I didn't want to work with my hands ever again. McCoy and his wife, Marie, became my lifelong friends and counselors. In short, my Saturdays were spent recuperating and looking forward to more abstract tasks; perspective was everything. And working with McCoy provided a ton of perspective, as well as his steady stream of x-rated Dad jokes that proved handy at school the following Mondays.

Learning at Jesuit was no laughing matter, however. Teachers' quivers had the usual arsenal of tests, quizzes, homework, and papers that got progressively rigorous as the semester passed. Instructors' personalities inspired their methods, of course, but some emerged larger than others, making the class—and more importantly, the material—easier to remember. You never questioned grading methods unless you needed to learn how to correct something. Except for Fr. Keller's World Religions course, there wasn't much attention paid to diversity, unless you count some of the Sicilian/Italian that Coach Cicero used in Physical Sciences. Cicero, the longtime baseball coach/manager, called us each "Champ" (so you'd never know if he'd forgotten your name), and weaved his way through human anatomy and mechanics during sophomore year. Jovial by nature, he had several baseball stories to tell, but insisted you master the material; he was sternest with the baseball players in the class, so he had no favorites, and he'd throw an errant eraser in your direction if you gave bonehead answers. In hindsight, much of the material was basic scientific facts about such things as light, energy, and physical force, infused with a fun, playful attitude toward the universe's capabilities. Coach Cicero was, indeed, a champ among teachers.

Normally, if you ask anyone about their high school classroom days, they'll have some wild story, especially about 1 or 2 teachers, or they'll wax nostalgic about "the good old days" they spent day-dreaming or working on a specific project or assignment. My favorite English teacher, Ms. Linzy, wasn't the greatest, most likeable, or funniest instructor. In fact, her attitude could border on disdainfulness or fixed at times, especially if a student thought he was going to trap her into some joking matter or other sophomoric pursuit. It was as if she knew her tight skirt and great-looking legs commanded attention, but you better not get carried away with idol-worshipping or objectifying her. Yes, I did admire her physical bearing—after all, I was 16—but beside the usual repetitive, interpretive appraisals of the boring classics we had to read (Huck Finn, Sister Carrie, Return of the Native, Beowulf, The Canterbury Tales, Madame Bovary) and the analysis of the poetry of Rod McKuen and The Beatles, she encouraged something I hadn't really had a chance to develop: writing. Obviously, the lesson stuck, but the big reason was Ms. Linzy's encouragement via constant writing assignments—descriptive, persuasive, narrative, essay—stuff I had never tried before. Not only was it a challenge, but it also gave me a path to express my thoughts, as well as to mimic styles I'd read elsewhere. It likewise provided my first real opportunity—besides letter-writing my cousins—to *communicate* with another human being in a way other than speaking (at the time I was inarticulate as hell). I could relay the sensory detail—colors, verbs, feelings, tones, and plots that were only in one brain, mine. I imagined Ms. Linzy—after a hard evening of reading the usual bilgewater from the usual knuckleheads—grabbing a glass of Chardonnay, kicking off her heels, placing her feet atop an ottoman, sitting near an end table and mellowing to some Bach as she read my superior work, or so the so-few red comments on my returned papers suggested, with no one the wiser. Seriously, I was serious about pleasing this instructor.

WAS BLIND, BUT NOW I SEE, SORT OF

In stark contrast stood Fr. Horstmann, whose favorite phrase—the notorious and much-copied "you damned fool"—belied his caring nature. Sure, he taught the hard sciences (biology, chemistry, and math), had a laugh to rival that of Bela Lugosi or Vincent Price, and his wire-rimmed glasses, lack of hair, and lazy eye reminded us of "Colonel Wilhelm Klink" on the '60s TV show Hogan's Heroes. But at heart, away from the classroom, he was a gentle soul. One of my jobs was as telephone/office receptionist on certain nights and weekends at "the residence", where each priest had his own private room. Father Horstmann often stopped by the office to chat on his way in or out, occasionally spying on how I was doing or sharing advanced tips on the main course on that night's dinner menu (one of the job's few perks). Of course, he had an impish side as well, such as the time he explained acidity by fooling the class into thinking he had taken a sip from a test tube (he held two such tubes (with us thinking both held urine), dipping a finger in each, using a magician's sleight of hand to make us think that only one finger had been used; the non-urine tube held simple, colored water). Behind the lectern and in the lab, though, he was all business, coming around to each lab table to further explain the assigned techniques while getting a yuk or two from seeing how squeamish we were in handling frogs, cow eyes, and fruit flies. Each time the lesson was to affirm what the book said, but in a much more three-dimensional method. Each lab was an exercise in discovery, communication, bravery, and teamwork. In Algebra, in asking me a question about a formula he'd just written on the blackboard, he discovered I was near-sighted before I even knew (when I replied, "Where is it?").

Self-discovery was harder to come by and—when it did—it was in another aspect of identity separate from race. Sometimes it was impossible, such as in the physics class taught senior year by Fr. Bradley, our newly appointed principal at the time. Part of it was that he had a hearing problem, cupping his ears with his hand while saying, "Please?" (imagine the mileage the class jesters got out of repeating that one word in odd situations; plus, the distraction it presented in the form of the nervous giggles it triggered across the room). But a large part was the material scarcely proved relevant to those of us who weren't mechanics-oriented or were word-minded: It was hard to wrap a 17-year-old mind on the speed of light waves in water, how to use surveying equipment, the amount of material stress in bridges, and the like. Moreover, Fr. Bradley was as bland and devoid of personality as anyone on the faculty. Not only did he not have a sense of humor, but he also was stiff, never drifting away from the overhead projector. Add that to our senioritis and you get the picture. More disappointing, though, was I knew him to be a great explainer of things—again from one of my work-study Jesuit jobs that I had two summers prior to the class. Likely because he himself understood the "how" of things, he was put in charge of renovating the priests' residence's study room—where the priests relaxed, conversed, watched TV, or whatever. Yours truly did the lion's share of the tile and adhesive removal and the painting, as well as helping to replace the tiling in the main classroom building. I knew nothing about how to do these things, but—thanks to Fr. Bradley—I learned by watching and listening to him, and by lots of trial and error; I never knew priests had knowledge about other things besides religion and Mass. Combined with McCoy's backbreaking ornamental iron tutorials, Fr. Bradley was making me into well-rounded handyman, but also a student of human nature by seeing the merits of repetitious action (second coats, grout removal and all) and the satisfaction of a job well-done. For the first time I could see the similarities between skillfulness (from Mrs. Malarcher, my once-a-week art instructor who insisted on experimenting with repetitive, broad, and layered pencil strokes and continuous clay sculpture texturizing) and honest, at times boring and repetitive, and hard work of men, such as Daddy and McCoy, who were artists in their own ways. My self-and racial awareness hadn't progressed much as I reached junior year. But I caught glimpses of future-me from time to time and learned a few things—some even early.

For example, Mamoo developed cervical cancer prior to my freshman year. She did her best to shelter me from the impact, but I felt it nonetheless, from the time that Dr. Sarpy—her physician and first cousin—visited the house to share the news, up to the time of her successful (which was how surgeons termed hysterectomies in those days when it came to cancer) surgery. In between, I worried off and on about what it would be like to lose her, especially with my first year of high school coming soon. Fortunately, Ree and Joey (Ree's then-six-year-old son) came to Shreveport to help during the latter months, with Joey temporarily enrolling in the nearby St. John's Elementary School and riding the bus everyday with me during that time (luckily—again—the school served as a feeder to Jesuit and was next door); in fact, acting as Joey's *de facto* big brother for those two or three months in Fall '68 helped me to largely forget my worries. Still, Mamoo's illness made me try to be as helpful as possible to Ree and Daddy, taking in the early days of Jesuit with a grain of salt and humility, but also by being a little more passive than I might have otherwise been about my identity, and more of an observer of my educational process at the time. In short, whether I should be a Frenchman or black or even white wasn't always foremost in my mind.

This is probably why it took a series of non-school events to bring identity matters more into focus. Let me start by introducing Mamie, a tall, beautiful, pink-skinned Frenchman a year younger than me; she lived with her family about a half-block down (sometimes "up" since it was at the top of the hill) from Cousin Sylvia. If you're starting to see a pattern, it developed because Mamie also was Catholic and a Blessed Sacrament student also in Sylvia's sphere of friends and playmates, as were her brothers and sisters (remember, we Catholics were to "go forth and multiply" in those days). Regardless, Mamie moved on to St. Vincent while catching my eye from the pulpit at Mass those days; she was drop-dead gorgeous, and Gianna had left Shreveport when her family moved up North. However, ignorant me spent months merely gawking at Mamie until one day—coinciding with the Shreveport release of Love Story—somehow, I worked up the nerve to ask her out; I recall thinking the confluence of dating and seeing a romantic drama would provide some heavy-handed hints as to my intentions. Plus, remember we didn't have a car at the time—we were still riding to 8 a.m. Mass with our landlords the Gallions—but Mamie's family had a station wagon, naturally. I can't over-emphasize transportation's role in my life, which was one of perpetual bus-riding and that—in Allendale—the neighborhood was a political afterthought in Shreveport leadership's mind. That meant taxicabs tread lightly there, we had no Starbucks or Baskin-Robbins in which to congregate, much less other places where you could meet with someone to informally get to know them; if you didn't get your point or your feelings across before dark outside, on the street or in a park somewhere, you were out of luck. So, the movie was our first real opportunity—or so I thought, not remembering that at a movie you were expected to largely sit quietly and keep your eyes screenward. Plus, we double-dated with her brother (Jonah, our driver) and his St. Vincent date, meaning there would not be much—ahem—interaction that we could have without disturbing anyone (Jonah had transferred to Jesuit from a seminary earlier that year, making me think this was his way of shielding his little sis from predators, or their mom's idea, take your pick). So, the whole date was sort of more like a group meeting and a comedy of errors; I tried, strategically but unsuccessfully, to hold her hand or put my arm around her. The whole thing made me wonder why she'd bother to come; of course, I couldn't compare to the actor Ryan O'Neal, but I had hoped as much. Did I miss something? In my post-date analysis, I assumed I had, but was clueless as to what. I was so gun-shy that I didn't ask her out again until about a year later, thinking, "OK, maybe she hasn't given up on me entirely." The venue was the junior-senior prom, I had just gotten my senior ring, was feeling special and thus had the will to scrape away the memory of our first encounter. Mamie wore a long green, sparkly dress and had her hair up in a sensuous bun with curls down each side—drop-dead gorgeous. I felt cautiously better about things as we enjoyed dancing to popular tunes covered by two of our instructors and their bandmates (Jesuit spared no expense) and I introduced her to as many classmates as possible. I can't remember if I received a goodnight kiss or a handshake, though, which says something, I guess. Maybe my "vibe" or aura gave off too much of a dorky patina, but I had—for me—a good time, leaving my classmates with the knowledge that I at least knew my way around girls (as if I was saying, "See, I can get a woman, too."). Still, this Frenchman-to-Frenchman thing seemed too heavy to overcome between us; we couldn't really hear each other over the loud music, and I think we were both worried about how we came across—at least I was, given the Love Story debacle. Afterward, our group went to a local Chinese joint for some late-night banter; but not knowing how to extend a conversation made for several awkward silences. I should have stuck to the safe subject of events at or surrounding the prom, but no, I had to try to get to know her right then and there or tried to show my cultural knowledge—not that she was "cold" or whatever, I just came across as the anxious group deviant. I think I wanted to seem "higher class" or bougie, but it felt slightly false and uncomfortable—it felt as if I was too afraid to be myself; I lacked the self-confidence. This dating business was a double-edged sword.

I had similar doubts earlier that spring when I took a car ride with Blair and his uncle one spring Saturday 60 miles east to Grambling College, a historically black college known more for its football program, coach, band, and other athletics than for academics. I thought we just were going for a basketball game, which was to feature Fred Hilton, North Louisiana legend and scorer extraordinaire. But when we got there, we visited a friend of Blair's in the school dorms. It was the first all-black place I'd ever visited and was hopping with coed activities—there was heavy, bass-oriented music, people were walking fast everywhere, and I was getting an eyeful that evening before the game. Blair started to transform his speech and physical mannerisms when we entered the dorm; he had started to comb his hair out to accentuate his growing Afro, his handshake was elaborate with his friend, starting with a high-five and then into a specialized hooking of fingers, something new to me. And there was what we now nonchalantly call "code-switching"—the casual usage of the n-word, again with loud hand slaps, double negatives, and much "blaccent". Blair's uncle—also a Frenchman—and I silent-ly took it all in, as if we were the audience in a show. Blair had more of a black "bent", ever since Blessed Sacrament, but I didn't know it existed to this extent. Yeah, we'd occasionally drop "is" and "are" from our conversation, or place "fixin' to" somewhere in there along the line, but that intentionality was "on speed" in Grambling. Later, at the game, in the college's 1950ish, archaic, barn-like gymnasium, I had the greatest time watching Hilton with those around me as he twisted, gyrated, spun, and quite simply fooled his opponents into awkward defense postures—it was as if I was sitting in a pew at a black Pentecostal church, speaking in tongues about the Holy Spirit, laughing, high-fiving, whooping, and dapping everyone in sight. I had only problem: How was I going to write about the experience to the extent that Ms. Linzy, a white woman whom I imagined had never heard of the NAACP or ever been to Grambling, would under-stand the magnetism for those moments? I doubted her hipness, but I wrote the essay anyway, strategically omitting the "funky details," as you might call them or leaving out the black English. Still, I felt somewhat like a covert traitor doing so, letting the white world dic-tate my words, as if denying the authenticity of the whole trip.

But the Grambling trip was not my only baptism into any kind of established, structurally strong blackness. I still had Blessed Sac-rament on Sundays, of course, and a side benefit, as I've mentioned, were all the mentors and contacts I made. Fortunately, those gains extended to girls, particularly to my first serious girlfriend, Valerie, the Notre Dame High School black coed I previously mentioned. She was short, impeccably dressed, often wore white gloves, and had these almost-luminous (to the point of glowing) white eyeglass frames that made her really stand out. The summer before my senior year, we'd initially just chit-chat after Mass in the parking lot, talking about sports, music, movies, and the like. Plus, I knew from my Blessed Sacrament days that she was a year younger than me, she was incredibly smart, the smartest of her class. Before long, our banter graduated to joking, teasing, and school matters, and I began to look forward to those meetings, finally getting up the nerve to ask her out.

I really liked her sense of humor and her familiarity and similar feelings about things we discussed—particularly when it came to pop music, which we both liked, for example, The Beatles, Carole King, David Cassidy, Bread, Chicago. I thought here was someone unafraid to like or know something about something beyond her own culture. Plus, she hailed from the professional black middle class; her great uncle was principal during the start of integration at the first black high school in Shreveport, while his wife was the first black female teacher in the segregated public school system and a pioneer in helping build Shreveport's black society, otherwise known as "the black bourgeoisie," to locals. Both were civil rights legends in the local black community. They also chauffeured us anywhere we wanted to go; I'd never met a kinder and more gracious couple. I didn't know it at the time, but—to use an antebellum metaphor—I was in "high cotton" when it came to meeting and interacting with Valerie's family. Our courtship would open my eyes to people, events, and experiences I never imagined would exist within Shreveport's boundaries.

Valerie lived in a very modest, wood-framed home owned by her grandmother, Gram, who came across as very loving but somewhat strict, as I was Valerie's first real boyfriend. All requests for outings had to be run by Gram at first. When I'd make the six-block walk on Sundays, however, Gram was lenient enough to allow us alone time in the living room, with an occasional appearance for refreshments. I thought the whole arrangement was a bit ludicrous for the early '70s, but I played along. Anyway, Valerie—besides being cute as a button—was a great conversationalist, especially on the phone weekday nights. It was the first time I didn't have to have a list of questions ready for a discussion with a young lady, even if the whole Gram situation made Valerie come across as being a bit immature or babied to an extent. Still, our nightly discussions were lively and fun, as we each dished out the day's happenings at school, our teachers, and feelings. Much of her gossip would be about who was dating whom, and how that was playing out in Notre Dame life, which included—no doubt because it was a small school—commentary from the nuns about their students' love lives. I paid no attention to it, except shock at its existence and its effect on students who paid it more attention than it deserved. Unfortunately, Valerie was part of that group, although she valiantly tried to assert herself to this one nun, whom I'll call Sister Floyd. This lady—if you could call her that—was super critical to Valerie when she discovered I was a Jesuit student, which Sister Floyd roughly equated to treasonous behavior, frequently beseeching Valerie to find another, more suitable male. I don't know if I wasn't black enough, or because I was a Frenchman or because of class status, or why, but the reports went on for a couple months, climaxing on a fateful night when some relatives and I took Valerie to a Notre Dame—which often used Jesuit's gym for its home games—basketball contest. Unbeknownst to me, the nun was there, too, biding her time to approach Valerie when I went to the vending machines and again give her two cents about my lack of proper qualifications as a boyfriend. I didn't find out about it until we were discussing the game on the way back to the car and Sister Floyd's unethical behavior that night came up, at which point I turned around, heading back toward the gym, ready to slug my first nun; I didn't care about the possible ramifications of an inter-school incident because this was going too far. Fortunately, Mamoo and Valerie held me back and Valerie never mentioned that monster again.

Coincidentally, that also was around the time Valerie had drafted me into her sorority affairs. Besides numerous charity events, the group sponsored civic activities, health fairs, and numerous women-empowering experiences, including recruiting and teaching young members-in-training, of which Valerie had been persuaded to join. This involved the usual volunteer opportunities, tea parties, and "debut" occasions—initial, formal presentations including a fashion show, dances, and culminating in a debutante ball, of course. At the time, I was going through an identity phase involving, of all things, my hair—which, if I'm being honest, never satisfied me. From the tight, curly days of grammar school to the parted days at Jesuit when I couldn't decide which side was better, to what I'll call the "afro-part" combination style I sported when I met Valerie, my hair was a mess. Although girls found it very attractive, it annoyed me because it refused to be neatly corralled and made my head look misshaped, thus having no small role in my identity woes. One Sunday, Valerie and I went to see the 1972 blaxploitation film *Super Fly*, a story about a New York cocaine dealer trying to change his criminal, hedonistic ways and go straight—with the help of one, last, big, heist. The film was not bad, but the hero's hairdo—dynamite: a light-skinned black dude wearing his hair high, straight and long, as to almost look carved. And, of course, it fell into his face—a la Elvis—during his several fights. I fell in love with his hair, to the point of asking for the help of any female I knew as to how to get my curls to respond. Valerie agreed that the hairstyle might suit me and volunteered her hair stylist; long story short—I wore the hairdo for about the next three years—but slightly worried all along to whom the action would classify me as a racial "sellout". I was particularly anxious around all the people I met during Valerie's debutante progression, but especially black males. But everyone was either quiet or approving, never giving me a moment's hesitation about adopting the white man's hair style. If Chuck Berry, James Brown, Nat King Cole, Johnny Mathis, and Duke Ellington could do it, so could I, but I still felt like the Lone Ranger without a tribe. Once again, I felt like a stranger in a strange land, where there's this mysterious dichotomy going in which black people applauded their achievements, but only with black people. Blacks had created an atmosphere to mark and encourage other blacks who had matched or topped the values that whites held in high esteem, with intelligence and training that were highly prized. But they had done so within their own closed groupings that perpetuated inclusion of only the professional class; there was even a nun at the local black Catholic high school misguidedly pushing her own version of divisiveness. I wondered if much of it mattered when Valerie decided to move away to her Northwest roots to get a degree in deaf education. I saw her sparingly thereafter, and never after she started college classes.

Before then, back at Jesuit, things got a little surreal again as we lost a classmate, Rhett, the spring before graduation. He and his girlfriend lost their lives in a car accident on the interstate after a

Me sporting my Super Fly hairdo for a senior yearbook picture.

Three Dog Night concert at the Fairgrounds over the previous week-end. The school put the seniors on a reduced schedule, to give us a chance to digest the details and, if needed, request counseling. I felt the old feelings—how to deal with a person who's there one day and gone the next—about my brother Pete and his drowning return a bit that day, but mostly dealing with the guilt of my mixed emotions about Rhett's death. On the one hand, it's always sad when someone young dies. But Rhett was mostly a prejudiced pain in the ass when I was around him, regularly dropping the n-word, calling the meeker classmates "dip-shit", and mostly because he routinely found a way to lead his threesome over mine in PE basketball. He was quite the athlete for someone who didn't participate in any of the varsity team sports, the MVP of our intramural sophomore basketball champs, in fact. Otherwise, he could be any other quiet, subdued, thoughtful student in the moments when he'd stare straight outward, listening to one of his groupies chatter on about some inane subject while Rhett chewed on the same piece of broom straw he'd been chewing on all day; in those moments, and in the classroom, he didn't seem all that bad a guy. But was I going to miss him? Hell no. Did that make me a horrible person, or just a racist one? Was it OK to not miss a racist who dies a tragic death?

I didn't give it much thought, but, as with everything else, the answer was probably something in-between. Just like the feeling I had on graduation day, the ceremony for which was held downtown at the Convention Center. I had looked forward to this day for four years, through all the ups and downs of crass remarks, academic achievements, good and bad teachers, proms with two different girls, gradually improving study habits, greater appreciation for my Blessed Sacrament family, and much more than I have time or space to list. Now it was time to ask: What's next? What should I do with my life? Scary questions, for sure, but no scarier than the transition to Jesuit. As the only dark-skinned person to survive the hurdles and tribulations, I certainly was proud—with National Merit Finalist and Attendance Award-winner at the top of my resumé. I certainly could ride the damn bus by myself. But I still had doubts as to what awaited, particularly as my parents had no money to send me to college; I was going to have to get there on my own. There wasn't any big graduation party for me, and no classmates mentioned any celebrations; I wound up watching The Godfather that evening with Ree—great film, but still a letdown from all the prior buildup surrounding graduation. That's probably because my collegiate snooping consisted only of reading catalogues and wondering how much was true. I had applied to the local private college, Centenary, but they offered little in the way of financial aid. As a National Merit scholar, I received many inquiries and potential offers flowed via mail, but I had nagging doubts about leaving home simply for the sake of that being what people expected; what did *I* want? After Jesuit, I knew that college was what you could make of it, not just the allure of ivy and Saturday afternoon football. Many of my classmates—especially those with science and

business pedigrees—were headed to LSU, Tulane, and big, prestigious schools. But I wasn't like them—I wasn't sick of my parents, I
simply wanted to get away from any more mental comparisons with
Jesuit guys and go where I could be anonymous. Daddy wanted me
to look hard at offers from the service academies, but I got a taste of
systematic discipline at Je-
suit and found it unbear-
ably macho and slight-
ly mean-spirited. And I
liked being at home—I
had a girlfriend (Valerie
had her senior year still to
go at Notre Dame), a new
stereo player I had just
bought, almost enough
savings to buy a used car,
was still rocking the Super
Fly hair, and was enjoying
life in general, if I didn't
think about anything for
too long.

As the search for my-
self had only recently
started, I knew I still had

My woeful senior graduation picture, taken in 1972.

time to figure out things regarding careers. Since Mr. Johnson was
my favorite teacher, I used him as a model for my college applications, suggesting that I wanted some kind of math or science teaching career. Not really a bad choice, because I loved the precision and
the mental gymnastics that math required and I loved the man, Mr.
Johnson; still, the choice of major wasn't something I felt strongly
about, either. Despite obvious overtures from Mamoo and several
others I knew at Blessed Sacrament, I categorically quashed any rumors or inquiries about becoming a priest. Besides, without saying
it aloud to anyone, I liked girls too much and didn't want celibacy or
additional all-male schooling in my future. I had received a broad,

well-rounded education at Jesuit, but perhaps it was too broad, as I found too many things to be interesting as to for a future occupation. I couldn't see myself like Duck, who was building a family and working in a wax production factory, or Ree, who was busy raising Joey and working at a clerical job for a health insurance conglomerate. And, using my hands like Daddy, McCoy, and a lot of other people was out, if I could help it; unfortunately, that was the life I knew many—if not most—Frenchman males pursued after high school. Or they got married and found a job later; but I was nowhere near ready to settle down with anyone, much less Valerie, who had her own, definite career aspirations. And I didn't know anyone in the professional world except Mamoo's physician and my second cousin Dr. Sarpy, but medicine struck me as something that you needed an aptitude for, a strong stomach (in order not to faint at the sight of blood), and you had to really have a head for science, which I didn't, as evidenced by the D+ I earned in physics. But none of the college applications or catalogues gave a definite cultural sense of attachment. There were no descriptions that so much as said, "If you're a Frenchman, go for this major." If I wanted something easy, I could major in English, I thought, but that would mean a lot of reading Shakespeare and other authors I hated at the time; the mature part of the decision was that there was little to no job market for English teachers. Plus, teaching never paid much, but science teachers were among the highest in demand, especially as computers became trendy and people saw their value in the working world.

So, my goal was to have some kind of professional job that paid decent money and interested me enough to keep me going for a while—not what the Jesuits intended as a motto for their school publications, I'm sure, but the best criteria I could foresee at the time. Besides, what 18-year-old knows how to go about tackling society's great issues and ills while simultaneously making a livable wage? Nixon was running for re-election, people were tiring of Vietnam, four college students had been killed in Ohio, The Beatles had disbanded, and the Dallas Cowboys won the Super Bowl, so how could I have any answers? Instead, I did the only thing I knew to do: to continue pushing, just as I did after Pete died, and to hopefully have my eyes opened by the whims of chance.

I was not looking forward to choosing a path. Being wishy-washy was beginning to feel more and more comfortable. College and the '70s had other ideas.

4

Real-World Problems

Ever the "safe decider", I chose to go to college at tiny little Louisiana State University in Shreveport (LSUS)—cheap, small (only 1,500 students and two classroom buildings), and nine miles away from Allendale. Best of all for me, the school had said I would qualify for financial aid, in the form of grants and a semesterly work-study program such as what I'd had at Jesuit, except I'd get paid. And the school had just that year been upgraded from a junior college to four-year status, a move that attracted an additional 400 students the fall that I started. As a bonus, I'd been assigned a full-time summer work-study job. Mamoo was delighted and Daddy, though not thrilled that I stayed home, was happy that I was working.

The job was with other college students and would entail some unique skills for one of the little-known federal government "action" programs—emanating from the national Civil Rights Movement fallout—dedicated to improving local economic conditions in the Shreveport metro area. The umbrella organization mainly ran Head Start, a federal program for kids up to 5 years old to nurture early learning and development, health, and family well-being by encouraging parent and family participation—like a kindergarten primer for kids, most of which were black. Of course, there were other "actions" that the agency ran, including job-training services, health-related assistance, adult literacy—things badly needed in American minority communities then. I was assigned (with three other collegians) to the Cooper Road community—a ghetto-est ghetto in Shreveport—services facility the summer before college. I was somewhat familiar with the area as Uncle Tuff and his family had resided there for years, and I had visited and played there many times. As far as I knew, it was just another normal neighborhood with mostly black families.

Politicians occasionally tried to indirectly meddle with the program throughout its early history, mostly around the issue of who would represent the community on—what else?—its governing board; they wanted to determine who would decide how all that new, federal money (more than $1 million, akin to $7 million today, but slowly being cut by D.C. Republicans) would be spent. However, the real "action" happened at the neighborhood level, where I was hired as a "program aide," a fancy term for intern/grunt worker who helped implement programs. I was one of four college students hired, the others came from Grambling (Shirley), Louisiana Tech (Donnie), and Southern University's Shreveport-Bossier (SUSBO) campus (Ollie Faye). We were all beginning or midway through our freshman years, so we knew next to nothing about community work; Ollie and Shirley knew the neighborhood best; the SUSBO campus sat squarely on the Cooper Road and Shirley lived in the area when not going to school.

We were met at the center by Hugh Bradford, who oversaw all the program's neighborhood centers. He was a tall, thin, athletic, goateed black man in white jeans and tennis shoes; he could have been mistaken for any high school coach. He gave us the usual spiel about job requirements and said we'd be spending most of our time outdoors, mostly at a nearby park as well as surrounding neighborhoods. Then he introduced us to the black ladies who ran things, including Mrs. Eulalia Francis, a congenial, dynamic woman who seemingly knew just about everyone in Cooper Road and who was the center director. There also was a lawyer (Mrs. T) and a counselor (Ms. G) there. Before long, though, Mr. Bradford whisked us away to the park that essentially would become Ground Zero for the interns and where we'd learn the most about the neighborhood.

But I'd be remiss without mentioning how I'd get to the job every day, which paints an interesting story about that neighborhood itself. I'd been able to save most of the money I'd earned on the job with McCoy and combine it with the money from relatives congratulating me on graduating from Jesuit. The resulting $650—about $5,000 today—bought us our first car, a used 1965 navy blue, standard-shift Chevy Impala; to 18-year-old eyes it looked like a well-conditioned tank, with bucket seats and a roomy back seat. I was ecstatic but, of course, the bus rider that I was, I knew nothing about driving, much less driving a standard shift; Mamoo and Daddy did all the negotiating, assuring me they'd get us a good deal. Daddy would later teach me how to drive a standard; meanwhile, Mamoo was the sole driver, primarily driving to her work as a maid and, eventually, driving me to my college classes. Back to Cooper Road: I couldn't take a bus there, since none served the area (and would not for another five years or so until Shreveport annexed it). Plus, Mamoo's job was in the complete opposite direction, meaning she'd have to drop me off downtown on those days that I had to leave early for work. Otherwise, I'd bus to downtown to what we called the "jitney stop".

A jitney usually is a small bus of some kind, which usually meant of the Volkswagen kind or a variation thereof in the early '70s. There were a small number of locations that such buses would call their originating stop, usually an abandoned store front or—if the stop was part of a multi-stop system—a repurposed small business site. The jitneys charged a cheap amount—usually a dollar or two—and I'd find whatever jitney was heading to the Cooper Road area next. On any given day, the jitney would carry anywhere from 4 to 7 passengers other than the driver, each rider going somewhere in the same general neighborhood or vicinity. The trip would usually take 30 minutes or so, and on the way, you'd meet nice folks—most coming from working a graveyard shift in the city or heading to the few Cooper Road area businesses. Not the same as the bus, but jitneys got you to where you wanted to go. And the places you would go—I saw homes that I wouldn't sell to my worst enemy: dilapidated porches, weeds for grass, dogs roaming inside worn or downtrodden fences or small kids playing on dirt driveways, makeshift drainage ditches running parallel to the street, and very seldom a new car—if a car at all. It made Allendale look like an upscale, middle-class haven. Not understanding racial politics at the time, most times I couldn't help but stare and wonder if my (young college student) presence would create any embarrassment or feelings of shame in the deboarding passenger. At home, it never felt as if Mamoo, Daddy and I were poor; but Cooper Road showed me that there were many manifestations and levels of poor—no wonder the federal government was trying to take "action" when it came to poverty.

But I never viewed the job as carrying any sense of some charitable intervention of any kind. If nothing else, Mr. Bradford—whose bachelor's degree and prior experience was in physical education (and thus explained his amazingly great shape for a man of 45, which the interns unanimously categorized as "old")—made sure we knew we were there primarily to help the area's kids have fun. He dropped us a couple miles away at David Raines Park, a then-sketchy-looking park with barbecue pits, picnic tables, some basketball courts, lots of trees, unmown fields here and there, and an odd group or two hanging around open cars that seemed up to no good. And he left us there with a duffel bag full of sports equipment, and some sign-in sheets of paper and a pen. "Y'all pass these things out to the kids, and I'll be back in a while," he said, jaunting back to his car.

So, our routine normally would involve a visit to this park, situated off one of the busier roads in the area but backing up to a newly developed neighborhood. We didn't know it at the time, but our bosses were amidst planning an expanded facility there that would include a Head Start program, a health center, a swimming pool, a gymnasium, meeting rooms, offices, picnic shelters, tennis courts, and walking trails; so, in a sense, we blazed the trail for that scenario. In our visits, we most often interacted with teens and, later, younger kids. We'd try subtly to discourage loitering at the park and would help "referee" any contests that participants would start, to foster sportsmanship and skill development. Normally, Donnie and I would take over refereeing duties and occasionally interrupt for teachable moments. Shirley and Ollie would encourage game-playing—Mr. Bradford eventually added a trove of card and parlor games to our duffel bag. It wasn't all idyllic and benign doings, particularly for Donnie and me; neither of us were athletic nor menacing-looking enough to scare away would-be thugs, especially with our "college boy" credentials. Usually, we'd turn a blind eye to the usual glue-sniffing that occurred or challenge the potential offenders to a game of basketball—not always successfully, but to the point that we got to know most park visitors over the summer.

But there was work to be done before reaching that point. One of our immediate supervisors—whom I only recall by the name of Mr. W., a tall, stout, bespectacled but extremely athletic Grambling graduate who thought he knew everything we didn't—took over the daily duties from Mr. Bradford and early that summer sat us down around a conference table to explain a project. Up to that point, he'd been mostly concerned with getting the kids into team sports. There was a problem, however; the baseball field wasn't suitable for anything remotely resembling that sport. So, Mr. W bought some shovels for us and announced we'd be creating a baseball field, by fashioning running paths between the bases. I wish I could say there's nothing better than digging up weeds in North Louisiana in June, but I'd be lying. So, the interns bonded—among other things—in our general dislike for and distrust of Mr. W., especially since he seemed to have a roaming eye on Ollie and Shirley. But, in contrast to his hopes for the baseball diamond, his planned project had its merits.

First, our service center wanted to show what it could do: serve the community in a big way. So, we interns would do some door-to-door canvassing of the various neighborhoods surrounding the park. We surveyed the residing adult (usually the mother) of the neighborhoods' homes and—if kids resided there—question the adults about the likelihood of their children participating in a week-long park event featuring games, art, face-painting and other age-appropriate, entertaining-but-educational pursuits. The center would provide transportation to and from the park. Second, for a few hours in the morning, the event would give the adults/parents some alone time for other activities, errands, or whatever they needed while their kids enjoyed and gained supervised, recreational and education experiences—a "school away from school" for a week in the summer. What normal, overworked adult would turn that down? Third, from our viewpoint, it gave us some inkling of what the home life of our primary clients—the kids—was like, to better understand and serve them. What we saw would be about what you'd expect to find in poor homes: A living room filled with a couch and an armchair or two; a TV loudly showing cartoons, game shows, or soap operas or a radio blaring gospel or rhythm & blues music in the background; a mother (or grandmother) still wearing her robe, curlers, and slippers; children (when not on the couch watching TV) running around—inside or outside—playing with the assorted toys (or makeshift household objects that served as toys) scattered on the floor; and the smell of cigarettes, coffee, or both. The adults often mistook us for the mailman or Jehovah's Witness recruiters, sometimes wouldn't let us in—guiding us to some porch chairs or only slightly opening a crack in the door—and seemed cautious about being questioned by college students holding clipboards and paper. They had a non-committal smile and wanted to know more than once "Just who y'all work for, now?"

At first, we thought the whole exercise was going to be easy because we were promising something honest and fun to the community, but by the end we were glad when our knocks wouldn't get answered. We had gotten wary of their wariness. Aside from the obvious lack of trust in door-to-door pitches, these people rightfully were skeptical about anything having to do with government or the word "free". At first, all four interns would approach a house; later, we split into two gender-based groups to more quickly cover a block or a neighborhood. But we gained some insight: For example, "poor" doesn't necessarily mean "poor judgment". While we gleaned personal info (phone number, number and grade level or age of kids), the adults were checking *us* out as to not just our employer, but details about the event, who was going to watch the kids and when would they be home, where we went to college, what we were studying, who they could call for more info, and why my hair was so long ("Don't you get hot with all that hair under your hat?"). Personally, I learned that you needed to converse with adults (regardless of their color), especially if you wanted to gain their trust. A sense of humor helped, so did speaking the prevailing lingo (hey Jesuit dude, we code-switch when we're talking to our people) and, particularly, showing respect no matter the condition of the house or the yard or the clothes the kids wore. Although Mr. W drove us to these neighborhoods, he never was much interested in the results, since the idea was really that of Mrs. Francis, who was overjoyed to have all that info to help her plan the event. If we had known she was the one who wanted the data, we might have tried harder to get more kids recruited. Still, the event went off without a problem, drawing three or four buses full of happy, excited, and boisterous kids who proved that if you build it, they will come, even to an understaffed, underdeveloped neighborhood park.

The entire Cooper Road experience brought home a few lessons. First, after four years of attending a predominantly white institution in Jesuit and seeing it execute its mission at a highly effective level, I discovered the same could be said for a black organization—and not just a religious or educational one. The service center, as run daily by Mrs. Francis, performed admirably, holding many social, educational, economic, legal, health, and administrative courses and meetings in its little building, in addition to the various public facilities in the Cooper Road area. This resulted from tapping into a dedicated, trained, certified and empathetic staff that truly cared about its mission. I saw first-hand that whites had no monopoly in knowing how to get things done. Moreover, I could see the competence and dedication in other black college students who used their mental and physical resources to deliver services to young people and heighten their expectations of their community; things got done through will power and dedication. More importantly, we used our organizational, planning, interviewing, and motivating skills to enable kids to see what a park could mean, and that there were behavioral expectations of patrons, regardless of whether they lacked the prior wherewithal, experience, supervision, or even family to know what to expect. Despite the inequality of the surroundings of these patrons—whether young or adolescent—we persevered and put the service center on the intellectual "resource maps" of many people we encountered.

I imagined our work as akin to that of a domestic "Peace Corps" of sorts; it wasn't two years but a little more than two months of preparing, organizing, staffing, surveying, teaching, babysitting, and encouraging people to get to know and see how to improve their area. I was not treated any differently from the other interns, although you could tell this light-skinned, long-haired brother had to jump through linguistic, physical, and cultural hoops before he gained full acceptance. Mrs. Francis, our de facto "job mother", laughed, cajoled and pushed me as hard as she pushed Ollie, Shirley, and Donnie, although I was "the black hippy" of the group; authentic authority to me translated into "black female"—no offense to the office men, but they were invisible that summer. Riding the jitney everyday gave me an appreciation of the lengths that black people would go to make a living to support their families; I also learned to appreciate the air-conditioned city buses. Most of all, I gained a more nuanced empathy of the black experience, the long-tread process of climbing up from massive and prevailing victimization to honest parity and economic improvement, no matter how small, although it was clear that blacks had to work harder than whites to get there. This didn't make whites evil, just privileged. And although I didn't foresee it, I felt blacker than ever as a person because I was treated as such. I never mentioned my Frenchmanhood and no one gave me an Ebonics test; as at Jesuit, my environment categorized me without asking me what I was. And I was too busy doing my job than to take the time to correct anyone. Besides, at this point, most of the Frenchmen I knew simply accepted black culture as part of life, for that was the predominant culture of our surroundings and the culture that largely accepted us as part of its own. So, the transition to working in the service center and in the Cooper Road area was almost seamless.

Making the move to LSUS was just as smooth in the first semester. Academically, it seemed no different from Jesuit; my courseload consisted of largely familiar territory—English composition, algebra/trigonometry, speech, and French. Jesuit-style joking had been replaced by adult seriousness, especially considering many students worked part- or full-time and their academic success meant more, whether it entailed a precursor to career achievement, or a ladder rung up from a previous occupation. Walking around campus, many of the folks who I had assumed were teachers were students seeking a second career, occupational promotion, or second act after early retirement. Many older students usually took the mythic prize of "best student in the class" and added great context—and no small amount of angst to many students whose main goal was having classes end early—to certain class discussions. Learning—unaccompanied by any semblance of immaturity—took a backseat to nothing; in fact, it wasn't unusual to hear summer-only students from LSU-Baton Rouge say they had never had such hard courses in Baton Rouge. Of course, that wasn't exactly the case, as you could find some bad teachers if you tried; the school was so new that there was a group of freshly graduated doctorates who essentially were experimenting as teachers or still trying to find their niche. There was one potential plus, albeit possibly only to St. Vincent and Jesuit alumni—the coed environment: real, live girls sitting next to you in class! Of course, their presence could result in additional stress, depending on how your dating life progressed. Socially, the biggest drawback was the relative absence of traditions or any extension of "campus life", since most students abandoned the small campus around 1 or 2 p.m. every day to return to work or whatever regular diversion they had. You were lucky if you found any upperclassmen who could mentor you. The campus was surrounded by a circular driveway, which meant traffic jams—this was before the ecological movement, when the ratio of students to cars was nearly 1 to 1—for 9 a.m. arrivals and early afternoon departees. The latter and LSUS' newness meant dreadfully little in the way of student clubs or groups and what few student government-associated organizations that existed probably reminded too many students of their high schools or bad high school experiences. But every drawback had its silver lining: Afternoons were great for studying (particularly in the library) or completing assignments and made it easier to make friends or visit profs in their offices (the school mandated one-per-term visits to your major advisor/prof about your career/schedule plans). I quickly latched onto a spades-playing cadre of black students in the "snack shack" a three-temporary-building solution that served as a coffeehouse/gathering place, lunchroom, bookstore, and vending machine hub; the custodian there, a black lady we all called "Ms. Odessa" became a surrogate mother figure/confessor to many over-caffeinated students. Probably the shack's best feature was its jukebox, which played Elton John's Tiny Dancer or Levon too often. Still, the afternoon quiet and the shack's lack of ambiance did occasionally make me wonder if I had made the wrong choice in schools.

Oddly enough, respite again came in the form of my new work-study job, in the school registrar's office. I say "oddly" because I just thought it would be some "go-fer" type job, or filing or something dreadful or boring. Even the words "registrar's office" sounded boring, reeked of administrative hell, as in the department of motor vehicles. The first few days *did* seem somewhat of a dead-end, as most of what I did involved filing transcripts, the central form that held a cumulative record of each student's grades. Don't get me wrong: There was some-

Still sporting long hair, here I'm entering the LSUS Office of the Registrar.

thing cool and devious about knowing how well some people were coming along, grade-wise (of course, I didn't let anyone know this was what I was *really* doing, although you'd be an automaton if you didn't occasionally glance at some of the records). But that exercise could carry only so much excitement. More challenging duties included answering the phones, but at first all I could do was announce the office's name, place the person on hold, and listen while a full-time clerk fully answered the inquiry; it took a while before I knew the ins and outs of the office.

I learned as much from the staff, which was smoothly run by a duo of white, middle-aged, beehive hair-styled women I would come to love: Mrs. Graham and Mrs. Booras. They ran the records and the admissions areas, respectively, and had been with the office from its start. This meant not only college transcripts, but keeping high school transcripts, recommendation letters, standardized test scores, course registrations (and, subsequently, requests for course drops and adds, resignations and dismissals), all graduation and registration processes, student IDs, military admits, and course schedules. They also had to perform *ad hoc* advising whenever a student had a request, no matter how irritated, privileged, illogical, or cantankerous the customer or the request; that necessity usually stemmed from the amazingly little amount that students bothered to read the school catalogue. Both ladies had abundant reservoirs of common sense, were extremely patient, and their styles bordered on deliberate, nurturing and easy-going. This was particularly the case when it came to my dealings with them.

For example, landing at LSUS, I thought I was a prize catch—a Jesuit High grad, National Merit Finalist, receptionist, altar boy, math whiz, etc.—but I simply was an unpolished kid from Allendale who'd been taught by religious instructors all his life and who still hadn't learned to drive. I was unfamiliar with how college really worked. Mrs. Graham recognized this early on; under her direction and tutelage, I began to see connections between preparation and results. For example, early on she handed me off to another supervisor who showed me how to run an offset press, which published the office's semesterly tentative course schedule right before pre-registration. I began to see how old-fashioned keypunch cards figured in the grading system, the depth of the involvement of the faculty, and every exception or loophole in the process that you could imagine. It wasn't as if she sat me down and womansplained everything to me; no, she would throw me to the wolves, I'd come back with a problem, and she'd send me off again to the person with the best answer; so, she "farmed" me out to do as many tasks as possible in the office. Because of the office's reach into the academics of the university, I got involved in the accreditation process, working with another student to calculate classroom and technical space. I learned about the public information and library functions, as well as about faculty governance's role in the catalogue, and the power of the registrar's office in university affairs, particularly course offerings. In addition to becoming my own little reservoir of LSUS data, I learned much more, in terms of my personal development, which I will address later in this chapter.

The impetus came as I learned more and more about the facts behind being a math major. First, becoming a mathematician or math teacher meant much more than taking math-oriented courses. Math majors had to take a computer science course; at the time, this meant learning how to *program* a computer to get it to do what you wanted. They might as well have enrolled me in a foreign language course, as learning Fortran—a combination of English and math equations—is ideal if you're working on engineering problems or running math simulations, nothing I ever intended to do. So, I dropped the course immediately after the first exam so I could save myself some embarrassment, learning that I should research a course before blindly enrolling or following an advisor's advice (although my instructor later lamented to me that my exam answers had given me a decent score). Compounded—do you like that math speak? —with my foray into Calculus (I can't remember if I got a D-plus or a C-minus) in my first spring term, and I started getting an uneasy feeling about my math-making plans. The year 1973 wasn't getting off to a good start and although I was enjoying my registrar gig, making $1.60 an hour was beginning to be a problem because I had gotten wise to how the market for college books worked: They start out expensive and they spiral up from there (imagine paying $50 ($378 in today's dollars) for a dictionary for an English class in which you never used it), if you catch my drift: In short, many people might say it's a racket; I prefer "never-ending escalator". Making $1.60 an hour wasn't much help; I needed to make more money.

This resulted in a trip to sweet home Chicago the following sum-·mer, when Duck and Ree pulled some strings and secured jobs for me—first at the small, South Side wax factory where Duck was the loading dock supervisor and next about a mile southwest of there at a Fulton Market Meat District meatpacking plant. Neither job lasted more than six weeks, but both added to my repertoire of "places I never want to work for again". The country was in the throes of infla-tion—thanks to rising energy and food prices and Nixon Adminis-tration regulations—and I was probably ill-prepared for either task. At Yates, one of the four wax companies in the U.S. the that provided wax castings for parts for dentistry and the foundry industry (Mc-Coy's job field, oddly enough), I had to mainly master two things: handling a forklift and mixing colored paraffin pellets. Neither came easily. The forklift I could drive rather well—just like a golf cart or something similar. The difficult part came in navigating tight spots in the warehouse, putting the lift's two prongs—the two, long, flat "forks"—into the slits in the bottom of the recycled wooden pallets that carried several bags of the paraffin or resin. After mistakenly slitting several bags, instead, I was quietly moved to the mixing de-partment, where I had to carry the 50-pound bags to an open-air, industrial-sized kettle, wax melter, pot, or cauldron—call it whatever you want—that had a scaffold on which I stood and from which I dumped the bags' contents. Finishing the job, I used a long, wooden stick to mix in the pellets. Easy, but back-breaking work, and the recession forced the company to lay off a small few of us about six weeks into the job.

Fortunately, Sam—Ree's husband—got me another manual labor job at the meatpacking plant. We rose at 4:30 a.m., and after break-

fast traveled to the Fulton District, home of several meat-related pro-
ducers. My main task consisted of taking a metal "hook"—it was a
small, rounded wooden handle with about a three-inch hook about
midway—and when the refrigerated sides of beef (commonly called
the "brisket" or bottom breast-shoulder part of a cow's side) arrived
at the loading dock in a truck, I would empty the truck by "hooking"
the briskets and tossing them to a co-worker who hung each side
vertically onto a multi-hooked metal cart or linen-covered basket.
The cart/basket was then lowered onto the actual loading dock and
rolled into the ice-box climate of the bloody-and-entrails-filled cutting room of the highly paid butchers, which included Sam. They
then would carve the brisket into various desired parts shipped to
local or regional meat markets or grocers. Occasionally, I'd deliver
some of the less-than-prime parts by foot down the block to a place
that made, among other fine delicacies, hot dogs; read into that what
you will. Again, the job was phased out and I was laid off, leaving me
little time to find another one before fall term started.

I took enough money back to Shreveport, though, to help buy
some new clothes, a couple albums, and textbooks. More importantly, I learned to even more appreciate non-manual labor and the fact
that my future college degree would help me avoid such jobs. Most
guys that I got to know in my few Chicago working days seemed to be
amidst a string of such jobs, as the usual after-work activity included
a trip to the local, corner tavern—of which Chicago has thousands—
to have a cold one or shoot a couple games of relaxing billiards. I sort
of felt sorry for them, although I wasn't sure why, perhaps because I
knew I was there only temporarily. Or maybe it was because many
of them gave off immigrant or ethnic vibes (my first time meeting a
black Puerto Rican). Or maybe it was the bloodied white coats they
had to wear, in AC or heat. Their lunch opportunities left something
to be desired, usually consisting of last night's leftovers (eaten most
likely as a cold sandwich, given the pre-microwave days), or a warm
sandwich served with fries from the corner deli restaurant, which
also served breakfast and donuts before work started. Such a diet was
a great way to put on weight and cynicism, as most of the day's banter

consisted of sarcasm aimed at some local councilman, the governor, and/or Nixon. And, of course, sexual-related jokes also made the rounds. In a larger context, it seemed that many of the Frenchmen I had known before were all busy working, raising families or finding larger, more affordable housing; work left little time for visiting or for learning much more, aside from eating, shopping or movie-going. What faith I had in the economy, and business in general, was slightly shaken with the shifting job market—why were my people even moving up North, I wondered?—and cemented by my last, one-day stint, as a contracted apartment crew assistant doing temporary repair on ceilings (I learned, again, oddly, that you could use newspapers as a temporary stopgap for a ceiling material until the painters came) that needed electric rewiring. I got $25 and a stiff back—ever work with your arms up the whole day?—for my eight hours of trouble and, not surprisingly, never received the promised call back from the foreman. I finally saw Chicago as the economic engine that my ancestors had envisioned, albeit with a little faded luster, and realized that growing up wasn't going to be the fun it had been in my earlier days. Making money was serious business, something to which I needed to start applying sober planning. Had I stayed at the wax factory, my view might have been substantially different. The Yates employees sort of reminded me of the medics and related staffers of the TV show M*A*S*H—war could be hell, yes, but that didn't mean that the *job* of war had to be hellish. There were only 45 or so (mostly) men who worked there, and everyone seemed to be having, if not a good time, a playfulness about them. I don't know if it was the fact that the place was run by Uncle Doc (my cousin's dad) and my relatives (Duck, and cousins Charles and Bootsy were the three day-shift supervisors), or if there were few non-Frenchman or non-black employees, but Yates seemed to embody a collective effort that was somewhat jovially executed. Perhaps the small staff nurtured a closeness not found at the meat yards, but it did seem that everyone knew everyone else and usually had a wisecrack to add in passing. I recall one guy asking me if I was a Frenchman, too, using that exact term. Things at Yates were often serious, but I also remember one of the floor supervisors more than once jokingly having to say to a crowd of two or three workers, "Break time's up. Get y'all's asses to work." This attitude certainly could have trickled down from my cousins. But I bore no ill will to my meatpacker colleagues; getting up at 4:30 a.m. every day to handle beef seemed to have had a numbing effect on me, until at some point I started thinking about the cattle, and what they had given up by being there. Before I had given it too much consideration, the job was over.

Although returning to campus that fall felt freeing, I was imprisoned by most of my courses. My advisor had scheduled me into some rough mathematical company—Calculus II, linear algebra, physics, and physics lab—and a breather with the second part of U.S. history. I won't bore you with what each course was about, except that I didn't fare well. I won't even blame my math or physics teachers, although I used to. The truth was that I no longer cared about studying these topics; toward mid-semester, I was burnt out on the abstractions of math and the laws of physics and my instructors' lectures began to get more and more complicated. I did not care about the concepts, their functions, or how neatly they solved Earth's scientific issues, as "the real world" was beginning to teach me other values. That world included women—who I rarely saw that Chicago summer—and the greater and greater distance growing between my high school sweetheart Valerie and me. Our correspondence dwindled as we both navigated colleges and rediscovered long-distance calls, and my eyes started to wander to the pretty girls at LSUS, although I was too afraid to ask any of them on a date and I still lacked confidence in my stick-shift driving skills. My mind also had started to wander toward other, more serious matters—particularly as I started to read more and enjoyed scanning magazines in the free hour or two that I had waiting for Mamoo to pick me up. I began wandering the aisles of the library and grabbing random books that caught my eyes or piqued my curiosity. Aside from the fine collection of Playboys (half of which were missing centerfolds), one juicy item was An American Dilemma, by Swedish economist Gunnar Myrdal—the title basically said it all: The U.S. racial problem was in direct contradiction to Americans' supposedly long-held belief in the basic equality of all people. Somehow the book spoke to me, showing me how outsiders viewed the problems facing most people I knew and that these views were no different from those of most blacks: Something was inherently wrong about how America treated blacks, and that the whole educated world knew about it since before World War II. Say what!??? Of course, I already knew as much (I had, after all, made an A in U.S. history last term), but it sort of shocked me to read that American racism was this well-researched thing that people knew a lot about, not just something that had recently spun out from LBJ's Great Society agenda. The whole notion of the existence of an established historical and social dialogue surprised and motivated me to learn more, and that meant that I began to pay more attention whenever I heard of unequal treatment somewhere in Louisiana, and particularly in Shreveport. I don't know what I thought I would *do* about the subject, but it struck a big enough nerve to lessen my interest in math.

It also made me want to write—something, anything, albeit I had no idea what or in what form. I just suddenly found self-expression cathartic and self-revealing. Aside from the dwindling pile of letters I'd sent off to Valerie in Seattle, most of what I'd written to that point were sweet, overly sappy poems that I'd occasionally share: a thank-you to Gram on raising Valerie to be as sweet as she was, a birthday poem to Mrs. Graham, a funny ditty to one of the ladies in the registrar's office about her love of fast food, or some freestyle lyrics emulating something I'd read in Esquire. Everything was fair game, especially since Ree had given me her old Smith Corona typewriter from her early '60s Chicago high school days; the keys for the "O", the "D", and the small "e" were gunky and dark, but I didn't care because I still could read most of what I typed. Plus, I liked the feel of words emanating from my fingers to a page, being readable and sounding intelligent, even if a tad unoriginal. This was even more fun than reading encyclopedias at my cousins' homes, almost like reading the newspaper in the mornings, and more interesting than my math and physics texts. Just imagine if I found something worthwhile or important to say!

There's an old saying that without failure there is no growth, and I had failure in spades that fall semester. While my Blessed Sacrament and Jesuit schooling had led me to consider myself more so as a man of learning, I wasn't doing awfully much of it at the time. Not that I wasn't enjoying college; the shack had become a second home—with Ms. Odessa, in her softspoken way, providing a calm, non-academic presence and listening support system. Plus, our gang of black students occasionally whooped it up playing each other in spades and chess, and while I learned to love hot cocoa and cold ham and cheese sandwiches from the vending machines. The registrar's office provided a friendly place to work and get to know various campus officials. Add in the library, and I felt extremely comfortable. But the classroom was dogging me: I was making no progress in physics, and the instructor was even more than oblique as Father Bradley had been at Jesuit, his cornpone countryfied accent and rolled up short sleeves notwithstanding. I earned an F, only slightly lower than my Calculus II grade of D; although I studied, I just couldn't remember everything for the exams, even though there were only three of us in the class. I blocked out my grade in linear algebra, but I'm sure it was close to a D. I made As in history and physics lab (go figure!) but my overall grade was close to a low C. The real world kicked my ass.

"You might want to consider changing your major," Mrs. Graham advised shortly after grades were released; she wasn't joking, and she gave off the most serious look I'd ever seen on her face, as if to add "you poor schmuck" to her advice.

"To what?" I said, having no clue as to the next step or its destination. I also was afraid she'd suggest something even more difficult than math, such as chemistry or biology.

Fortunately, LSUS was small enough that Mrs. Graham knew everyone. She couldn't answer my question but knew who could—Dr. Brashier, the school's academic dean known more for his award-winning rose-growing prowess (Shreveport is the seat of the American Rose Society, so any rose-related news often made the first section of the local newspapers; thus, so did he) than for his smarts. The tall, red-haired, freckled man was easily visible on campus for those reasons and commanded a room whenever he entered. Mrs. Graham always spoke in hushed tones whenever she mentioned his name, as it was clear he was instrumental in laying out our office's policies and procedures. Whenever he walked into our office, he always went directly into the office of our mysterious, seldom-seen Big Boss—Registrar Fabia Thomas—as if he was entitled to, which he was, as he was her boss. So, when I visited him after speaking with Mrs. Graham that December, I had butterflies for sure.

In early January, I stood at his huge, rose-decorated office, directly in front of his desk, afraid of what he would say. Why was this guy meeting with little old me, a failed math major? Didn't he have better things on his plate? After he invited me to sit, he looked down at some slim sheet of paper for about 15 seconds—oh my God, he'd been briefed about me—then he asked me what I intended to do about my academic situation. I hemmed and hawed, muttering something vague about not being aware of too many other options out there, and my own indecisiveness as to what I could possibly learn at which could excel. "Please help me," I said to myself.

THE BUMPY ROAD AHEAD

"**H**ave you thought about journalism?", he said after listening to my weak offering. He added that it might suit my talents.

I had blanks; still clueless and a bit embarrassed, I had to ask what journalism was; I'd never heard of it. He, surprisingly—because I thought he only knew about roses and his own field of chemistry—knew; that blew my mind. People made money for doing that kind of writing, he said. It made sense, but I had little knowledge of, or inclination toward, the subject, never hearing or thinking about it prior to our meeting.

"I guess I could try that," I sheepishly volunteered, although I'd have said *anything* to get this serious-looking dude off my case, leave his office, and head to my shift at the registrar's office. I was not at all comfortable dealing with important people, especially tall ones.

"Well, then, why don't you think it over and let me know what you're going to do or if you have any questions, OK?"

I agreed, hastily stood, shook his hand, and left; I was glad more about the fact that the meeting was over than I was about my future. This "journalism" sounded somewhat interesting, but I didn't know how I was going to handle this "option" or what to do next. I had to speak to Mrs. G and see what she'd say about it.

She was ecstatic. "Oh, goody!," she said in her sweet Arkansas accent, clapping her hands together, after I told her of Brashier's suggestion, adding, "I hoped you'd say that. I knew journalism was the thing for you!" I couldn't get why she was so happy, though, and I felt like I was set up somehow. "I've seen your writing, George, and journalism was just made for you," she said, her eyes twinkling, pooh-poohing any of my worries and reminding me that her husband, Don, was chief of photography at one of the local newspapers—as if that would somehow seal the deal and provide the greatest possible encouragement. "You're gonna love it," she said. I'd never seen such joy in a white person regarding something involving me. It reminded me of Mrs. Merchant pre-Jesuit, and how that had seemed at the time—as if other people knew well before me what my path in life would be. What's going on? I asked myself, not entirely satisfied with the situation.

I forced a faint smile, blurting, "Well, I hope you're right," and exited her office with a slight bewildering feeling, again as if I'd been a bystander in my own life, standing in front of a blank canvas. The next few days were a blur—submitting the paperwork to change majors, setting up a meeting with someone from the communication department where journalism was taught, and feeling a little flustered to find myself in a situation where I thought I'd be starting the whole college process over, worried about any graduation delays and money setbacks "my decision" would create, not to mention explaining the whole thing to Mamoo and Daddy. They had no clue about college, its enrollment process, curriculum electives and requirements, or, for that matter, journalism—although they were avid newspaper readers and news viewers. Oddly enough, however, "If that's what you want to do," was all Mamoo said of the matter. "You know Mama don't know nothing about journalism, cher." I assured her that people made a living writing for newspapers and magazines. She then, a day or two later, announced my decision to Daddy in the middle of a Cowboys game on the TV. "What's that, Son?" he said, on the edge of his seat, half-crouching, one eye on the game, dipping an inch of cigarette ashes on the floor. After I explained, he said, "That's good, Son," then, cigarette in lips, he continued to yell at the referees.

Switching to writing and communication courses was a breeze compared to math and physics; in class, it was like night and day. Whatever the teachers tried to get across seemed so much common sense, as

Mamoo holding our kitty Fat Chance and relaxing on the front porch.

did the volumes of writing that they required. The Smith-Corona got a good work out, and my instructors seemed generally pleased to have someone new who could spell, elaborate on a point, understand the nuances of beginnings, middles, and ends in content organization, and kept up with popular culture. Most of the graded marks I received asked me questions about the substance of my arguments or the completeness of my thoughts; I'd get ahead of myself, so eager was I to share them. Mostly, I felt personally connected to teachers for the first time at LSUS, because the feedback felt personally directed, often with a "you" or two included, toward something *I* had created. My grades, outside of multiple-choice tests, reflected my never-lost passion for exploring ideas.

But I discovered journalism wasn't only about writing. Despite my writing abilities, writing was the easy part of the job. What was I going to write about? How to decide? How was my news judgment? Could I think of interesting story ideas? Reading the morning and afternoon newspapers—Shreveport was blessed with both—was a good place to start, but I had to cater the ideas to a college-aged paper, as our stories would be submitted to the LSUS student weekly publication, The Almagest. So, your story had a better chance of Almagest printing it if you could *report* something related to the campus or college life in general. The word "reporting" suggested where most of the work was involved in journalistic writing—and most of the "outside of class" work, because class meeting time involved listening to lectures about subjects related to reporting and writing.

I wasn't the most imaginative beginning journalist; because I worked at the registrar's office, I thought I could double-dip and cover the office as well. Bad idea, as I discovered most of what the office did—acting as a repository for grade-related paperwork—was dry stuff to most students, except when they had a personal matter to handle—changing or dropping courses, changing majors, or sending transcripts to potential employers or other schools. I couldn't very well write about those subjects unless it affected someone noteworthy—a school or state official, which almost never happened. So, that meant I had to really hustle to find something newsworthy to report. At first, I had it easy since everyone wanted to know the size of student enrollment in the first month of the semester. Afterward, crickets. Mrs. Graham was of little help, unless it was something that made the office look good, like a new filing system. I had to explain that news usually involved problems, not solutions—unless they were meant for huge problems. It pained me to shoot down her ideas, since she had been so helpful in my choice of major; fortunately, she understood, no doubt thanks to her husband. So, I struggled to make newsworthy contributions that merited more than a couple of paragraphs, the equivalent of turning over rocks only to discover no worms. I also discovered that if I truly imitated what I read in the newspaper, I would probably land on the bad side of the entire registrar's office, endangering my job there. Math never once presented such a possible ethical quandary, and I didn't have the maturity at the time to give it deeper thought.

Particularly pertinent was one of my first pieces for my feature writing course the following fall. I had had success in the class imitating Mike Royko, the then-famous dour, politics-loving columnist for the Chicago papers; I imagined my style as the wise guy of LSUS journalism who, like Royko, called it as he saw it with a slight sense of humor and a wickedly sharp tongue. One of my submissions involved something near and dear to my heart. I thought as a black-influenced author, it was my duty—as a recurring member of the group of black students in the snack shack who had a great, sometimes unusually vocal, time playing cards between courses on certain afternoon—to bring our happy times to the attention of the entire student body in the shape of news, as I had occasionally witnessed many white student passersby looking at our group with, if not disdain, then bemusement or concern (or was I just feeling guilty?). I was afraid on two fronts—being classified as lazy or laissez faire by other students, or for what I had witnessed as too much of a good time among the group. OK, I was a downer of a kind, but with good intentions.

Unfortunately, those good plans didn't come through in the column that The Almagest published that Friday in October. Up until then at LSUS (and likely because I was observant at drop-out time at the registrar's office), I noticed the abnormal numbers of black students who I thought were "one and done" in terms of their attendance—here for a short time and then disappearing. I did an informal, unscientific survey of black students, asking why they chose the school; their answers centered on the academic challenge and course transferability at other schools, although I raised the possibility that the academic challenge also could be a problem with the dropout rate. I know I went wrong with the snack-shack reference, but then I quoted one black coed saying you must go after what you want. And then I added this suicidal ending: "Maybe blacks should try harder," implying that familiar complaints of racism weren't cutting it.

Ouch. Dumbass! For the next week or so, none of my black friends spoke to me, although I had several white students (and more than one professor) say it was a great column. Still, seeing it—in black and white in the newspaper—gave it more of a "hit job" air, one for which I duly paid until my friends *did*, fortunately, start to talk to me again. I'll never forget having black eyes on me in the snack shack for a month or so. I was an idiot, albeit with what I thought were good intentions, i.e., helping to solve a problem that appeared to me to have been caused unwittingly by having leisurely fun, but without any hard proof. I had used the power of the press to address what I saw as a problem and received a swift kick in the ass. Lesson learned about why certain topics are taboo, why appearances can be deceiving, and, more importantly, how much good reporting—had I done any—would have made a difference. I knew what it felt like to be considered a traitor: I treated my own social group as if I was an outsider looking in, and now I truly was an outsider—for a while, at least. So much for relying on my observational skills or copying what I thought was good journalism. I swore to do better.

And I did, studying longer and deeper, attending summer school, performing more duties at the registrar's office, and earning increasingly higher grades, repairing the damage that my math and physics doldrums had created. Then, at the start of my third year, I took a step that would turn my professional life—not to mention, my personal soul—in a positive direction: I joined The Almagest writing staff, rewriting press releases, composing headlines, proofreading stories, writing columns, and eventually reporting original stories. None of the stories were world-beaters, but it was a great ego boost to see other students around campus reading content that I had helped to assemble. Particularly meaningful feedback came from faculty who said they either enjoyed my columns or had a comment about a news story; it was especially cool and gratifying to receive little, personal notes from the dean of my college, Dr. McBride—an avid newspaper reader and English literature scholar—who became our strongest supporter. Not only did her messages reflect well on our staff, but my pals also took notice that I was the most frequent recipient, helping to burnish my reputation and make them a little envious. An extra benefit—probably the biggest bonus—came in our development into a cohesive collective.

As an oft-times weekly, we had to adhere to a rigid production schedule to have the paper printed and distributed by Friday noon or thereabouts, before the mass auto exodus created by the many students who either had to go to their jobs or were getting a jumpstart on the weekend. This meant we had to get the content written and edited by around 8 p.m. Tuesday, in time for delivery to The Tribune, the professional printer across the Red River in downtown Bossier City. The entire process sounded simple, but it was anything but: Getting journalists to work together as a unit is akin to herding cats—stories, ideas, photos, releases, cartoons, and ads carry their own idiosyncrasies (e.g., when they happen, when they're over, who's involved, where they occur, etc.) that their originators (usually members of the public) decide and then later inform the news organization. That randomness plays havoc for planning and producing content. Add the fact that the newspaper staffers doubled as college students, often with additional, part-time jobs, and you have the potential for chaos. And that possibility makes for an interesting, messy, deadline—or, as we called it, Tuesday night. Mixing our individual personalities, temperaments, work habits, egos, and eating practices made for lively, at times shrill, opportunities for personal development and, oh yes, journalism. Tempers often attached to short fuses, poor dietary habits, and conflicting personal agendas often created tension, or at the very least, rough sledding for either the editor or an offended or tardy underling. Who played which role varied by week or by whatever Wednesday exam or important project was scheduled.

Still, we secretly looked forward to Tuesday night, because there was no more fun than the non-journalism stuff that would occur: exchanging punny potential headlines, gossiping about sources' personal lives, or arguing over which musical group was better or "less commercial". And it seemed there always was a rush to proofread a story, edit a grossly overwritten story, or fret about whether (or how) to include a good quote that only halfway related to a story. In the process, we shared pepperoni pizza, lamented a pending class assignment, swapped tales about unruly sources, or salivated about how to get more eyeballs for an upcoming story. Throw in the random flirting, double entendres, and someone's latent juvenile tendencies, and you had the makings of a fun evening—or a recipe for a good argument.

The Almagest had that and one more key ingredient: humor. Not the immature kind of laughs that usually were made at someone's expense at Jesuit, but the more satirical, often-times pessimistic, culturally laden witticisms that many people used to expect from Saturday Night Live. Mostly our humor was "inside baseball"—minutiae about journalism, music, race/racism, celebrities, faculty, and sex that everyone thinks about when he or she *thinks* that he or she recalls when waxing nostalgic about SNL's "good old days" but when they're conveniently forgetting about the many bad or awful sketches that come in SNL's last hour. Most of it I couldn't repeat without libeling or slandering someone or some organization; plus, I doubt it would be all that funny. Besides, the best jokes were told in the context of a story or journalistic situation that only journalists would entertain. In addition, the group's core shared a love of dancing—line dancing, disco fingering, swinging, electric sliding, bumping, hustling—you name it, we'd try it, using our best imitations of couples we'd seen on TV, and fail. Our faux pas were seen mostly at several downtown places, where we'd dance to a cover band that would play Saturdays until 2 a.m. Good, daiquiri-infused fun. And when we weren't dancing there, it would be at someone's home. We could be ourselves without worrying about how we looked.

This went on about three years, without nary a hitch—surprising me and no doubt my newfound friends, who were all white except for me and Carlos, a frustrated Puerto Rican poet who could pass for white because of his limited dancing skill. As the lone person with any darker shade of skin, I had had some trepidation about joining the group—especially since my car still was mostly at Mamoo's call. But I and our mustached editor, Randy, became fast friends, riding his ugly, yellow Ford Pinto just about everywhere it would take us—malls, theaters, dance clubs, pizza places, or to the girls' houses, where we'd turn into two or three couples looking for some dance floor to slay. I had no romantic interests in, and got none from, any of the girls, since we usually were working buddies or had developed friendships. And, honestly, I had no clue how to court a white woman, what were the right moves to make, or how it could not be hazardous to your health in places where drinking was allowed; this still was Shreveport in the '70s. Music, however, seemed to smooth any "savage beasts" who might have been itching for confrontation. Of course, there were "looks" from those stunned to see me in the group, but nothing ever happened, even after slow dances! I don't know if I looked too inept, too innocent, too white, or if the lighting of most places was insufficient to warrant a glance in the joints we integrated.

That didn't mean that we weren't aware, however. Randy and I often made racial jokes with each other: He'd offer an imitation of a black celebrity such as the singer Barry White or Soul Train host Don Cornelius, pretending reactions from our neighbors when he'd come over to visit ("Your neighbors are probably wondering, 'What the *hell* is that white boy doing over here?'") or the like, I would crack wise about his "dorky white boy" attire or something similar. We knew we constituted the "odd couple" when we went places, but we'd simply clown about it—as if we were both black (or white). This became our running shtick when we couldn't think of anything else to humor us or satirize, to the point that some of the others, particularly Carlos, would join in and we'd soon have each other doubled over in laughter, like schoolgirls. But we'd engage in serious conversations, as well, particularly about journalistic coverage of sensitive issues. Randy often would jokingly mimic the rednecks he grew up with in the rural suburb of Haughton and recounted the countless times he heard the "n-word" in school, church, or the workplace. I would just shake my head and tell him of the distrust most people I knew had of whites and of the pervasiveness of that word in the black community. We hated Nixon, and his demonic alter ego, George Wallace. Journalism brought us together on a plethora of issues: local policing, self-righteous hypocrites, Louisiana politics, rednecks, disco, blue laws, TV news, people who tried to sell useless things, and East Texas. We had some great times in our mutual dislikes. Randy and I considered ourselves as equals in most things journalistic, and the wisest of the wiseacres on campus. A not-so-old man sitting in front of us at the movies once got so irate as we cheered for the reporter characters in the film version of their Watergate scandal book, All The President's Men, that he threatened to throttle us if we didn't shut up. The proverbial "peas in a pod," we often commiserated about our own failures (mine at my internship, his with his attempted dating life, mine with my then-girlfriend (a Blessed Sacrament organist with twin girls who we derisively called "the widow woman"), his with his dysfunctional relationships with everyone in his family). The girl thing was a particularly sore spot as we simultaneously grasped that no amount of intellectual intelligence or college-man *savoir faire* would help you feel as emotionally mature as the current women we were dating. In a moment of youthful ignorance on the subject, we pledged to a forgettable, new campus fraternity; to our chagrin we didn't care for any of the other members, their parties were lame, and their vibe nerdy.

It didn't hurt that we took several classes together, some with Almagest staffers, and shared similar opinions on the quality of instruction at LSUS. We idolized the political science professors, who were barely older than us and who seemed incredibly liberal and hip (for '70s Shreveport). Norm (from the Northeast) and Marv (of Kansas) were always saying outrageously liberal things about local, state, and national politicians and came across as the coolest of the cool; plus, they challenged us to write papers that questioned the status quo (and greatly informed our columns). We also had a journalism advisor who everyone loathed and whose idea of teaching was reading from the textbook; to boot, he liked to confide in us how miserable he was, sort of like the comedian Rodney Daingerfield. Probably the most dynamic teacher from a journalism perspective was our department chair, who had no journalism experience but instead a speech background that informed his teaching of a course on persuasion and propaganda—how not to succumb to their ways, i.e., how to be a critical thinker, a core skill for anyone aspiring to be a journalist. There's not a day—in journalism or out—that I don't use what I learned (sometimes too much of it) in that singular course; it made me a certified skeptic

This photo of derby-wearing me was taken in Frierson, Louisiana for an Almagest staff photo.

Fittingly, as my time at The Almagest came close to an end, it was time to spread my wings and begin my internship. I had two influences on my choice of newspaper: I had made a connection at the Shreveport Journal, where Mrs. Graham's husband was chief photographer, by stopping by one day and introducing myself to the managing editor (head of the entire newsroom) and sheepishly trying to chat them up about a possible job. It also helped that their Executive Editor Stanley Tiner had lectured our feature writing class on what it took to succeed in journalism, inspiring me to write an op-ed, anti-smoking column. Armed with those connections and my Almagest experiences, I felt I was ready for anything. Wrong again.

The first few days they wanted me to rip copy—literally—off the teletype machines feeding the newsroom. Don't feel bad if you've never heard of such things; most people haven't. They were, over-simply stated, usually four-foot-tall, electric typewriters connected by special wires to the dominant global news services of the time, the Associated Press and its then-competitor United Press International. The machines constantly typed the latest news gathered from across the world on this continuous roll of coarse paper about the width of an iPad. Once a story came across this "wire", the machine printed it and then advanced the paper in position for the next, or "breaking" item. My job, starting at 5:30 a.m., was to rip the latest stories off the wires every few minutes and separate the individual stories into a pile for the managing editor or, more often, the Page One editor, who then would read them and judge each's importance for that day's paper. Or that was the plan, anyway. But remember I wasn't the best at manual labor, even the daintiest kind. Ripping the pages in "clean"— not rough, jagged edges with story parts torn or missing—took ol' soft-hands George at least a couple days to master. I put it down to the early hours, at first, or at least my lack of caffeine intake. So that's what I did—or, more accurately, tried to do—the first part of the day. Suffice it to say, it was mindless work that did little to boost my confidence before I started my main purpose—which was to write, or so I thought. I had heard that many a newspaperman had gotten his start this way—lacking a college degree, at the organizational bottom, happy to run copy or whatever else to an awaiting editor until he earned that first, big break (a story assignment). Journalists visiting our classes often had made it sound noble and romantic, as if such grunt work was equivalent to serving your country. I didn't mind it too much, if I got to write.

Well, I did write—obituaries, which I discovered constituted the next-to-lowest rung in the newsroom. Obituaries, or death notices as they were often known, were a staple of every newspaper in the United States and Europe, mainly because a key readership demographic audience viewed them as must-have and sacrosanct, right up there with the comics and the crossword puzzle; you know who you are—senior citizens either checking to see if anyone they knew had died or trying to compare their own lives to those of the dead to see whose was better. That's all well and good, if you're a senior citizen. But to a 21-year-old, this might as well have been the *kiss* of death because you not only got a taste of what was in store for you down the road of life, but you'd get semi-depressed after composing so many similar notices; it's disheartening to learn so early in the morning that life had pretty much the same things in store for most people. Newsrooms' dirty little obit secret is that rules and procedures exist to make obit-writing easy: Start with announcing the date, time, place, and deceased's name, adding who was the officiating minister/rabbi, priest. This was followed in the next paragraph by the cause and date of death. Finish it off by listing survivors and any family preferences regarding flowers or charitable causes. After compiling obits for an entire semester, I understood why news people drank so much coffee. Bummer, dude. Add the fact that all this was typed on ancient, clunky Underwood typewriters using lifeless, gray paper that—in the cases of many notices—had to be glued together with the most-hallucination-inducing-smell of glue housed in brown jars on every desk, then you get the idea. Oh, and Monday was the worst day for obits; it seemed the elderly (or the foolish) died more often over the weekends. But it wasn't all awful: There was the great repartee you would develop with the funeral home directors, most of whom had great senses of humor about their profession and its trappings when they'd feed you updates, corrections of obits in the morning paper, or new notices to insert before your deadline; many were white guys who liked to call themselves "southern planters", or say that crematoriums made their blood boil. I also secretly delighted in using my formal, telephone voice with these gentlemen, wondering if this guy knew he wasn't talking to a white guy or if they would ever agree to handle my funeral plans. Whenever one of these guys visited the newsroom in person to drop off a notice, I could see the surprise in his eyes when he greeted me. I would eventually get used to such instances, figuring that running into prejudice was going to be part of the job.

Speaking of which, I could tell that Butch, the city editor, really didn't trust me. Maybe it was my copy-ripping fiasco (that only lasted a couple weeks, thank God), my lack of conversational style

(I was still trying to overcome my bad habit—developed across the years, on many jobs—of not asking questions when given an assignment) that made me come across as passive, or the fact that he was a Louisiana Tech grad in a room full of Tech grads (unbeknownst to me at first, the Shreveport newspapers were traditionally the first stop for many Tech newspaper grads; their program director was a Shreveport Times weekly columnist). Many of my assignments were event-based, meaning that some organization had submitted a press release to the paper describing the event in advance, thus the name "advance"). As a result, I wrote many of what were called "news features"—not controversial or late-breaking hard news, but quasi-soft, or "fluff pieces". Think of the retirement of a postal clerk, or a female Army mechanic at the nearby National Guard station, or how amateur radio worked, or the rationale for an LSUS bicycle-riding course. Others might include the state of bad-check-writing, or an immigrant industrial engineer at a local ammunitions plant, or the job market for new grads, or an alcohol-prevention seminar—in the '70s we used to call that "lifestyle news". Seventy years ago, it would have been "women's news". In fact, many such stories were assigned or guided by women in that section of the newsroom. Valuable advice and experience for sure, but nothing that would make the front page. Meanwhile, the Tech students—also males—were receiving what most journalists would consider much better, more newsworthy, more serious assignments: covering government meetings, public officials' actions and decisions, health, business, runaways, police and fire, court testimony—stories that often resulted from covering a regular, vital beat. In a self-defeating way, I somewhat understood what was going on: The male editors, whose responsibilities usually included hard news, were so busy guiding and shaping the breaking news that this priority precluded them from taking time with me and my not-so-newsy subjects. So went my last semester—a learning experience, for sure: I subtly discovered that good, complete story guidance was more likely to come from a woman than from a man. But this was not the bright, sparkling, front-page future I had created in my mind. I suspected my male editors' lack of use of my talents was simply because no one knew how to train a person of color or was afraid to (I never had any formal feedback from any of the male editors except to correct mistakes), or didn't expect much from a commuter school project like me. If I had known then what I knew now, I would have had an easier time accepting such an arrangement because research has shown that women and minorities have significantly more roadblocks to overcome in fighting white-male editor bias in many newsroom-related matters to this day (more insight about this will come in the next chapter). But lacking such hindsight, journalism was beginning to disappoint me, and I was thinking I maybe should have stopped that first day as a copyboy. Graduation day would soon be upon me: I had to have a plan in place, or else go empty-handed to my parents when I disappointed them at the end of college with my jobless status.

Naturally, I turned to Mrs. Graham, my confidante, my rock. Her bosses noticed that students adored her so much that they put her in charge of job placement, so she was invested in helping me land on my feet. She suggested hitting all the local potential journalism outlets, but she also had a public school-related prospect ready for me while I pursued writing jobs. I don't know how, but she also knew Tom Marshall, one of my Jesuit classmates who was in his senior year at the University of Missouri's top-rated journalism school; Tom and I weren't exactly best buds, but we did have our joint time on the basketball squad. By the mid-'70s, the job market for journalists had gotten severely restricted, thanks to the public's discovery of the heroism of Washington Post reporters Bob Woodward and Carl Bernstein, who you'll recall broke the Watergate scandal story and had recently written All the President's Men. The book and the scandal's publicity made journalism jobs a hot commodity, drawing several college students for each journalism job, making for extreme job competition at the better newspapers and TV stations. Mrs. G had suggested that perhaps that maybe there was something more that I needed to know about cracking the news job market or positioning myself as a good journalism candidate—that I may need some polishing in one or two areas. She knew that the good journalism schools were not only turning out competent candidates but there also was competition for admission to them, making it sound reasonable to check them out for tips as well as potentially having a fallback option if I didn't land a job. I decided to write Tom, who was finishing his degree at Missouri at the time, to see what his thoughts were for someone in my position, as well as how he would rate "Mizzou", as its grads called it.

To my slight surprise, a few days later I heard from Tom, who waxed glowingly about Mizzou j school, the quality of its curriculum, and how well-prepared he felt because of it. "That's nice," I thought, and filed it away in my mind. I had to scrounge up my admission materials (grade transcripts and faculty recommendations) and the required fee, as well as set up a date to take the required standardized graduate admission test. A decision wouldn't come until March or so, and I sort of left things there for a while as I finished my Journal internship and occasionally filled in at The Almagest, to keep my skills fresh, just in case a job came up. Meanwhile, I still had my registrar's office job and my on-again, off-again dating of Mary Louise, who was almost a decade my senior and a real sweet girl. As members of our ragtag 8 a.m. Blessed Sacrament choir, we had vaguely known each other for a while, especially since she was our organist and co-planner (with me) of our Mass hymn lineup. She was shy and seemingly innocent for her age, especially considering she was the mother of twins. She had moved back in with her Frenchman parents after she was widowed and returned to work; I knew her parents before I knew her, seeing them most Sundays in some service capacity. She liked most things I did—dancing, movies, pizza—but she didn't shed her quietness whenever we went out, as if she was intimidated or non-conversant. We hardly ever talked on the phone, either; I put it down to a combination of our age difference and her being a working mom with little to no free time during the week. Still, we were comfortable in every other way. Otherwise, in the rest of my life, I sort of cruised on auto pilot—going to school, the office, The Almagest, The Journal, dancing, and church; life was semi-good. Then came the news that Mizzou had accepted my application.

I was thrilled of course; it's nice to be wanted. But, on the one hand, mental conflicts started to create doubts in many areas—I would be starting all over again. Would I fit in with other grad students? What did grad students do that undergrads couldn't or didn't? Was a master's degree simply an undergrad degree without electives? Would I be bored by essentially retaking courses I'd already taken as an undergraduate? The whole world knew that Louisiana education wasn't Top Ten-worthy, so would I find Mizzou courses harder than those of LSUS? Missouri was north of Louisiana, but not that far north; should I expect more racism, a la Shreveport, or would it be a brand-new ballgame? What about my friendships with Almagest staffers; would they quickly forget me? Was their friendship with me truly just one of mutual convenience (i.e., dancing partner), rather than a lasting, real bond? Would my relationship with Mary Louise go the same route as that between Valerie and me: Would she find a more mature stud and drop me like a hot potato? How easy would it be to make friends in the middle of the Corn Belt? It certainly would again mean being in the minority, so could I duplicate the comfortable relationships I had with my LSUS mentors? What about dating—could I ever find the right Frenchman or black girl? How could I keep in touch with Mrs. G? Not least of all, how would I afford two more years of school? What would Mamoo and Daddy think?

On the other hand, I had just passed 22 years of age. I was a grown man—maybe not in Mamoo's and Mrs. G's eyes, but technically speaking. I could do anything I wanted, right? Maybe. I had felt emboldened by having my parents as a fallback; I'd still had the assurance of three meals a day and a roof over my head, no matter what choices I'd made at LSUS. Mamoo and Daddy were just glad that I was trying to make something of myself; I never thought they had high expectations. But Mizzou would be a slightly different matter; the university said it had no more dormitory rooms available (even if I could come up with the money to pay for it), so I'd have to solve that issue myself. I didn't know anyone in Columbia (home of the main campus), so arranging housing would be a challenge. In addition, I had applied later than normal, missing a few deadlines, particularly financial aid and scholarship; so, of what money I could qualify for, much of it would have to come directly out of my pocket—sooner or later. I also would be considered an out-of-state student, so tuition would cost more than for an in-state student—meaning less money for regular expenses such as food, clothing, rent, books, and so forth; by the way, a college education in Missouri cost considerably more than it did in Louisiana. When I started LSUS, tuition was $90 a semester and $120 when I graduated. At Mizzou, for an undergrad in 1976, tuition cost $300 (about $700 in today's money), and $600 for an out-of-state student, grad or undergrad (that's about $3,300 in today's money).

So, as is my usual, passive manner, I stewed over the decision until shortly after LSUS graduation. I still was hoping for another, paid internship at The Journal, but the editor told me chances didn't look good, that he'd already made budget decisions that didn't include a third intern, which would be me. That forced me to pay a visit to the Caddo Parish School Board office to its personnel department, to investigate the full-time job opening that Mrs. G had mentioned to me as a stopgap. I met a tall, white-haired, slow-spoken black man named John Washington, who was an assistant administrator.

He looked at me, and then at my resumé, and with a slight giggle and a rub of his clean-shaven chin asked, "Are you sure you want this job?" Not wanting to come off as timid, I said "Yes. Why? What's wrong with it?"

"Well, I don't want to undersell it, but it's a bit of a bad choice of words," he said, looking around for the right description.

"What do you mean?"

"Well, it's called a teacher's aide job, but you really would not, in fact, be a teacher's aide."

"What would I be?"

"Well, let me explain," he said, again with a half-smile. I was beginning to like this guy for his candor, and for his realistic assessment that the job was a little beneath me. For quite some time, there was this classroom in a South Shreveport, predominantly black junior high, that served as a *de facto* textbook depository; that was where the job was and—I was to learn after we got there—the bulk of what it entailed.

"Do you have time to take a ride with me? I'd like to show it to you before you make your decision." he asked. What else could I do? I wasn't about to look a gift horse in the mouth—not me, who'd done foundry, painting, landscaping, and office work. No job—especially a paying one—was too good, considering the alternative of spending money I didn't have in a place I'd never visited with no roof over my head. Besides, I was extremely curious; and Washington's brutal honesty and likeability sort of made me hope that he had been exaggerating, and that the job was this cushy position that I'd come to eventually learn to love.

No such luck. The room was about 35 feet x 35 feet, with windows in the rear and two sides each with blackboards. The fourth side was a standard bulletin board, loaded with faded bunting from years gone by. And then there were the books. Dozens and dozens of textbooks, raggedly and unevenly piled on top of each other, with piles ranging from two feet high to about six feet high, spread out over the entirety of the room. Nor were the books neatly closed: We're talking disheveled, messily opened books—some covered in dust, others with pages half-torn, and silverfish feverishly gliding from page to page as if they were having supper and it was a continuous, ongoing event. John and I looked at the piles and then each other, and I said, "I'm your man." And so I was, for about a month, in which I cleaned up and stacked my way through half the morass, until Journal editors rescued me with a last-minute offer of a brief internship for the rest of the summer. The money I made would help at Mizzou, but it wasn't nearly enough without a place to live—these were pre-apartment locator service days—and significant financial aid of some kind. Enter Mrs. G, again.

She had one last trick up her sleeve. Without telling me, in late July she telephoned the Missouri financial aid director, George C. Brooks. It so happened that Brooks was the university's first black administrator and had earned his master's there in 1958; the experience still must have been fresh in his mind as he listened to Mrs. G talk about me and my dire financial situation. He didn't have much time to talk and explain, but he told her to "Send him up here. We'll get him a place to stay, and we'll take care of him." I had only about $700 saved, but she sounded so hopeful and had gone to all that extra trouble, that I swallowed hard, said, "I'll try," and proceeded to break the news to Mamoo, who less-than-enthusiastically said to do what I thought I needed. Before I could think much further about it, two weeks later this Frenchman was on a flight to St. Louis, thanks to an enterprising white woman and an inventive black man.

THE MISSOURI BREAKS

I saved all my worry after I boarded the flight in Shreveport, retracing the blur of the previous four years—from that momentous Cooper Road experiment in which I participated, to the fact that I was truly on my own for the first time in my life. I thought back on all the people I'd met along the way. Indulge me here: There were the folks riding with me in the jitney, the other college students forming our neighborhood team, Mr. Bradford and Mrs. Francis, Mrs. G and the registrar staff, Ms. Odessa and the snack shack card-playing gang, the guys at the wax factory and meat-packing plant, Dr. Brashier, my LSUS teachers who made good (or bad) impressions, The Almagest staff (particularly Randy, my "brother from another mother"), the Jekyll-and-Hyde Journal managers, and all the Blessed Sacrament folks I'd miss—they constituted quite a journey. Of course, I was too young to come to any synthesis or conclusion about what it all meant, but I knew that life got more complex with advancing years. It made me think back to that lonesome, unsatisfactory Jesuit graduation night, watching The Godfather with Ree and wondering "Is that all there is?" And knowing that, had you asked me, I could never have predicted that the next four years would play out as they did. I certainly wouldn't have known that I would heavily rely on older folks—black and white and Frenchman, alike—to help guide me. Then I thought back to Myrdal's classic book and realized my life was just a drop in the bucket compared to the lives of other people of color and what they had historically endured. All they fought for—integration, civil rights, voting rights, educational parity, adequate food and housing, among others—was slowly heading toward fruition and I, little old Frenchman George, was a primary beneficiary of it all. Then I saw the cornfields outside Columbia airport and wondered if I was about to throw it all away in a monumental blunder. It was Sunday and I needed to pray, but I didn't know where. I found the lone pay phone in the small lobby, called Mr. Brooks, told him I had just arrived at the airport, and he told me to find a hotel, relax, and he'd see me that coming Monday, after I'd registered for classes. I spent the day sprawled in my hotel room, double-checking my clothing, underwear, and shoes to make sure I had everything I needed, then double- and triple-counting my money: Yep, there it was—500 dollars to get me through to when I'd find an apartment. I'd see what happened to my stash after registration. I walked the block to the Pizza Hut on the corner, grabbed a magazine, and savored the pepperoni pizza that was my first decent meal since leaving Shreveport. The next day, I suffered through the various lines that composed the registration process, departing with a few dollars' deposit to keep the bureaucracy away long enough to speak with Mr. Brooks.

He was a genial enough man, mustachioed and dressed for the part, complete with the cigarette-and-cologne smell that quickly wafted my way. He asked me how much of the town I had seen; I staved off fears that he would say he'd made a mistake ("Do you have enough for airfare back to Louisiana?") long enough to reply, "Just from the hotel to the registration area to Jesse Hall (administration HQs)." Then he gave me directions to another hotel, Tiger Towers, that he thought would have rooms available; "the Towers", as they were called, were a glorified off-campus dorm (by about by a block or so) without the food service and probably not as quiet. Their management often offered financially challenged students the chance to share suites at a reduced price—perfect for me, I thought. Once I was moved in, he wanted to see me again, presumably to talk about money. Long story short, I was awarded with three roommates—all freshmen from the St. Louis and Kansas City areas—and allowed to apply for government-financed loan assistance that set me up money-wise for a year until I could qualify for in-state tuition via scholarship. All of this is to say I made it to firmer ground—and then school started.

DQ, Richard, and Kyle were good, reasonable (for freshmen) roommates in most respects. They loved to eat, smoke marijuana, borrow money, play music, and stay up all hours of the night. Two of them—IDs will not be revealed to protect the innocent— occasionally liked to shoplift, while the third made the track team. "Study" slowly disappeared from their vocabularies as the semester progressed and I don't know what happened to them after that fall, when I took my talents, my grades, and my record collection to a real, on-campus dorm, on the other side of campus. Still, the four of us had great times together, especially when trying to fool the building's Weed Police (hint: wet towels), but I really spent most of my spare time at Jack In The Box (may the Bonus Jack rest in peace), the School of Journalism, and the campus movie theatres (free or $1 movies were my go-to move when I wasn't enjoying the free shows of singers performing in the Union). Thank goodness that women did not enter the mix because, well, freshmen. Besides, I was too busy getting acclimated to a different academic way of being. But I paid a price.

My transition to Mizzou at first wasn't great. The campus paper, The Missourian, was not at all like The Journal or The Almagest, for several reasons. First, the immediate editors were teaching assistants (TAs)—many of them graduate students with substantial internships or prior professional experience under their belt—and their bosses were the faculty editors who sparingly made appearances two or three times a week, mostly days. I mistakenly thought I was too good to really adhere to the story advice of the TAs, as it was either obvious or too authoritatively delivered (I'm sure they thought I was a pain in the ass, too). Second, our coverage area was Columbia—home to three universities (Mizzou, all-girl Stevens College, and Columbia College, a liberal arts school), each with a journalism program, and nicknamed "College Town, USA"—a very small town of about 60,000 in a metro area of about 102,000. That meant that at any one time, there were far fewer original story ideas than there were journalism students trying to think of them. It was so bad that editors recommended looking in the morgue—home of clippings of previous stories organized by subject—before planning a story; and sometimes it meant a lot of time in the morgue. Third, and as a result, many of the town's folk had been interviewed several times by student journalists by the time they had become adults, meaning these sources could often turn hostile if they didn't like your line of questioning. Fourth, and again, as a result, you could be unlucky and be assigned to a team of students tackling a topic; talk about possible chaos getting those cats herded! Fifth, The Missourian competed against The Columbia Daily Tribune—often staffed by former Missourian reporters and editors who found Columbia too attractive or too cheap to leave for their first jobs. Sixth, The Tribune's editors and reporters stayed in their jobs longer than the semester for which most students reported, meaning Tribune staffers had greater knowledge and institutional memory of the city and of events and the better sources; and the town's folk preferred talking to them to talking with students. Seventh, it wasn't unheard of to have your story butchered by Missourian copy editors/students who were too busy trying to showcase their editing skills—think outlandish headlines or splicing and dicing paragraphs to the point of unrecognizability—to their bosses instead of caring about what *your* story said to the reader. It's enough to make you think twice about telling any editor about what story idea you were working on or when it would be completed. Eighth, and finally, The Missourian had a policy of fact-checking every story before publication—again signifying that your story might not be current by its publication or, worse, it would be so nitpicked by TAs (again, in showing off their editing skills to their superiors) that it might be delayed several days for re-reporting. Don't even get me started about calling sources you've already interviewed, thus making them angry about being asked to repeat themselves or, worse, giving the wallflower types a chance to retract or change what you reported they said—even though you have them saying it on a recording!! Don't get me wrong: There's a valid reason for each one of these conditions, the best being that you want students to strive for accuracy and fairness—the twin towers of the journalistic holy grail. And I tried to follow each rule to the best of my ability. But honestly, there was a time or two when I ignored one of these rules if it served the purpose of truth and didn't mislead or shortchange the reader. So, shoot me.

Still, those hurdles frustrated me, the newbie on the Mizzou journalism block. Reporting took up so much time: We also had to have weekly meetings with the course instructor, who had dozens of us to meet. Sometimes I put less effort into stories, especially if I knew they wouldn't result in a byline, than I did in others that were of stronger interest to my prospective editor that night. This is horrible to say, I know, but I'd worked my butt off in Shreveport on *all* my stories, both front-page material and those ending in less-significant sections, but at times I felt I was being harassed and that I wasn't being given the benefit of the doubt that I thought I had already earned before I arrived at Mizzou. In hindsight, I was probably wrong to think this way, but grad school in a new arena was kicking my ass.

On top of the reporting class—to which I'd been assigned an elementary school and municipal court (two known insignificant beats in any town) to cover—I had the distinct displeasure of having to enroll in the most boring class I'd ever taken: advertising. Not only was the teacher the most milquetoast, sleep-inducing speaker I'd ever heard (and I was putting in late hours at The Missourian doing stories or editing sports or writing headlines the nights before this morning class met), but I couldn't get interested in a subject that had little to do with reporting. I already knew advertising paid the bills/salaries, but so what? Yes, I was a little arrogant, but at 22 I thought I'd earned some arrogance—probably another pitfall of going to graduate school too soon after earning a bachelor's degree. None of any of the people I'd met at the J School—they were all white—understood, or so I thought in moments of self-pity. I didn't realize that I was effectively sabotaging what Mrs. G and Mr. Brooks had worked to create for me. I had spent the Thanksgiving holiday alone—my roomies had gone home—and stayed up all Sunday night writing a term paper that I hated for the advertising course. On my behalf, I loved my other courses—mass media with world famous scholar John Merrill and copy editing on the sports desk; those grades reflected my enthusiasm for media's intersection with social issues and trying to turn football and other writing about sports into standard English, without clichés and without crimping the writer's style. I was enjoying J School: The pizza was a cut above, the weather was slightly cooler, the school library subscribed to The Journal so I could keep up with things in Shreveport, and I wasn't bothered by money issues for a change. But matters didn't sink in until I got the grades that December, and realized my grades averaged below the magic, mandatory "B" level for grad school. Oops!

Being on academic probation placed a fire under my behind and, from experience, I knew that I could surmount the problem with the right decision-making and strong work ethic: Thanks Mrs. G! As I mentioned earlier, my first action was to escape Tiger Towers hell, which I later discovered was full of younger football players, creators of the constant noise that drummed the halls after sunset. Fortunately, I'd only stay there for my first semester, and settled into the Loeb Hall dorm group, happy not to worry about the source of my meals and grateful for only one roommate, an extremely quiet, mild-mannered electrical engineering student named John. The dorm was only about a block from most of my classes, on the edge of downtown and two blocks from the student Catholic Church. One bonus came via my neighbors, a fourth of whom were women, and who hosted the only working TV in their recreation room. At first, I was a bit leery of being in a dorm teeming with young boys, of which I'd had my fill in the fall semester. But, oddly, having young ladies around seemed to keep most of the rowdiness at bay; I took advantage and spent quite a few hours watching TV after studying, meeting other residents in the process and learning more about social hotspots, administrative procedures, and the non-urban part of Missouri. A second, unexpected bonus came from the fact that many dorm residents also were journalism majors—giving us a shared experience, hope, and expectations, and probably lessening the possibility of any week-long disappearances facilitated by alcohol. A third bonus was that I had spent that first summer, in 1977, in a fairly new journalistic environment: The LSUS Communication Department Chair passed on an opportunity to me as I roamed the halls that summer, visiting Mrs. G and a few other old haunts on campus. There was a part-time opening at The Bossier Press, the second fiddle newspaper in the city across the river. Even though my friend Randy grew up in that area, I wasn't too fond of it. I always envisioned it as a small town that thought it could rival Shreveport for things to do, trying to out-Shreveport Shreveport. The fact that it was home to a huge Air Force base or that its school system always had superior rankings to Caddo Parish seemed to have flown over my head. It always seemed small-townish, sort of like Mayberry on the TV show. I interviewed and got the job working for the publisher, Don, a portly, casually dressed man who seemed only interested in one thing: good news that drummed up good will for the newspaper, which subsequently meant more revenue.

Leery at first to being in a place where the advertising content took precedence over news, I did a lot of copy-editing and headline writing, as well as stuff similar to what I had done to start at The Almagest: news briefs, descriptions of photos, drawing art to accompany editorials, taking information over the phone, and whatever else the staff could think of to give me. Fortunately, their requests started to pile up because—as anyone who's worked for a small paper or small business knows—there's always too much work to do and not enough people to do it. Finally, I was assigned to write about the school board, interview with the local racetrack general manager, interview the newly elected mayor, interview the LSU football coach, and interview the city judge. There also were varying city government issues, the local community college, other light features, and movie reviewing. As I said, it was a small town. The towns folk, who weren't very used to talking to reporters, were nice as could be—a welcome change to the jaded "veteran sources" I'd often meet in Columbia. By the time August rolled around, however, I was ready to return to Mizzou and my new residence hall friends, even my staid, quiet roomie John, the only person I knew on our floor who brushed his teeth morning *and* evening.

Loeb Group's stability—it even provided a nightly study hall in the cafeteria— gave a more academically conducive atmosphere, enabling me to meet my own expectations in my courses. Plus, the semester away from The Missourian meant having a more do-able and practical schedule, allowing added time for reading and re-reading boring material, as well as breathing time for intellectual thought that was expected by a more cerebrally centered course slate. For the first time at Mizzou, I became recognizable to my instructors because I was able to engage them more in class discussions, with the resulting mentorship with the person who'd eventually become my thesis advisor, science journalism expert Joye Patterson. A rather small, wiry lady who always wore pantsuits, she took time to get to know me, volunteering to advise me and imparting many questions that got me thinking more deeply about potential topics. In short, she was a godsend—just what I needed, in other words. Mizzou was no longer faceless and useless toil to me; I had gained purpose and direction. I had also begun to parlay my TV night visits in Loeb's girls' residence Francis House into acquaintances and friendships that also felt oddly nurturing, thanks to my interest in the miniseries Roots and Saturday Night Live, which always drew a crowd. I think it helped that I was there to watch the TV—not for the normal, preferred male intention of hitting on the chicks behavior. I also made a point to learn more about dorm life, attending Group Council meetings and volunteering (my older age gave me a more benevolent, advisory view of many residents and endeared me to the group admin staff—the head resident and his group of assistants). I had even joined a Bible study group at the student Catholic center. Altogether, my first two semesters were night-and-day experiences.

With a successful second semester under my belt, I also created an active letter-writing sideline to all my friends back home. Not only did it help me to maintain my friendships, I got the sense that

I wasn't missing too much, and I felt able to jump right back into things when summer rolled around. That meant the two Ds—dancing and dating, of course—but also a feeling of being different, somehow. Going away from home had shown me that I could be friends with black *and* white people, not only in Louisiana but also in Missouri; but in Missouri I didn't have any racially oriented conversations with anyone. Maybe things were better in Missouri, or maybe I'd just been accepted for who I was because that's what everyone else wanted, too? Even having three black roommates my first semester didn't seem to make much of a difference, although the music we played fit into the jazz-funk-soul area. Two of "The Tower Three", as I'll call them, were unafraid to throw around the n-word when they felt the urge, and others they mentioned were either "brothers" or "sisters" or ""white chicks" or "white dudes". At no time did I feel unwelcome because I had somewhat lighter skin than them or my curly hair was a little "finer". We were too busy being students to have heavy dialogue, it seemed, and with Nixon and Gerald Ford out, there seemed to be hope for Jimmy Carter's administration, Star Wars came out and Roots opened millions of minds about slavery. Missouri wasn't the Promised Land, and no one was declaring racial peace. But being back in Louisiana still felt the same, however.

Which was why I really looked forward to the coming fall semester. If I was honest, however, I was somewhat fatigued by the sameness of going to class and writing, although its routineness provided structure. Life was looking up, financially speaking. I'd been awarded a scholarship for the year (translation: a stipend and exemption from out-of-state tuition), so I'd have a little extra spending money. At Loeb, I'd also succeeded in getting the daily job of co-mailroom coordinator, which meant I'd be co-responsible for distributing the mail and whatever packages arrived. The bonus was getting to peruse all the magazines—Rolling Stone, Time, and Newsweek were the big draws—to which residents subscribed, and I received some extra, psychic income by being instrumental in delivering happiness or disappointment, depending on the day's haul. I also knew just about everyone's name. I wished I had a dollar for each time we were asked, "Is the mail all out?" To that, I added Sunday morning janitorial duties on each hall floor (enough to cure me of ever wanting beer); I wasn't flush, but I was able to continue to send Mamoo money every month for the long-distance bill.

At J School, my horizons broadened widely. I took advanced courses in history, journalism history, and specialized reporting, to name a few, expanding my mentoring circle of faculty members and learning procedures and information that I would never have known otherwise. Dr. Patterson expanded my black journalism orbit—we'd decided that I'd do all I could to learn about educational and career patterns of black journalists—by including me in a focused trip to Chicago where I'd meet some of the top black professionals in the business, and by introducing me to more faculty experts in the subject. With that experience and trips I'd make later, I began to work on a survey that would provide the brunt of my thesis, which also would become one of the most-circulated works in the journalism library's history. In the process, I became familiar with other libraries on campus, as well as other facilities, and was well on my way to identifying more as black or with blacks, when it came to journalism, at least. I began to see a calling, at least, in mass media when it came to the welfare of black Americans and of black journalists.

Simultaneously at Loeb Group I started to help develop a circle of what you might call "movers and shakers" when it came to group activities. Our group—mostly made up of concerned Group Council members, not one of them black—did informal surveys of Loeb residents, to discover that most had no sense that there even was a council or agency overseeing group concerns. Using those results as a springboard, we appealed to the campuswide council for funding for a publicity or awareness campaign to educate residents about the council and its potential to help them. Then we started doing things—a game day for kids, the publicity campaign ("Are you a Loeb Lover?" anonymously placed personal ads and flyers across campus), administrative changes to make daily dorm life easier (think extended study hall hours) and the food better, and a huge, Saturday night blow-out dance off-site to cap off the year. Although it seems I should have been a little perplexed or bothered by my interactions with the racial spectrum, I never gave it a second thought. It seemed completely natural, actually; in each case, with each person, I never felt inauthentic or as if I was forcing things. For example, simply because the Tower Three had all the stereotypical problems that some people might pin on minority students, I didn't think of them any less. Nor did I panic when I first saw their shoplifting expertise at the local, big-box grocer. Although I was not inclined to join them, neither did I believe their futures would involve jail cells; they were just my roomies, and we all were scuffling to make it at Mizzou. In addition, my ignorance of Missouri's racial habits seemed to fit right in with my search of the backgrounds of America's black journalists; in both cases, I was learning and, for the first time since my Chicago childhood, the student in me felt free to experiment and grow. It probably was no coincidence that I also dated a handful of white girls while there, none too seriously, but just enough to discover they were no different than the black and Frenchman girls of Louisiana—not just pretty, but also much more emotionally mature and wiser than any guy, ready to discuss even the most esoteric of topics, and knowing much more of what they wanted out of life, one they'd already partly envisioned for themselves.

In the process, they served as good role models. When I had left Louisiana, all I knew was that I wanted to get a job that paid decent wages for good writing. I was going to be a crusading journalist, impacting things, righting wrongs, educating readers, and making the world a better place for people less fortunate. But meeting new people, interesting individuals with their own ideas and plans, opened my eyes to new, nuanced ways to go about doing things. For example, there was Ruth, a New York white girl with some decidedly black traits, whom I didn't date but whose journalistic independence and connections to other people came across as decidedly enlightened, advanced, and hip. She and I drove to St. Louis one weekend for area black professionals teaching early journalism skills to black St. Louis high schoolers; her conversation was so fluid and vibrant that I've never had a two-hour drive go by so fast. And Dr. Patterson was the most sincere, calm, and insightful professor I had met up until then. Her interest in social justice and how that affected blacks entering the profession was never more on view than our two-day Chicago trip, where we visited pioneers Francis Ward, Vernon Stone, the offices of Ebony, and the world-famous Billy Goat Tavern. We got into very meaty discussions with our guests, and I was struck by how intently she listened to each one, without ever talking about herself. Then there was Dr. Merrill, a Mississippi native, former Shreveport Times reporter, a prolific writer, vagabond rockstar professor and whom I first noticed on my first flight to Columbia. He had several degrees, but his master's in philosophy really made him stand out, arguing with anyone about anything. I had the honor of interviewing him for a story that I never got around to writing, but he was a joy to listen to, a half-smile always on his face, and a penchant for gently teasing people as he taught them. Finally, I met George Curry at the St. Louis workshop and interviewed him for my thesis. At the time a St. Louis Post-Dispatch investigative reporter, Curry was caustic about the job ahead for black journalists. "We tell them (students at the workshop), 'Nine times out of 10, you have to be twice as good as a white reporter. First, you can cry and call it racist, or secondly, you can say, 'Yes, it's racist, but I'm not going to let it stop me,'" he told me. I'd never heard a black journalist say these words so defiantly, as if they were absurdly obvious. I sensed a great deal of moral outrage sparked the words, but he, too, had a half-smile, as if all people knew this. There were too many other influencers to name here but suffice it to say each one taught me something about being assertive but not aggressive, a listener without judgment, and a critic without being harsh.

May 1978 approached, and it was nearly time to make another decision about my future, plus I was putting the last touches on my final thesis draft. So, I had two choices: send letters to numerous papers in locations of which I knew little or contact The Journal— which I wound up doing. I had visited the newsroom during the holiday break between semesters and had gotten a very warm reception from everyone and ended working a three-week "mini-internship" to help fill in gaps where regular staff had taken vacations. My work-load was heavier and more topical—including covering a family's tragic Christmas fire, a police crackdown on the sale of pornograph-ic books, a cab driver's murder, the search for the perpetrators, a local judge's dalliance with the upcoming mayoral campaign, the behind-the-scene's maneuverings to get a convicted killer paroled, an upcoming bond issue election, freezing rain conditions' impact on local streets and power lines, and an explanatory piece on zoning procedures. I guess I showed growth and skills, so much so that they quickly responded to my application letter with an enthusiastic in-terview invitation before I had even left Mizzou. The Journal offered me a probationary, three-month salary of $175 weekly (that would be nearly $900 now) plus benefits to cover the education beat—with which I was delighted and feeling vindicated, after my first go-round with the paper three years prior.

You'd be OK in assuming here that all's well would end well. But journalism is a strange mistress. That saying—"You can never go home again"—lurked in my mind's rear-view mirror as I started remembering all the things I disliked about Shreveport: The south-ern racial mentality, the small-town mindset of many, the police, the slowness of change, the fascination with sports, segregation, conser-vative politics—by what you've read here, you can probably deduce a few others. So, naturally I had my doubts, particularly about whether all I had learned at Mizzou would apply to Shreveport. And I short-sightedly considered the job an ending—my first, truly adult respon-sibility—to a list of experiments that started when Mamoo and I left Chicago in the mid-'60s. This was *it*, or so I thought. No more child-ish meanderings and reading books for fun and visits to the library and courses and teachers. Young adulthood had begun, and I had to prove up to the task. How to proceed with old friends, mentors, and the "Pookie" or "George" that they thought they knew? How could I show them I'd grown? Should I? "New kid in town" or "old book-end"? My Mizzou days made me feel as if—for the first time—I was a genuine human being; was I returning to those less-than-legitimate days or was I going to be allowed to be fully me? Had things changed at The Journal—much less Shreveport—to the point that I would get my full due, i.e., what other, white reporters expected, or would I be left to my own devices? Would I have to sport a facade—using the twin- or triple-perception that served me during my Jesuit and LSUS days—or could this new, more subtle George emerge from my first experiences as a full-time reporter? What kind of safeguard or cushion could I build if things went crooked?

I never expressed these feelings to anyone because I didn't know that I needed healing. My recovery would come in fits and starts, and I would need the advice of several would-be therapists who could help me trace the origins of the problem. I in no way assumed I was a finished product, "God's gift to journalism" or the Bob Woodward of Shreveport. But I also knew that I certainly had that goal in mind because, as per George Curry (and others who'd answered my thesis survey), I had to be twice as good as everyone else. But I didn't want to do so by code-switching—acting white to white sources and then acting black to black sources. If writing all those features at The Journal, The Missourian and then The Bossier Press—other than you couldn't depend on editors to always set you on the right course—had taught me anything, it was that people appreciated you if you were honest with them—saying you don't know when you don't and spitting out the truth even if they didn't want to hear it or had ignored it in forming their words or opinions. Trying to fool people or manipulate them into saying something they wouldn't otherwise say was a fool's errand, and eventually would cost you, either in trust or substance or something else down the line. It wasn't that I learned to ignore racism—that's impossible, because people, by nature, compare themselves to others, and comparison nearly always leads to a judgment of deficiency on someone's part. I wasn't exactly going to accept racism, either; that would be self-defeating or let sources get off too easy. Of course, this is much easier to do as you become more mature or older or both. This, too, requires an honesty of a sort—a self-honesty, if you will.

That means having an openness toward how people behave or how they relate to you; you try taking it in, examining and reflecting on it. This doesn't mean you have to code-switch, however. Code-switching is a form of lying or pretending to be someone else when you're not. Sure, it doesn't mean that some code-switching minorities don't survive or even succeed. But eventually, for your own peace of mind and to enable your own success, you must look at yourself from your own thoughts, rather than those of others. That doesn't mean that you embrace selfishness; how could you if you're a diligent, responsible journalist, whose first loyalty—if you're doing your job—is to the truth? Being a journalist, in my mind as I began my career at The Journal, I was to continually search for who I was while I simultaneously sought the truth for my readers. If that sounds pompous or pretentious, I didn't see it then, in 1978, as such. I simply thought I was being a solid citizen, a good human, trying to develop as many sides or aspects of myself as possible, meaning I wanted to do a lot of things, and show my editors that they made a good decision in hiring me. But just who was this guy that they hired? I'd come a long way from that high school kid working in the Cooper Road community. Developing human relations skills in our door-to-door neighborhood canvassing efforts gave me a feel for people that would serve my journalistic advancement, helping me to pull myself out of the self-created morass of becoming a math major and jump into the unknown that was Missouri. I thought I was ready for my final act in Shreveport. But Louisiana had, as always, other plans.

The School of Journalism facilities at the University of Missouri-Columbia.

5

I Am The Egghead

When I entered The Journal newsroom in June 1978, I didn't realize that I wouldn't be spending all that much time in it. For instance, my editors had rethought their initial idea of assigning the federal courthouse beat to me, switching me instead to the education writer job. As I discovered, that would mean covering all schools—public, private, colleges and universities, and anything that smacked of education—in the Arkansas-Louisiana-Texas region, as well as anything significant happening in the rest of Louisiana. Moreover, covered topics would range from policy changes, politics, school administration, teaching, teacher unions, parents, educational innovations and trends, and everything in between. Boredom would very seldom be an issue. Fortunately, the reporter I succeeded was there to orient me, providing tips on personalities, issues, logistics, helpful minions, and obstacles. On my first day I got a softball committee assignment, took an inordinate amount of time working on the lead (first impressions and all), filed the story, then settled in at my desk.

The backbone, or the essence of the beat, centered on covering the Caddo Parish (county) School Board, which at the time was the largest employer in the county and had more than 50,000 enrolled students. That meant going to extremely long meetings twice monthly, in addition to committee meetings, principal meetings, and gatherings of any substantial or powerful group in the school district. Given the 18 members of the board, plus the superintendent's staff, and the times of persistent desegregation and instructional change, no two meetings were ever totally calm, subdued, or orderly. Each board member—many of them former teachers or administrators—believed he or she had the most telling insights or critical concerns about most issues, which made for no shortage of interesting quotes or lack of emotional discussion turning points. It was a reporter's dream—or nightmare, depending on your tolerance for redundancy, pontification, or just plain silliness that emitted from the members' mouths. "For the future of the children of Caddo Parish" became the most emphatic catch phrase during the typical meetings.

And that was just the oral commentary. The politics could devolve into name-calling and personal hostility; "racist" and "socialist" weren't uncommon adjectives, with "shortsighted" and "misguided" often thrown in for good measure. More commonly, however, politics came in the form of reform (usually those coming from business background) vs. tradition, teachers vs. administrators, staff (and those board members so inclined) vs. board members, parents vs. administrators, and the old reliable: conservatives vs. progressives ("liberal" was hardly ever used; this was the South, after all). Fisticuffs were never raised, but several members would occasionally walk out in a huff, allegedly for restroom or smoking purposes. That was the Caddo board; its Bossier Parish counterpart prided itself on being the exact opposite: jovial, back-slapping, guffawing, paternalistic, and staff-trusting—if not exactly transparent. In fact, neither governing body much cared for the press and often had to be cajoled and occasionally coerced into sharing data, budgets, and the like. The Bossier group was particularly opaque as the meetings rarely lasted past an hour, discussion was at a minimum, and dissension was almost non-existent; furthermore, as the smaller group (12), the Bossier board members most assuredly had already had informal, individual meetings or intra-group phone calls of some kind about agenda items as their meetings almost never featured any extended, critical questions (what I discovered is a small-town mentality); it wasn't until about three years into the beat that I discovered they had committee meetings, the time and place of which no one ever thought to divulge. I always felt guilty when I departed the Bossier meetings, because in my heart I knew there was something I wasn't being told. Also, the fact that the group held its twice-monthly meetings several miles to the north of Bossier City (in Benton, population 2,000, or 50 times smaller than Bossier City) helped that body keep a low profile. Prior and subsequent education reporters had similar concerns.

Despite these obstacles, I developed a natural affinity for the school beat. Aside from spending most of my lifetime in schools, my foray into graduate school and extensive experience I had with teachers—mine and those who were friends and mentors at Blessed Sacrament—meant that I understood what the basic unit of all schools was: the classroom and its context within a school. Several of my Blessed Sacrament co-parishioners worked in or often visited the Caddo headquarters to meet with supervisors or attend meetings of various sorts. So, I had this built-in subset of sources I could usually use to confirm or discuss ideas—instructional or political, although not all were that forthcoming, as employee fear was rampant in Caddo schools in the shape of retribution, retirement outcomes, supervisory conflicts, and the like. But I strategically drew upon this knowledge base when it served to gain insights into sources' motivations and, thus, their Achilles heels. In addition, I developed a reputation for fairness, often visiting individual schools, writing soft features on classroom innovations, calling upon particularly secure and courageous principals for context, and always remembering that the folks at the ground level were certainly overworked and vastly underpaid for what they contributed.

Colleges were a slightly different matter. Professors have a great deal more autonomy than classroom teachers, building on the (often uninformed or outdated) materials through their advanced reading and study, plus their own research. They are somewhat like independent contractors who—while required to occasionally teach a "core" or basic course in their respective areas of the curriculum, also are expected to improve on a field's knowledge by doing independent, creative study or "research" in a specialty within a field, which is the reason you'll find an English literature professor who knows the ins and outs of American Jewish writers, or people in the classics, such as Dante, Shakespeare, London, Dickens, and Chaucer. As a result, professors have a split mission: to teach, to research, to help administer the university; this last part usually means having to serve on administrative committees, task forces, or projects to which they either get automatically assigned or volunteer. Of course, the teaching and research take precedence, but covering a college means keeping track of all the moving parts, including any supervisory, advisory, or trustee groups' actions—which often are rooted in politics, but in which most participants are smart enough not to be so obvious about it.

That primer, which I of course learned on the job, hopefully shows the extent to which education means so much. I haven't even discussed the financial aspect—the property tax debates, the bond elections, the sales tax collections, the awarding of grants, the state legislature's role—that sets the whole thing in motion and is itself affected by policy, politics, and demographics. Add to that the influences of the economy, and you come to appreciate what a homeowner or a parent must go through, in addition to worrying about their children's personal advancement. Education is central to American life, meaning that if any journalist or person tells you schools news is for mothers or sissies or those who can't become investigative reporters—you can tell them they don't know what they're saying.

As a result, I learned that there was always a political or a money angle to a story that could land my story on the front page of the paper, or, at least, the front page of the local news section. For example, after attending the Caddo board meetings for a while, I noticed that special education—the teaching and development of children with special physical and emotional needs—often was treated like the proverbial "red-headed stepchild" of education; no one on the board delved deeply into its procedures of placing students in the appropriate classroom. It took my suspicions that forced me to revisit the number of students awaiting what's called an IEP—individualized education program—and a subsequent internal disagreement as to what was causing such alarming numbers, before I convinced my editors that special ed's model of evaluating the students (largely involving the use of IQ tests) was on its way to becoming extinct with the passage of U.S. Public Law 94-142, the federal law requiring the mainstreaming of all special ed students into regular classrooms. IEPs became part of the newsroom's vocabulary afterward and we started receiving numerous calls from parents regarding special ed issues, of which there were many, and about which board members thereafter became more verbal.

There's also something to be said about the role of parents here. At first, I resented any of the ordinary citizens who would appear before an agency to discuss grievance or a matter of some personal concern. Most of these folks mean well, but living busy lives, they usually appear before the board or a council without any preparation—from understanding what the agency does to not knowing how to clearly convey their message. That's because it's probably their first time addressing a public body with possibly dozens of other citizens listening intently. And their nerves get tighter because everyone loves to watch when a well-intentioned speaker goes off the rails, letting their emotions escape, unable to modulate those feelings, and broadcasting wild conspiracy theories. Often such well-meaning folks must be reminded either that they're out of time, or that the concern is already being addressed, or even that they have the wrong agency. Not a pretty picture and as frustrating as talking to an inattentive teenager. In essence, they're likely wasting their time. Either way, it delays the group's ability to address its stated agenda and makes everyone else retreat into what I call "meeting hell"—visibly or metaphorically shaking their heads, looking down at the floor so they don't have to watch the train wreck anymore, coughing or sighing deeply as a plea or signal for someone in authority to do something to move the meeting along, or running to the restroom to decompress from the sheer boredom created by the speaker. Of course, the solution is to speak with the appropriate staff person ahead of the meeting to get all your feelings out and find out what can feasibly be done to solve your issue.

In any case, in the controversial '70s—when local people really began to have suspicions about government at all levels (called "the accountability movement") and didn't have Google to provide them with ready-made background information—schools were starting to engage with many social issues, which made many homeowners and parents of young children nervous. I've already mentioned special education, which legislators and Congresspersons tried to remove from the dark shadows and the closed doors of institutionalized settings and into the public schools. As with every government innovation (some might instead call it "intrusion"), there were usually unintended consequences that riled certain segments of the public. One of these was racial segregation which—while rightly deserving of the federal government's ire—often was a logistical, as well as a policy, nightmare. The central problem was a question of how to implement integration to the satisfaction of all involved parties; and in the South, that also meant logistically avoiding "white flight," in which dissatisfied or suspicious white parents would withdraw their kids from public school integration efforts if it meant lowering the quality of education or, frankly, having to send their children to school with black kids—although no one ever would use those words. Often, they objected to losing the "neighborhood concept" central to most school organizations or putting their kids on buses for rides into "undesirable" neighborhoods for integration's sake. So, educators had their hands full—and that was just with the white parents. Black parents also had their concerns, of course, as desegregation plans often meant busing more black students away from their home-district schools into white neighborhoods, adding considerable transit time to their school day. And we haven't even addressed the quality of the academics affected by such plans.

Knowing this scenario will help you understand my first big mistake—just a month into the job. After a long, dreary June Wednesday covering the normal Caddo board meeting, I witnessed the members decide late that evening to break for an executive session—a closed-door meeting to discuss personnel or legal matters, one of which was the current, ongoing desegregation lawsuit against Caddo. As I was a relatively new reporter, I knew that most such sessions were never discussed once the board returned to its regular session, and that only personnel promotions remained on the agenda. So, I and other reporters decided we'd had enough and called it quits for the evening. Unfortunately for us, a board member had decided to open a can of worms, introducing a controversial motion to defy the federal court's standing order to hire teachers on a 50-50 black/white racial basis; the motion failed by a tie vote, 7-7. The matter became public thanks to someone calling our editors. Of course, I was mortified; missing a momentous public vote is a reporter's worst nightmare. I stupidly compounded the problem—after being asked about my whereabouts—by lying and saying I left because I thought the meeting was over. In my defense, the closed-door session was three hours long—you probably would have left, too; why should I stick around for some insignificant personnel matters? Surely the newspaper didn't want to pay for three hours of twiddling my thumbs. My boss, city editor Bill, already knew my answer was a lie (first law of investigative reporting: Never ask a question without knowing the answer), so he then was furious for *two* reasons—leaving my post *and* lying about it. Fortunately, he let me off with a stern warning— and I never again left a meeting before it ended. But I also never truly trusted my city editor again; let's just say I didn't know for sure where his loyalties rested. Truth be told, Bill always made me anxious. I'd been on his bad side, and I'd also seen how red-in-the-face mad he could get with the other reporters if they got on his bad side. I'd often get a knot in my stomach, knowing that any assignment from him could wind up with a tongue-lashing if I didn't meet expectations; other times, he was OK with you returning to the newsroom empty-handed. It was like dealing with the nuns—not much good would come of it if you failed, but you wouldn't be sure if that's what they had in mind. That plus some of the assignments he handed down at times could come off as kind of goofy if you weren't exactly looking at the task through Bill's eyes—like the time I wound up in one of the city's worst, poorest, crime-ridden neighborhoods after dark, knocking on doors, and asking whether the residents knew of any vote-buying activities that Bill suspected. I was a skeptic about which Bill I could expect, to say the least—and with good reason: About two or three weeks later, the bomb dropped.

Bill decided to run for the state Senate. He was a maverick to start, going to school at a private Evangelical Christian liberal arts college in Wheaton, Illinois, running a cattle ranch before he went into investigative journalism and conducted a police corruption probe that landed him a Pulitzer nomination—and the job that brought him to The Journal. He also had a master's degree from a Baptist seminary and was a crusader of sorts—I recalled covering him as among the leading doubters of a pro-fluoride activist the city had invited. To our amazement, Bill subsequently won the election in a runoff and went on to becoming a leading proponent of creationism in schools and has explored his own Cherokee heritage in a book about a Native American sculptor. We were flabbergasted that he would leave us, but the upside was that everyone loved Mitch, his interim successor.

Before Mitch's permanent appointment, however, I tried to lay low and simply do my job, not knowing who would replace Bill. One of my goals, besides fully covering meetings, was to complement the subsequent barrage of stories about racial matters whenever I could and try to familiarize myself with the schools themselves. So, I made a point—with the help of the schools' PR staff—to find one school or teacher every week or so that was doing something innovative in the classroom. For example, I found a principal who'd introduced the "club concept" to his school, getting kids to join extracurricular clubs that helped students learn the fun side of their regular subjects; a space exploration club might complement a science class, for instance. Another time, I watched as a PE teacher, good with his hands, introduce a mini-gym he had built to his students to help them master basic physical skills. And there was the second-grade teacher who made basic reading skills fun by inserting them into game-playing activities. In short, not only was I gaining entrée into the schools, but I also got an inkling of the structures and work-arounds that teachers had to devise, as I simultaneously developed an admiration for the teaching process and how much love many teachers provide in doing their jobs. I also gained insight into exactly how curriculum standards, pay schedules, teaching goals, teacher motivation, and classroom teacher-pupil ratios worked their way into everyday classroom life. All teachers were interested in our coverage of the School Board, but over time I realized they were mostly trying to balance day-to-day resources with their responsibilities to their students, hoping that they wouldn't come up short most of the time. It made the racial and political hot topics that we gave so much attention to most days seem a little removed from what was important. That The Journal was concerned with racial matters in Shreveport was natural, given our publisher Dr. Charles Beaird's leading role in the court-appointed committee that was looking over the board's shoulders; naturally he wanted matters correctly presented to readers and to the influencers he knew. And our editors went out of their way to remember that—impressing upon reporters that The Journal would report all significant racial complications. But that emphasis felt at times as if it almost overruled all other considerations, which was why my school visits felt refreshing; the people I talked with were not as professionally or politically invested as those who directly dealt with School Board-related fallout.

Taking a break from deadline at The Shreveport Journal, circa 1979.

Using that involvement as a measuring stick, I noticed more and more differences among my sources. For example, at first I thought that Caddo School Superintendent Walter Lee was just another dumb southerner, because he talked so slowly. But when I heard myself agreeing with some of his statements, I realized his slow cadence was for my benefit—to assure that I got every…last…word…he…said…accurately…written…down. I also realized that, at times, he felt hen-pecked by the persnickety board, which seemed to find fault with everything he proposed. So, yes, I discovered people liked you to listen to them and would respond positively if you could reliably show that's what you were doing. That spurred me to constantly ask for examples, and, when they were finished, to briefly summarize what they had said back to them. I guess you could say that I was growing up, but I liked to believe that I simply was more attentive and not as self-conscious as I was at the start of the job. I also noticed that blacks—particularly those in positions of responsibility—were reticent to definitively go on the record at first, consistently—with a joking smile—responding with something akin to, "Now, wait a minute; don't go writing everything down yet. Let me explain something to you." I didn't know if this was because they previously had been burned by an incompetent or deceptive reporter, but this began to rankle me because white sources had no such reservations or fears, and I almost started to believe that these black sources just were too dumb to recognize a good opportunity to educate the public. But, after a while, I appreciated that this was more a show of fear—of repercussions, consequences, retribution. After all, despite the advent of the federal government's integration mandate (or threat, depending on your view), if you were black, you probably thought nothing in the way of promotion, raises, or positive reinforcement was guaranteed in the Caddo system. Whereas Walter Lee's verbal slowness reflected an eagerness for accuracy, his black assistant superintendents and administrators almost came to represent publics pillars of possible panic—at least that's how they came across in board meetings, to the point that they almost seemed "Uncle Tom-ish" in complying with board requests or deferent in responding to its questions. This really puzzled me since I knew these people were highly respected (and well-paid, for '70s Shreveport) and not at all like their white counterparts in these respects. But I was really embarrassed for them and for me and all black people. "Hell," I thought, "are we still back in slave times at this damn place?" I remembered, though, that I'd seen this act before—at my dad's place of work, with McCoy at the foundry, with every black custodial worker at LSUS, and at Mizzou with the cafeteria workers at Loeb Hall: the age-old act of fear, of a superior or bigger or greater foe or adversary. I'd foolishly believed that higher placement on the organizational chart would give you a seat at the autonomy table; but it took a while before most of the black supervisors felt truly at ease with me, despite my darker skin and quasi-Afro. Today's me would have pushed them more, so that I could understand better; but in the 1970s I was more concerned about obtaining facts and understanding decisions, rather than picking up on the human nuances among the people with the facts.

Determined to get to the bottom of the school system's decision-making process, I took the risky step to use the privilege every journalist enjoyed and decided to selectively grant some sources— particularly those fearful of their superiors' likely revenge tactics— anonymity, freedom from identification, if what they told me could be verified. This effectively put many sources, especially black administrators, somewhat more at ease in revealing how things worked in the system. Mostly I discovered, as you could imagine, that not all that happened in the schools was for the benefit of the students; personal agendas, alliances, preferential resource allocations, state politics, and board member patronage and their tendencies to want to reward faithful staff confidantes or certain constituencies in their districts came into play—no shock there; just people doing what people usually do. Such influence-peddling remains prevalent in Louisiana politics to this day but largely remains invisible until someone finally gets fed up or excluded until they've reached a breaking point. This is the stuff of the prize-winning reporting that we students always heard about in J school but rarely could practice because of our youthful inexperience and lack of patience. Long story short: I began to trust—i.e., grant complete anonymity—to one particularly offend-ed source, who would share the board's real thinking, what it would only share behind closed doors or in personal, hallway discussions. As a result, I began to ask more informed questions in questioning the staff and the board. In return, I gained the trust of what I con-sidered "inner circle" persons in the school district—from parents on up the food chain, simply because they had come to realize that I now mattered to the process, and that I might also help them, usually by sharing some or all of what I knew about a subject.

TAKING J101

Journalism 101: This kind of access obviously marked a turning point in my technique, but also in my productivity. It's amaz-ing how a faucet that was running at a trickle's pace could be adjusted by using a little leverage. What had been a succession of simply covering speeches, press conferences, and meetings gradually changed into me being able to synthesize and analyze and then *determine what would be more interesting for the reader*. I put that last part into italics because much of a beginning reporter's job usually involves completing assignments given to him or her by a supervis-ing editor. A beginning reporter can't match the local or institutional knowledge of the local area of the editor, so early on, necessary cov-erage gets dictated by the editor, who usually will refer you to the newspaper's library for background because the editor has too many other things to worry about, specifically, keeping you and the other reporters busy enough to supply an adequate amount of stories to keep readers reading. The exception comes in a beginning reporter who has a good deal of prior reporting experience or who spends more than a normal amount of time learning about his or her des-ignated beat and, as a result, knows ahead of time what needs to be covered. Or, as a reporter, you can get to that level of expertise by having an exceptionally good feel for the people important to your beat. Good or decent salaries can keep a reporter motivated to stay on that beat for a longer time than, say, an average TV reporter who's underpaid and overworked and itching to work in a bigger city or more prestigious beat and who usually quits a beat in less than a year. And the fact that the schools beat is not all that visually friendly only aggravates the situation for the TV reporter.

However, with greater knowledge came greater responsibility. I began to see the school system as one of the big cogs among other, semi-big or smaller cogs in the education system of Louisiana. Other major cogs included the state's LSU system, its Southern (a historically black college or university) system, and all the "directional colleges" nestled in every corner of the state and elsewhere, depending on a region's political pull (this last group was well-known for rampant duplication of programs among its members). These colleges not only supply the teachers for the state's local school systems, but also the key members of specialized, politically savvy populations—not least, the state's legislators, but also the prestige professions (with vocal white *and* black memberships), the state's teacher unions, and most of the leadership (think business owners and executives) of the state. Each has an opinion, and chances are that where they went to school will account for some part of that opinion. Nowhere was this truer than in the controversy surrounding the use of standardized testing to determine who could be certified to teach—a political football if there ever was one in Louisiana. Of course, there were myriad explanations—some test critics saw testing as an attempt to confirm beliefs in disparity of racial capabilities, others saw the cutoff scores as unrealistically high, others said some teacher programs should be dismantled, while others said testing was a necessity to combat what they saw as inadequate Louisiana teaching (at high school and collegiate levels). So, I took the test, scored well, then set about examining all the criticisms, upsetting both racial camps along the way and providing valuable background for readers, instead of self-serving quotes from experts. I had to do this for my own sanity, if I was going to know who to believe and having more to relay to readers than simple, "he-said/she-said" quoting. Doing so would be basically giving up on finding the truth, and sort of capitulating to the fact that since I had both black and white blood, to be objective I'm going to find out *only* what both sides say and leave it at that. No way; I hoped my Missouri approach—becoming my own expert or "egghead", as many in the public see educators—to get closer to the truth of important issues, would eventually set me apart from the other reporters in The Journal newsroom. At least, I would try it until I could no longer see its utility.

My drive to do so, however, suffered brief setbacks. Never one to pay that much attention to health matters, I jumped right into my reporting job full throttle after I left Mizzou. My only concern was not the job, but instead that nature—or whatever you want to call it—jumped into my headlights. At first, it was a brief, fleeting moment of I-don't-know-what, a sense that I was experiencing a weird, unbalancing, unsettling feeling in my head, as if my head was spinning when in fact, my vision remained fine; this would particularly bother me when I drove. My otolaryngologist (ear, nose, and throat specialist) said it likely was because of too much caffeine; forever after, many a good acquaintance of mine has doubted my manhood when hearing me order a decaf coffee or drink at a restaurant. I never knew that could happen with too much coffee or tea, but I drank the Kool-Aid, so to speak, cutting back on my three- or four-cup or more daily habit, and went on my normal, happy way. Not soon after, I developed an uneasy feeling when driving, especially on the interstate or in rural settings, as if the wide-open spaces felt threatening; it worsened to the point that I started worrying about oncoming traffic (Louisiana was notoriously full of two-lane roads and highways) possibly veering into my lane, feeling the fear in the pit of my stomach and progressing to the point that I would have to stop, pause, take a breath, and steady myself before I could continue. Crazy, huh?

With the help of some positive advice from friends (and even School Board staff), however, I began to realize such negative thoughts could be transformed if I willed it so and practiced positive thoughts. Problem solved—until it wasn't, and I began to feel down, defeated, and just plain despondent for no reason at all. I couldn't see the good in anything, everything seemed to have a downside. Oddly enough, these feelings started as soon as I started becoming more productive at work. Fortunately, they dissipated after about a month or so. I didn't realize I had a problem until a friend from my involvement with a social justice group (backed by the local Catholic diocesan office) just started giving me motherly advice—about my feelings, women, sports, Catholicism, being a good person, and anything else we discussed. My editor Mitch occasionally would assign me to write for the Saturday religion page, so covering the social justice group and this person, Nancy, became a regular occurrence. A white transplant from Mizzou and the chief organizer of something called Social Justice Day, and—it so happened—a close friend of our top editor Stanley's wife, Nancy also was the most compassionate person I'd ever met. It didn't hurt that she and her husband at the time, with their suburban brood of four kids, reminded me of my cousin Daughter and Doc in Chicago—good Catholics, including a stay-at-home mom who seemed always cool and unruffled, and a great sense of humor. And she was a natural writer, so much so that The Journal made her one of the four "neighborhood" reporters who'd have a weekly page to relay all the community goings-on in a specific city area; her civic involvement made her an innate reporter who also seemed to know everyone or know someone who knew everyone. You could go to her for any informal advice about Shreveport events and people. I overlooked the fact that she was a devout Catholic, because she loved a good nun joke as much as the next person. At any rate, Nancy was my go-to whenever life was stumping me, which it quite often did in those days. Looking back, and knowing what I know about my children's lives, I simply was having growing pains, trying to accomplish a lot in a short amount of time and not having mastered a work-life balance.

This attempt to have more command of things that mattered to me did, however, set me on a path to do more than simply doing my job. It meant I was starting to look at my career trajectory and whether I liked where it was headed. The whole thing was set in motion by a little letter I received in the mail from an executive at The

Boston Globe, directly asking if I had thought about journalistically moving up from Shreveport, professionally speaking. At first, I was flattered, seeing the letter as an acknowledgment that my reporting was starting to get noticed. But the letter caught me off guard because, up until then, I had never thought of working anywhere else except Shreveport. And why not—the pay was good (especially with regular overtime), and I had saved enough money to reach two goals: buying a new car (and letting Mamoo have the old '65 Chevy) and moving into my own apartment, finally leaving the nest. Having mastered the Chevy's stick shift, and the '70s oil crisis and gas shortage still fresh in mind, I stayed with manual transmissions and bought a little, new goldish yellow Japanese Datsun B210 from Randy's brother-in-law (he had gotten married to the librarian from the city library; more about this later), who gave me a good deal. I was turning into a real grownup: Witness the fact that the apartment also was the result of networking, learning about its availability from one of the Journal secretaries. The newspaper had also experienced a personal setback, losing one of our editors, a 25-year-old, only three months into his tenure; his history of heart trouble caught up to him. So, things weren't swirling but change was a factor, causing me to consider and eventually accept The Globe's offer to visit for an interview, although I wasn't sure exactly what it was that I was seeking in a job. Everyone I asked about whether I should accept a job there gave me neutral or predictable answers. "Gee, if you like it, sure!" or something to that effect; no one gave me an enthusiastic thumbs up or a definitive "No; it sucks". I knew Boston was a great town: home to Harvard, MIT, and the Celtics, never friendly to the New York Yankees, famous for its lobsters and other seafood delicacies, and site of some of the nastiest neighborhood protests of school busing. My trip, with my Journal editors' approval, occurred one cold wintry weekend; I didn't know a soul in Boston, but I had the phone number of a local TV newsman who was friends with a Shreveport broadcaster I knew. He was a rising black star in Boston broadcast circles, destined for one of the networks. Kind, considerate, patient, and honest, he pointedly told me the Boston job was a good place to work in terms of journalism, but it was not without racists and racism. The Globe had won five Pulitzers and was a known stepping-stone to The New York Times for many of its reporters and editors. But I wasn't impressed, maybe foolishly so. The newsroom looked like dozens of other newspaper newsrooms and some of the reporters looked old enough to be my parents. But I couldn't see myself starting over as a reporter, which was what they were offering; I was looking for a new challenge, not knowing that there was a lot I didn't know about reporting. Plus, I wasn't blown away by anything enough to push me out of the "maybe" category. It was as if they felt *I* should be the one who was blown away. They had the wrong guy that day. In a phone call a day later, and after speaking with our top editor Stanley, I decided to stay in Shreveport, unsure if I'd made the right choice, but certainly sure that I felt no impetus to leave when I felt I had it so good. I figured something better, more substantive would develop, even if I didn't know now what it would be. Neither did, it happened, my Journal editors.

As much as a reward for staying or a pacifier for understanding that I was becoming restless, Mitch sent me one weekend to Little Rock, Arkansas, of all places, to a National Governors Association regional meeting to cover state strategies for energy security. That thing was dull as dishwater; not even a chit-chat with then-Gov. Bill Clinton could move the needle on my dull-o-meter. I couldn't wait to return to Shreveport—and write a funny column about how dull the conference was. Maybe that's what my editors wanted me to see? That life could be worse? Or, that things would get better, meatier, in terms of our education focus? Meanwhile, life covering the Caddo School Board returned to explaining the financial pros and cons of a new early-elementary-level basic skills program that promised to end social promotions; the board was trying to backdoor some federal funds to help pay for the program, for which it had chosen the least-funded route. While I worked that story, however, I began to flex my investigative chops: I had stumbled upon a great scoop (journalese for exclusive) story revealing local state education employees had been coerced into buying testimonial tickets to help retire the education superintendent's re-election campaign debt. Although he denied the accusation, we put the story on the front page, citing and relying on anonymous sources. I thought I had done a great job until one of my sources, a black woman who was a friend of a relative, called, sobbing and saying she had lost her job because her superiors had manipulated others into finding out who could have possibly leaked the story. Of course, they didn't officially fire her for helping with the story, but on some other, trumped-up allegations. I felt foolish when she called, and I was powerless to help her find another position. So much for trying to show governmental corruption; I went back to school news, taking my frustration out on Caddo, reporting its second-worst percentage in Louisiana for those awaiting special ed IEPs; even worse, Caddo schools' rate was 10 times worse than that of Bossier schools—ouch! Such an easy target, but a routine that was getting old, and, if I'm honest, could be seen as unfair to Caddo: An urban school district isn't likely to win in a comparison between it and the neighboring suburban district. Caddo wasn't helping itself, either, by continuing to define a fourth grader as someone reading at or within a year of fourth-grade reading level—and infuriating the state because that definition didn't jibe with the state's (someone attending a fourth-grade class); this also played havoc for those trying to compare results across counties/parishes. Of course, this was a political as much as a curricular move: The district was under constant criticism for low assessment test scores (a movement in which The Journal played a large role), which largely could (and would) be pinned on its substantial black enrollment; this claim was often used by educators to soften the news of lower scores and heighten the criticism that assessment tests themselves were culturally biased against black students. Caddo's fudging of this definition also meant a percentage of Caddo's test-eligible students was significantly lower than students in other counties—creating contentious, controversial, highly publicized news in counties newly desegregated. Also, it didn't help that Caddo had significantly more students who had no racial identification on their testing materials. I also set my sights on higher education, particularly my alma mater LSUS, doing a week-long series on its political, staffing, and curricular shortcomings at a crucial point—the search for a new chancellor. All the while, I kept doing the weekly light-hearted features showcasing inventive teaching methods, and interest in local education matters began to pick up, a good thing for my career but only adding confusion to my search for identity.

PLANS IN BLACK AND WHITE

Then things got even more heated. One of my anonymous sources helped me to develop a story that reported that the Justice Department had hired an expert to configure a desegregation plan for Caddo. The story was published on a Friday and was the top story of every local news outlet in Shreveport; it helped that we copyrighted the story, meaning they had to cite our paper as originally reporting the story. The very next day, I was invited to a closed-door meeting of black delegates to the state Democratic convention being held in Shreveport that weekend; the message they wanted to me to hear was their disgust with current practices and leadership within the party and their feelings that they were being taken for granted. I had to admit that the two stories made it seem that a racial reckoning was coming to Shreveport in some form. It also meant that I had solidified my standing in the local black community as a friend, or at least a reliable mouthpiece, for black grievances. But more particularly for me, I had set myself on a path to continually pursue all things racial in writing about public schools. That copyrighted story gained notoriety for us, but also the expectation that we would be at the forefront of the issue of segregation/integration, checking for whatever influence could potentially do harm, such as if Caddo voted to accept NTE scores (i.e., what would happen to black or any teachers who couldn't make the cutoff) as partial hiring requirements, and then ask federal courts for relief from the 50/50 black/white hiring ratio mandate (because the NTE would hamper recruitment). People were beginning to get paranoid, or—at least—skeptical of others' motivations.

The resulting cloak-and-dagger atmosphere (in the minds of my editors, at least) made for interesting-yet-inconsequential updates. For example, while Caddo still had nothing in hand from the feds, principals were beginning publicly to worry about white flight. After being grilled one night by a predominantly white parents' group about desegregation matters, I got so frustrated by all the rumors that I wrote a column saying let's wait until we have all the facts before we begin sparking more rumor-mongering. I wasn't feeling all that reader-friendly, knowing that our all-consuming search for quality stories had wound up costing my competitor—a truly nice guy—at The Times his job because he wasn't keeping up with us. Plus, I was simultaneously covering so many other non-educational topics that I didn't have much time to think about that job opening, especially since I turned down a "name your price" unofficial offer for that position, my loyalty to The Journal overwhelming any inkling I might have had to switch to "the enemy". But I was conscientious enough about racial matters to lay out a story about a model example—from Little Rock, of all places—of how a school district learned to combat white flight, despite real estate agents' best attempts to the contrary. I realized that things were getting more contentious, after the Caddo board's mid-May 1980 meeting was particularly hard-headed. Members used dog-whistling terms—for example: standards, forfeiting quality for equality—in deliberating what to do when faced with a shortage of teachers, especially blacks. At The Journal, we determined that we might as well do a multi-part series revisiting Caddo's long history of fighting the federal government regarding public schools; at one point, I felt as if I was doing the local schools attorney's job for him, revealing how to navigate the ins and outs of getting an integration plan accepted by the courts. My research showed that the feds usually were foremost concerned with integration, *then* education—not really a good omen for either blacks or whites. I talked to lots of people on both sides: None wanted to piss off the judge who'd be making the ultimate decision, a Shreveporter named Tom Stagg. So, no one would give me a definitive quote except the cautious few who knew that a lot of negotiation would have to occur first. Anonymous sources once again helped me understand that white flight was really an issue of white parents' fear for their kids' safety and that teacher quality was made more complex by the outsize role of principals and how aggressively they pursued quality candidates in summer. And the School Board's insistence on standing firm on its NTE cutoffs complicated matters, leading to outspoken criticism from key black community leaders in the Legislature and the clergy, suggesting racist intent by the board and its administration. The board relented somewhat, waiving the NTE-passage rule for about two dozen teachers who were already certified—all of them black—and to appease the city's leading black minister and his colleagues, who attended a board meeting en masse to specifically to complain about how badly the board had been treating blacks. Although happy to be the servant of this verbal sparring, I was getting a little tired (and dismayed) at all the posturing and supposed, promised "showdowns" to come. Shreveport (and I) felt like a house truly divided. So, to amp my journalistic game, I resorted to a little confrontational trickery. It so happened that Gordon Foster, the University of Florida professor-expert charged with creating the feds' proposed plan, was meeting with Dept. of Justice attorneys in Shreveport for a day on a Thursday in mid-July—but that was all I knew. So, posing as Foster on the phone, I was able to get the number of his return flight to Gainesville. After discovering the departure time, I decided to rush my little Datsun west on Interstate 20 to the airport, where I promptly paged Foster because I wouldn't be able to pick him out of a crowd, having never seen or met him. Fortunately, he heard the page and came to the flight check-in desk to see who was paging him. Unethical? My Mizzou profs might say "perhaps", but I couldn't simply give up; confronting him face-to-face would at least yield a quick interview. The Justice lawyers around him were furious, but the public at least learned that desegregation planning was a long process, involving a lot of discussion, drafting, and re-drafting. Anyway, it made for a good story to use whenever I spoke to a journalism class on journalism and situational ethics. Meanwhile, I had become the *de facto* race reporter of sorts at the paper, drawing assignments to include racial results in the school district's annual student suspension data (blacks fought, whites played hooky) and to cover the local DA's allegedly biased handling of the legal case surrounding a controversial racial confrontation between a black city councilman and two white policeman (councilman pleaded guilty to a lesser charge). The "race card" divisiveness in Shreveport seemed to be seeping into daily life—Shreveport's and mine.

So, at times, the racial subject matter forced me to take stock. Sometimes covering the dissension on the School Board made me wonder if the reactions were more about concerns for quality education (which almost took on dog-whistling status in the minds of some). *Whose* quality of education were we discussing—for a specific race or for all? And where did I fit? If I figured out a source's intent, would that mean that person was just a racist or truly concerned or—and you couldn't put this stance past anyone—was it just something said simply to scare listeners and the public? Of course, I tried to make educated guesses, especially in the cases of white speakers, as *their stances regarding how to integrate* largely were being challenged by the presence of the federal government. But I also knew blacks could be conditioned to only be concerned with black students, as that was the population that historically was at a disadvantage and their political base. As a reporter, such back-and-forth, dualistic thought processes could, at times, feel overwhelming, detract from your focus and sometimes obscure some of the pertinent context. Again, that's one reason that reporters often just report what sources say, as you're likely to not break any ethical rules, while suggesting that you're simply trying to remain objective.

In any event, as the summer progressed, I covered desegregation in drib and drabs, most of it concerning speculation about the NAACP's possible involvement or the extension of Justice Department efforts to include Louisiana's dual higher education system. But the start of a new magnet high school, increasing school lunch prices, and a newer, more relevant basic skills reading program loomed as things that would also demand my attention in what looked to be an unusually busy 1980 fall. If you considered that Caddo teachers were going to enjoy a new 10 percent raise, the system's gifted and talented program was getting a makeover, and most teachers, principals and assistant principals had received satisfactory or higher evaluations, things might have looked a little brighter for the students *and* for the politicians, many of whom were up for re-election. But racial matters weren't unique to Shreveport—this was, after all, Louisiana. About two hours south, a small group of parents captured attention of a different sort; led by a failed candidate for Congress. This Rapides Parish group decided to turn a court-ordered closed school into an active one, holding classes for almost 200 students, defying a court-mandated desegregation ruling to bus their children 10 miles away to another school. I didn't know it at the time, but their actions would eventually lead to the end of my school-covering days. I'll speak to that a little later, but the existence of other desegregation-related activities, especially by parents, showed the depth of the political problem in Louisiana. In the minds of many Louisianians, the courts and the federal attorneys gave the impression of interfering with the status quo, upsetting the apple cart, if you will. This is particularly true when any proposed integration plan or approach proposed to use elementary school children as pieces of the puzzle to be rearranged. It's probably because of the young ages of these children—as young as 5 and usually no older than 12 or 13—that people and paents got so upset about what they see as the politicization of what should be an idyllic childhood experience. It's difficult to see such concern as racism—it's just being good parents, right? At least, that's what I tried to remember if I had to interview any such people (reporters sometimes don't like to interview those persons who have a personal, intimate stake in a situation—they can become emotional and extremely biased toward what they see as "protecting" their children). In most cases, these parents are white because, to date, *they're* the ones whose routines and whose children are being discussed for *possibly* bearing the brunt of the possible change although, on the opposing side, black or minority children are the ones who've borne the brunt of the likely inferior-but-well-meaning approach to education. This could mean that black parents may see potential student busing or pairing of schools as a *good* thing to be tolerated if their children were to be given help in reaching parity instruction with white kids.

No matter. I was dispatched the 145 miles to Forest Hill, sight of the takeover, which many experts boldly predicted soon would fizzle, expecting the overseeing judge to either send troops or to hold the group's members in contempt. The judge had devised his own desegregation plan to avoid what he thought was a worse plan—drawn up by the same academic, Gordon Foster, responsible for Caddo's upcoming federal proposal. The synergies in the case were obvious, and all strategies—no matter how flawed or bold—were open to public scrutiny and debate. If white parents in this smaller, more rural school system could develop such a response, what would those in Shreveport concoct? Speaking of which, things were getting hotter, not from resistance but from weather, which had forced some schools to close early and prompted outlandish cost projections ($50 million) for system-wide air-conditioning, of which only 17 percent of Caddo schools had at the time. In Rapides, as you might imagine, most objections were coming from the county's rural whites because blacks saw the plan as a no-brainer to give inner-city blacks (in the county's largest city of Alexandria) an integrated experience. Whites, on the other hand, saw the plan as disruptive, putting students on buses earlier in the day for longer times.

While we covered Rapides' issues, we also published Foster's Caddo proposal draft—with a front-page story—by simply printing a map with all schools listed with their projected feeder (supplying) schools, with cautions from administrators that the proposal really was an "approach" more than a plan. Foster and the feds even went so far as to say they hoped school leaders could devise an alternative or better plan; talk about saying, "Please don't make this another Rapides Parish deal!" He even told me that the plan omitted five additional components—such as teacher assignment, school plant, extra activities—that most plans usually have; so, we were talking the relative "baby steps" of plans. The immediate public reaction was slightly muted, with a few upset calls but not anything overwhelming. One public meeting in the north of the county was civil, with no one supporting the proposal; my first reaction to the calm reaction was to wonder if we in "the media" were all wrong in how we were covering the matter. Why weren't people more upset? Why *wasn't* this imitating what was going on in Forest Hill? Maybe if we or the school system adopted a systematic, non-racial, method-based approach we could decipher the common desires of both races and I could stop feeling like a ping-pong ball?

Meanwhile, it seemed as if school administrators started doing just that: analyzing the plan for loopholes, costs, incentives, and strategizing as to what would please the public and the board. A popular option included magnet schools—alternative schools that usually have a special curriculum that attracts (thus the term "magnet") students from a diverse population. The term had been discussed many times in board meetings, in other school districts, by experts of one kind or another. This was especially true in the case for gifted students (and white parents) and those who had seen Caddo administrators hold up the system's one magnet as an exemplary case and a good way to beat a court order. I had to admit that my visits to the magnet school and talks with its principal left good impressions, reminding me of the performing arts magnet featured in the then-popular film Fame debuting that summer. Aimed primarily at whites, these schools had a—pardon the pun—mixed track record, with success widely dependent on their curricula, locale, and target population. So, about a month after we published Foster's approach, I did a week-long series about magnet schools' pros, cons, and everything in-between. Even so, the board divided over whether any new plans, magnets, or alternatives should be presented, citing an earlier, temporary court ruling that the school system was unitary (i.e., it had no evidence of a dual (black/white) system) and that considering alternatives was a concession that it wasn't unitary. Yes, it seemed as if we had some real knuckleheads on the board, prompting me again to consider their personal motivations in the matter. But although racial division regarding the plans still was the public's primary fear, attendance figures showed no white flight. Not surprisingly, however, the board's attempt to get voter approval on funding for air conditioning all schools failed, mostly because of white voters, likely backlash against integration talks. Soon thereafter, the board found a moral victory in unanimously authorizing negotiations with the Justice Department without losing any legal rights to appeal or challenge any plan. This is the kind of recalcitrant attitude that the feds had to engage. I felt sorry for the board's staff, having to bite its tongue through all the hand-wringing and the wait-and-see foot-dragging as proposals were ferried back and forth. Plus, the board hoped Ronald Reagan's newly elected administration would offer any solace or relief—drawing a threat from local black educators to submit their own busing plan. Some board members didn't even want to discuss surveying parents about their opinions, fearing it might jeopardize the Justice Department's view of the board's position—in essence, negotiating in bad faith. "What a circus," was all I could think to myself as I watched this nuanced flirtation with alternatives. I was beginning to hate politics, especially when—after the board and the feds met in early December—everybody was happy and smiling and said there'd be more swapping of info and then more back and forth, perhaps even a couple more months. Oh, for the love of God! Could it be that all it would take would be a few smiles, handshakes, and knowing winks to get this thing settled?

Of course, it was going to take much more. My own analysis, which I never shared in the paper for fear of scaring anybody into doing something rash, saw the issue as bizarrely complex. First, my feeling was that any plan to duplicate the seeming success of the first magnet high school would have to find a damn good, multiracially oriented principal with a good eye for instructional basics and who had a good way with any kind of public or parental group. That was the vibe I got from Magnet High Principal Ascension Smith, a Spanish native and a warm, open, lover of learning. Trying a cookie-cutter approach to simultaneously open multiple magnets can be a recipe for disaster, depending on the curriculum, the principal, and the faculty; it's hard to get all three right in the first year. Second, community and curriculum need to go hand in hand when opening any magnet. The subject material—a less fancy name for curriculum—must have a natural constituency, hopefully one that is racially or multiculturally mixed. The community must be substantial or have terrific potential for growth. Let's say you're going to start a business-oriented magnet that requires a large enough business community with ample resources, possible mentors, and champions of education with enough intellectual diversity to help shape a diverse and multi-faceted course roster that can grow and change. That latter part means the faculty must be given curricular control but be advised—and potentially taught via continuing education courses— by business leaders who can spot subject areas too stagnant or ripe for reinvention; the faculty cannot be afraid to change what it teaches. That also suggests a significant role for students and parents because they are the target population, not local businesses. I could go on, like an egghead, but in sum, the creation of a school is not for a naïve or apolitical person; you don't have to like everybody, but you do need to listen to them.

I share this lesson in school organization because it posed issues for me as a journalist *and* as a Frenchman regarding the Caddo School Board. Indulge me for a moment: It was apparent that the members didn't like each other very much; they never socialized together in the hallways of the board HQ. Nor was there enough trust to go around the room. Was this the natural result of being elected by different demographic groups? From experience, I knew that blacks and whites could get along well, at least in the academic settings I'd seen; aside from my buttheaded classmates at Jesuit, people learned to trust each other in a variety of situations. Race didn't mean you weren't a human being. But why were black kids commonly thought to be getting an inferior education to white kids? As someone who'd lived in the black community, I could accept the reason that the cumulative effect of years and years of being taught by teachers who weren't taught correctly or didn't have the latest techniques and materials made the situation possible. But surely that wasn't happening any more since my Blessed Sacrament days in the '60s? Which part of me was clouding how I remembered my adjustment in relearning the value of note-taking at Jesuit and acknowledging the gaps in my own education, when kids who liked or excelled in school often were derided and teased for being (in boys' cases) sissified or effeminate or bookish? I remembered how I felt when it seemed as if I was missing something or had been ostracized from being in the know. So, I knew that some kids—because of IQ or lack of exposure to education or educating experiences—could be left behind academically; I'd seen enough examples in my own schooling. But because certain individuals couldn't cut it, did that apply to an entire racial group? The white members of the Caddo board certainly seemed to believe as much; so, if these folks couldn't agree on an approach to integrating schools or improving learning, then how to describe their seemingly political approach to solve obviously a learning problem? As a large school system, Caddo was having problems even getting to the point of developing individual plans for specialized children; so, was it surprising that black kids were falling behind? Would a new "basic skills" program that Caddo was intent on implementing in its earlier grades make a difference later, especially if the rate of school suspensions of black students continued to outpace that of white by a 2-to-1 ratio? Would such a program appease black parents into "going easy" on white schools by not accepting government interference? And while we're at it, if black schools' achievement was falling short, was the court-mandated 50-50 black/white teacher hiring ratio worth salvaging? Would higher NTE teaching test standards work to bridge achievement gap by forcing black teachers to somehow boost their scores to equal those of whites and learn to be more effective teachers? What would achieve testing parity? And how should I view it—as making blacks attend white-administered teacher-training programs? Was the answer in a plan that moved certain students and reprogrammed schools guarantee that—once they arrived at their designated schools—the same achievement gaps wouldn't persist? Could the board be trusted to engineer a structure to discourage "good teacher" flight to "good schools"? More importantly, could simply reporting on the board's actions and desires enable the public to force a just and lasting change in student achievement?

These "big picture" questions prompted journalistic ones: What was a newspaper reporter to do? Stand by objectively and let the dominoes fall? Engineer stories or a series of stories to hopefully prompt negotiations into the "right" direction? Speaking of "right", what's right: Stand by and record, or advocate for the obvious victims? And in the process, who do you expose as bad guys? The judge? Federal attorneys? Foster? The board? Its attorney? Certain board members? Uncompromising white parents? The bureaucratic school administration? The black elite (preachers, attorneys, teachers, old guard educators)? Or students, for becoming more visually oriented and less-reading centric? Could a Frenchman—being betwixt and between both side of this issue—adequately construct an approach to help answer these questions? Should his or her race even be a factor?

As I pondered such questions while dreading Caddo's board more and more, things were brewing anew in Rapides—this time in a high school where three white girls attempted to avoid the federal judge's order to transfer to another school; they wanted to return to their nearby high school in Buckeye. A local judge allowed them to do so, pending the other judge's decision—creating somewhat of a judicial kerfuffle—enough of one that I was curious as to how desegregation was coming. The Forest Hill area, along with Buckeye— about 40 miles away on the opposite or northeast side of Alexandria—were the main resistance pockets in a plan that had resulted in the loss of only 1,000 students (it could have been worse). Federal District Judge Nauman Scott had padlocked Forest Hill to keep out the squatting students; in this case, he slapped a $500-per-day fine on anyone defying his plan as the holiday break approached. After lots of motions and counter-motions by the state judge and the girls, federal judge Scott used somewhat Solomonesque reasoning, agreeing to let the girls stay at the school—for that semester. Eventually, to get the credit they'd earn at Buckeye, they'd have to transfer in the spring to their court-designated 9th grade school they were to originally attend. To compound matters, by year's end the feds were investigating not only several Louisiana county school systems, but also the LSU and Southern University collegiate systems, and the state's vocational-technical 50-school education system for desegregation or civil rights irregularities. Starting in 1981, things took a more definitive turn as the Caddo black educators' group and its affiliates had its first, in-person meeting with national and local Justice officials in Shreveport. Again, nothing definitive came of it, except the surprising comment that the Justice team reacted as if it had never heard that side of things from Caddo's official delegations.

Here's where things started to change for me. After attending the Buckeye 3 hearings in Alexandria for a week that January, I finished covering the hearings and I was ready to return to Shreveport. Instead of returning to my apartment, I went where I knew I could get a good meal and a sympathetic ear—back home to Mamoo and Daddy. So, I drove for the two hours back up the highway, trying to stay awake but also worried. Over the years, I'd heard horror stories about drunks often causing horrible, indescribable wrecks on the two-lane road (my classmates at Jesuit delighted in re-telling the gruesome crash scenes they'd seen on film in their defensive driving courses) by drifting into the oncoming lane. By the time I got to Shreveport, it was late, but I still had to write my stories, so I chose to drive to The Journal and write the stories then and there, instead of returning for the usual 6:30 a.m. shift. It must have been nearing 2 a.m. when I went to my folks' house. Daddy had gone to bed. Mamoo was up and had warmed up some leftovers for me. When I finished eating, then I went to sit in a bath and relax before I called it a night. There, I sat, enjoying the warm bath, but also feeling every muscle in my body ache. Then and there I admitted to myself that reporting was killing me slowly, piece by desegregating piece. I decided that I would try for the opening we had for assistant city editor, to give me something besides desegregation to think about. And it would be the second prong in my plan to make "a new me": The first gave me a chance to directly impact the profession via teaching—LSUS had asked me to teach a course in one of the very same old classrooms that I had sat in some seven years prior. The extra pay wasn't bad, but I wanted to try my hand at teaching as a way of perhaps having a later-in-life option, in case reporting didn't work out as hoped. It was going to be a small class, and I relished the chance to get some reporting techniques and tips into the students' heads. Plus, a few days later, I took it as a good sign when it appeared that the Caddo board was going to re-appoint its superintendent, meaning another four years of the same leadership—not something I particularly relished, as I had found him too political (wishy-washy) for my tastes.

Meanwhile, the Justice Department, in its latest meeting with the board, offered a counter plan, including pairing 16 schools that the board felt would certainly prompt white flight. Trying to read the entire plan, it would make your head swim; the only way to make sense of it all would be if you only concentrated on where your child(ren) would be assigned; there was no way to keep track of the 40 to 50 schools involved. Still, the feds said they were open to hearing alternatives, if more was done to decrease the number of one-race schools and to increase the quality at some one-race schools to increase their attractiveness and/or decrease student racial isolation. It sounded as if the board still had a way to go to finding its desired unitary status, or—if it felt the plan was part of a bluff—to come up with a quality "rabbit" proposal from its bag of integration tricks. To its credit, it planned several public meetings to get ideas and comments from parents and, more importantly, to let them vent. Covering such meetings, however, usually meant getting ready to have a lot of colorful quotes from parents but not useable insights; and that's what ensued for the next month or so—this or that group developing an alternative plan that so happened to leave something it treasured—usually a neighborhood school—intact or ignored the one-race school issue. To that point, I had given parents little credit for being able to decipher the parish wide school map, but they earned points at least for trying their best. Most of them—the white parents, i.e.—had no intentions of letting their children get on a bus headed across Shreveport to a black neighborhood. Many black parents liked the idea of school pairing, but with minimal risk to those in the earlier grades; of course, they were in the minority at most of the "town hall"-style meetings. As one black dad grumbled, "Busing isn't the issue. Busing of whites is."

He was only partially correct; *money* was the (unspoken) issue. If whites fled the public schools, there'd still be lots of black students. However, fleeing a school often meant moving to another school. I often thought the real, unspoken worry was losing white parents to the public school system across the Red River, to Bossier Parish. Physical flight from Caddo to Bossier would mean tax dollars—particularly sales tax dollars—fleeing to Bossier as well. At the time, Louisiana schools were especially dependent on sales tax (instead of the property tax that many school systems prefer) because the state often allowed property owners extra exemptions (think older aged citizens and those who served in the military) from state property tax. Besides, it was easier to raise sales taxes because they're usually pennies on a dollar. Federal (about 13 percent) and state monies (about 44 percent) as well went to schools; the rest is sales tax revenue. If Caddo lost sales tax revenue to Bossier, there'd be a hole the size of Texas in its budget, as well as its property and sales tax revenues because blacks economically can't match the dollar total coming from whites, and it would take some time to do so. Also, any loss of federal funds—say, for not complying with desegregation orders—would hurt the state to the tune of 30 percent of its annual revenue. So, money certainly influences the root of all segregation; meanwhile, the seemingly endless process of varying interest groups—ranging from the Chamber of Commerce task force to the local NAACP chapter to informal parent-affiliated factions—interested in sharpening or reshaping the board's counterproposal to the feds continued unabated. Regardless of what side they were on, everyone knew something needed to be done, as annual California Achievement Test scores showed predominantly black schools ranked significantly below predominantly white schools in most categories; and if you compared the same group of kids as they moved to upper grades, the black kids' rate of improvement lost ground to that of their white counterparts. A few days later, board instructional staffers tried to present a statistical case that—although the overall scores were low, Caddo kids' scores were higher than their IQ scores indicated they should be. But double-checking what sounded a bit like hocus-pocus, I discovered that—no matter how you spun the results—between 58 and 71 percent (depending what grades were involved) of U.S. school kids still were smarter than Caddo's kids. So, some kind of change in instruction of black kids certainly seemed necessary, for their future's sake. But April 1981 came with semi-bad news for the board: The Justice Department attorneys indicated that the board's plan placed too large a burden on black students while not significantly improving the quality of their education. Their letter prompted the board's attorney to respond that they had used inaccurate figures, and that increased integration of predominantly one-race schools was unworkable. Any way you viewed it, the Justice response was a warning to the board that its plan needed improvement, but also that negotiations weren't dead and that both sides needed to discuss the next step. I wasn't happy.

Meanwhile, and I think as a result, The Journal management's "ease up on George" campaign continued, with the understanding that the Arkansas/energy conference trip hadn't moved the needle much. So, I got sent on another junket, this time to Atlanta to attend a national education reporters' workshop put on by a Southern newspaper publishers trade group. Being among other, like-minded people was a plus, as was the food. It was nice to get away for three days. And it helped that, when I returned, Rhonda, our federal courts reporter, was assigned to stay atop of the Justice Department's movements in the Caddo schools case. Even better, the editors in late April decided to promote me to "the desk"—meaning I'd be City Editor Mitch's assistant; I'd won the assistant city editor (ACE) position over two other in-house candidates in a month-long competition, and would be designing pages, proofreading copy, conferring with news reporters on stories, editing the religion page, writing headlines, and being *de facto* managing editor of the Saturday paper (as well as training the next education reporter). It wasn't a totally perfect deal, but it meant eventually I'd be reading about desegregation and doing less (if any) reporting of it, as well as having Mondays off and writing a weekly column. Shortly thereafter, the board and the feds came to agree on an integration plan, and I wound up shepherding the reporting efforts of four of my colleagues, my first real editing assignment. I breathed a heavy sigh of relief when the paper was published that day. But the very next day, I did a story pointing out the agreement's shortcomings, pointing to housing and zoning patterns, fair housing regulations, and white flight; journalism was a ruthless taskmaster.

DEADLINES AND DILEMMAS

I started my new job earnestly enough, though, realizing that I could really make a difference. Besides improving reporters' writing skills, via subtle but positive editing changes to enhance flow and consulting them about said changes so they wouldn't be surprised, the ACE position gave me a chance to really get to know my colleagues better. Before, our only interactions were trading dark jokes across the newsroom, chit-chat over the water cooler, and occasional lunches together. Now, I had to industriously read their stories from start to finish (no matter how good or how boring they might be) and try to be helpful in suggesting revisions or additional reporting opportunities, as well as discussing upcoming stories. I genuinely had to become somewhat of a social butterfly, flitting from desk to desk, trying not to intrude but also trying to engage in light, interesting banter—not something you're taught in J school.

This meant I also had to be sensitive to the reporter's current activities, whether to interrupt them, as well as understanding their personalities and quirks. The female reporters always were the easiest, and the most eager to learn, even if I knew that they knew that I knew that they simply were tolerating my inquiries so as to not hurt my feelings or appear standoffish—which the male reporters often had no trouble doing, especially since we *all* knew that the assistant city editor had no real power, could be overruled at any second because I was low man on the editing totem pole. Often, I was left out of the loop on the "assigned order of things" on that day's agenda—usually set by top editor Stanley at that morning's editors meeting, to which I usually wasn't invited—rendering me occasionally ineffectual and misinformed about certain stories direction or future. And try though we did to avoid it, there was an informal hierarchy of reporters at The Journal, as the male reporters—with perhaps one exception—got the choicer assignments and beats. In any event, as the new ACE, having managerial egg on your face tended to undermine your abilities in other areas; I also (in the back of my mind) knew that I would have to fight any anti-black bias, even if it was as faint as I thought. I already had to beware of any latent, unintentional feedback with racist or sexist overtones, recalling my earlier days as an intern in a newsroom top-heavy with white guys.

So, I had to tread lightly when dealing with certain male reporters—for example, the cops beat reporter who also had been raised in segregated Shreveport and was so tightly embedded with Shreveport police that I sometimes considered him a cop first. Or, Mitch, my immediate boss, occasionally would have so many things on his mind that he'd forget to fill me in on what directives had been issued in cases of situations when Stanley or the publisher had their invisible fingers on the scales of certain extensive investigations or long-term projects—usually involving business or political topics. And then there were reporters who sometimes didn't think too clearly or were too new or green or had so many bad habits that they required direction, but they had to believe it was their own idea because they were either sensitive to criticism or got too down on themselves that their confidence wasn't that great. You'd be surprised at how many reporters go through such a stage; reporting—as I learned—is intellectually driven and draws many high-achieving types who can quickly wuss out when things don't go well or when they falter. In addition, some reporters may internally resent criticism from a black editor or from one they perceived as inferior in some way; they're more used to taking direction from white editors, who made up an overwhelming majority of editors then, and still do. As a result, they've built a long legacy as the stereotypical newsroom authority figure. Finally, as in any job where you're dealing with the same folks daily, it's only human to get to know their strengths and weaknesses, and to sometimes forget that you're giving assignments whose quality often correlates to a person's capabilities. Doing so winds up occasionally backfiring on you and perpetuating an endless loop of lower expectations and results. I often had to remind myself that not everyone was a Mizzou grad and just because they went to J school somewhere else didn't mean that they had less training or couldn't think as critically.

This little gem was considered a necessary evil if you wanted to be given press privileges. Like the 'fro?

Fortunately, I wasn't totally unprepared as an editor. Reporting also meant I had to deal with certain people on a routine basis and, honestly, I had to tailor my routines and how I handled sources accordingly. The education beat had been a tutorial in diverse personalities in sourcing and diversifying how I thought of the races; I had no one-size-fits-all glove to wear in interacting with sources. Women and men were different, obviously, education levels varied, race varied, political orientations varied, and values fluctuated according to birthplace, education, communication skills, motivation, and many other factors. So, I used every skill at my disposal, but people will always test you, intentionally or not. One of the more confounding things was the unofficial pecking order I mentioned earlier. Some reporters inherently sense their value, others you must spell it out for them. One example came early and frequently at first: My replacement at the education reporter position happened to be someone I was friendly with: Sarita, an extremely well-dressed and friendly

20ish black young lady, she had been on the staff twice, with time off to get a master's at a big Midwestern university. She got promoted to the job from the Bossier beat, which most newsroom observers thought of as the red-headed stepchild of Shreveport journalism. Bossier City was Shreveport's "little brother" of sorts: very provincial, mostly suburban, even whiter in population, home to the racetrack and a U.S. Air Force base, with a deserted former "strip" of nightclubs and bars, and traffic subject to the whims of railroads—dullsville at that point in time, in other words. That would change over time, with the increasing growth of Shreveport's black population and the blossoming of the riverboat casino industry in Louisiana, but in the '70s not many young people—who make up most of the journalist population—put Bossier City at the top of their "happening" lists. So, Sarita was thrilled to get the education writing position and leave "bummer" Bossier to some other newbie or unsuspecting reporter. But it also meant learning the basics, topics, and sourcing of education, which I provided with a heavy dose of hand-holding and mentoring—which initially consumed much of my non-editing time. We had to tread lightly, however, as we had been (and continued for a short time thereafter) dating when I was a reporter, and as an editor, I was considered one of her superiors on the organizational chart. So I probably—and would have done so, anyway, as I was a bit of a perfectionist—was more critical of her early work on the beat, often meeting with her for a coffee break or immediately after we'd finish editing the early edition, carrying a mental list of suggestions where she needed to take more care or consider alternative methods to, or aspects of, a story.

I did this with many of the reporters, because being naturally inquisitive, they often had questions about how I'd edit their stories. I understood their concerns because of my own (fortunately few) experiences with the editing desk over my stories. Our editors usually were pretty good at informing us of any substantive changes—it was, after all, a small newsroom where there was no such thing as a private conversation—usually quickly after the fact, so that any bent feelings could be eased or eliminated before anyone emotionally erupted. And that was an infrequent occurrence, as we had (for the most part) good, solid writers. Still, matters of style (preferred ways of spelling or phrasing) could be a sticking point with some, or, truthfully, a pet peeve of mine since most reporters would hardly ever thoroughly read through their *edited* stories after they submitted them; they were often busy with phone calls, updating their stories or chasing new ones after our early, first deadline at 8:30 a.m. It might not be until after the second, 11:30 a.m. deadline that they had time for such a thing. Besides, most errors usually came after the first few paragraphs—when reporters would misread or misplace information or when their senses of concentration had waned because of a lack of breakfast or not enough caffeine before they started writing. My problem (or theirs, to put it accurately) was that this demonstration of lack of care came almost every day, in almost every story that some reporters wrote. At first, I interpreted it as a lack of respect on their part, almost driving myself to an ulcer with rage. After discussions with Mitch or our sensitive, all-ears, all-knowing librarian Martha (and several walks around our downtown block to calm myself), I learned not to take such things personally. Besides, accuracy of content was everyone's primary goal, and writing style was the icing on the cake, especially when the content had to be generated (through effective, efficient reporting) and written within the span of three hours—no small feat for any reporter working on a daily newspaper in the '70s. I also confess that it took me the better part of six months before I grasped the skill and discernment necessary to edit 5-10 stories, write their headlines, design the page where they'd reside, and develop the patience and the good-naturedness necessary in dealing with the unionized copy setters in our printing room basement after each deadline.

Without going into too much detail, copy setters (usually blue-collar types) took all an edition's stories and the stories' designated layout guides, and ran the hard-copy versions (photo-facsimiles of how the stories would appear, width- and vertical-wise and typeface-wise) through a small waxing machine, placing them on life-sized sheets about equal to a sheet of actual newspaper. The stories would be arranged in the design that editors had stipulated and then placed the arranged stories on design tables for editors to approve before they were photographed and made into press plates. The ritual would involve going downstairs to the pressroom with a blue-inked pen to final-proof the copy, check the copy setter's work, wait for the copy setter to saunter by, and confer about any possible or needed changes. As you can imagine, this process could go smoothly or with great difficulty, depending on how each of you felt that morning, how well you slept, or how easily matters went upstairs in the newsroom—or if the copy setter wanted to be an ass about deadline or other procedures or, had too many pages from other sections to work on, or accidentally cut themselves with their cutting knives or, more likely, had picked up some new jokes (and/or a hangover) at the bar last night and just had to share. More often the jokes were not as ripe as the copy setter's breath. Still, this could be a fun time of the morning—fun in that the copy setters were a breed apart from the reporting staff. As I said before, they loved a good joke and could receive as well as they gave. It also seemed to be in their DNA to try to upset any of us editors with something outlandish—such as an earlier deadline, an absentee copy setter, a well-past-retirement copy setter, a hovering boss with an eye on the clock, or just out and out slowness. Either way, it was never a dull place to visit, and a good place to sharpen your "real people" skills, as their favorite comeback to something you asked for, was, "Hell, I don't give a shit!"

As a result, and more seriously, the ACE job unexpectedly got my intellectual juices going. I began to re-read my old psychology texts to see if I could find something to help me do better at handling reporters and others. For example, I mentioned the Bossier City beat as being one of lesser newsroom assignments—mostly because of something that I also discovered at the county's School Board meetings and from my time spent at the weekly Bossier City newspaper during the summer of 1977: the overly, aw-shucks, wink-wink folksiness with which the board members conducted their business. The members asked few questions, and they hardly ever had dissenting votes on most agenda items, as if they had already discussed the matters and that the vote itself was a mere formality. To a reporter, the lack of disagreement in a government body is near deadly and clear evidence of the lack of conflict and, thus, lack of controversy or divergence of thought, or, worse, the attempt to hide something—the stuff of news DNA on which many reporters thrive. So, it wasn't unexpected to see a female reporter on that beat seem somewhat—if not depressed—disengaged or lack the normal enthusiasm of the others in the newsroom. To put it lightly, let's say she appeared to not have the same outlook or attitude toward her job; sometimes, the cause could be salary or other kind of perceived inequity, although with her assigned beat you could see the potential for run-of-the-mill coverage that wouldn't spark editor fervor (which was like, in the words of Dr. Beaird, "psychic income" to reporters), much less reporter passion. Or maybe she didn't understand how to set her goals in such a manner that they might create greater internal excitement toward her job. Of course, it's always easier to see the problem when it belongs to someone else; as an editor, I wanted to explore the issue more, but I also realized that as ACE, I didn't have a whole lot of resources from which to pull or implement quickly or effectively; plus, I still was fairly ignorant of this person's situation, because schools and desegregation matters had consumed most of my attention the three years prior, leaving me next to no time to get to know my reporting colleagues and what motivated them. How do you make a person happier in their job when your bottle of "happy pills" isn't enough? Plus, I couldn't tell Mitch how to do his job, not with my paltry experience as a manager; he might think I'm on a power trip or might have his own, ongoing plan for the Bossier reporter that I didn't know about. Second-guessing the Cowboys coaches on Monday morning was easier.

Not knowing the answer to what made reporters tick, however, didn't diminish my desire to understand reporters' motivations, however, and realizing that hardly anyone else had definitive answers was frustrating, as well, to the point that it affected my career and the pursuit of my definitive identity. And here, please pardon the quick journalism lesson: Editors expect certain things from reporters; mostly, developing content for the newspaper or the TV station or web site. But once journalists are hired, it's usually too late to try to teach them new skills. At The Journal, our top editor Stanley was trying to make us understand that readers were valuable commodities to have and to cater to, mostly because we needed their eyeballs to please advertisers, but also because audiences were changing. People no longer just wanted news, but institutions—and universities, as well as newspapers—were slow to recognize this change, that audiences wanted more about their own community; thus we first created the Bossier page, then recognized we needed something for Shreveport, too. But Shreveport was so big, we divided it into four "neighborhoods," each with its own weekly page written by a "real" (read: non-journalist) person who would do grassroots level reporting—often as not, this was non-serious journalism: stuff for housewives, retirees, and homeowners. In attempting to create "community", many newspapers mistook neighborhoods for communities. Think of it this way: In any part of a city, there are numerous neighborhoods, each with several, distinct communities—such as older adults, adolescents, teenagers, everyday working people, fans of local sports teams, mothers—and each community has its own interests. The mother community, e.g., would be interested in maternal health, children's health, grocery prices, affordable toys, clothing styles, crafts, parenting tips, and the like. But such subjects didn't appeal to reporters, who were largely taught that their main responsibility was to monitor the government, publish what government officials said, expose corruption, explain the economy, and keep account of government agencies relating to the homeowner, usually someone 30 or 40 years older or older. Not to mention that reporters typically lived in duplexes or apartments—meaning their interests usually differed from most people. So, to get such "neighborhood reporting", editors hired non-journalists instead, saving the journalists from this new notion of news. This spurning of such "market-driven" journalism eventually would later signal the death knell for many publications and create major adjustments in the definition of news for those remaining, surviving newspapers.

As to my own work, I was a little ambivalent about this because my own desegregation coverage essentially showed that communities—if left unserved—would later rear their heads (through whatever economic decisions they possessed within their limited spheres of power—for instance, white flight) and create havoc for whoever ignored these communities. I knew we needed something better than our usual, government-driven journalism; if I found it boring, then the audience probably did as well. But as a lowly ACE, I didn't have much pull with the editor higher-ups, so I could only do something within the small sphere of my control.

Accordingly, I turned to one of the benefits of being the ACE: After completing my editing and design duties every day, I was free to work on any story of my own choosing—seen by my bosses as "lagniappe", or a bonus of sorts. So, I used that freedom to pursue things that interested me; I saw myself as different from the other reporters—not just talent-wise but interest-wise as well. Growing up in black Shreveport for the most part meant I took a greater curiosity in how the city and area worked; and covering schools I learned that many of them reflected a partnership or strong connection with their neighborhoods. The teachers' attitudes and approaches often came directly from interacting with motivation-wise parents or listening to those few good principals who'd taken the time to know the surrounding community. And, in covering the School Board, I learned that many times the parents knew way more than the board members about what went on in certain schools.

So, I started expanding my interests to things that, for lack of a better explanation, made me curious about the process or inner workings of a place, institution, or organization; aside from assigned stories and the residue from desegregation matters, I had free license to choose my own topics. I had to get used to my ACE editing and designing routines, so I took it slow. At first, I tried to flex my writing muscles in my columns, doing just enough reporting about a topic to make it half-way interesting. Unsatisfied with that approach, I then did "you-are-there" travel pieces for everyday things such as cleaning out a dresser drawer, or visiting a department store grand opening, or saying goodbye to a friend at a nearby train station; these still were heavy on vague description. Finally, I started to delve deeper into personal circumstances of my subjects. For instance, I finally got a chance, when visiting Ruston—home of the proud Louisiana Tech University biomedical engineering department—to understand better what kind of research they did and how it affected people, particularly computer aids for the physically challenged. Also, it felt good to see hands-on work by academics who could explain simply what they did—and students excited by the training they received. For another story, I finally got to chat about personal experiences with a former LSUS mentor, who told me about a heroic-but-unsuccessful attempt by his teenage son to save a drowning man off a jetty in Galveston Bay. The emotional toll that the near-rescue had on the boy (and his still-proud dad) was too interesting *not* to include and made for great, human-to-human storytelling in my weekly column. I also tried to be resourceful, piggybacking on the police arrest on the eve of Labor Day 1981 of a serial rapist suspect next door to a party I had attended with my friend Randy and describing the tense, harrowing reaction of the people closest to the action. I didn't forget about educators and desegregation parties, either, however—in a humanizing piece on the Alexandria man who had filed the original Rapides lawsuit, and in a light story about the Caddo switchboard operator, I felt I was trying to give back to all the sources who I hounded for months and years for bits and pieces of information. And my weekly columns took on a cornucopia of real-life drama, e.g., the trials and errors of a homeless door-to-door teenage magazine salesman.

I took what I considered to be a huge leap, though, when I started a multi-part series on the local fair housing situation, specifically, were people finding quality housing or were they being steered according to race. Fewer than 15 years earlier, in 1968, as part of LBJ's Great Society agenda—and prompted by Martin Luther King Jr.'s death, the return of black servicemen from Vietnam—the federal government passed legislation prohibiting sale, rental, and financing of housing based on race, religion, national origin, sex, (and as amended) physical challenges and family. The prevailing wisdom was that if you had non-racially based realty industry, you would likely have more integrated neighborhoods. But that law has not prevented more subtle forms of discrimination, however. Not only did Shreveport have no local enforcement ordinance on the books, but it also kept the federal government waiting for one. And there was no official evidence that minority homebuyers were being informed of their full range of areas in which to buy: In essence, school desegregation also was being abetted by the city and local real estate agents. I wanted to show how complex desegregation problems were and, I guess, solidify my role as one reporter in the city who gave a damn about the issue; I didn't care if that meant I was characterized as "the black reporter", if the public was to be fully informed. So the series revealed other, "problem" areas that today are no-brainers: How job choices meant blacks couldn't afford better homes in better neighborhoods or how job location affects neighborhood choice. Then there was how the city wasn't enforcing current housing codes; how metropolitan school desegregation plans affect housing choices more than citywide plans; blacks and whites have different incentives to move or remain in integrated neighborhoods; and public housing sites tended to be in predominantly one-race neighborhoods. What did the series accomplish? I couldn't say except that no one in Shreveport could say there wasn't much information on how to help integrate neighborhoods. And, again, I learned that housing—with an eye toward race—was much more tied to economics than I'd originally thought. In addition, Sarita and I tried to anticipate the feared flight to private schools that the new desegregation plan was supposed to cause, comparing private schools to public schools in another in-depth study. The series' upshot was that such things as test scores, teacher certifications, and curricula make such comparisons look stupid, and that "better" was in the eye of the beholder: Each school had its advantages and disadvantages, and enrollment choice resulted from unique circumstances. It began to feel as if all I was doing was "wheel spinning" when it came to trying to educate people on the state of Louisiana's education quality—although the series got quite of bit of airtime on the state's only public TV station.

One drawback of this hopping from subject to subject—especially considering how difficult it was to find worthy topics for my weekly column—was that it somewhat dulled my usually sharp senses. I went weeks at times without writing anything I considered substantial; I often literally used my own internal debates about things going on in the world as column fodder, creating imaginary, composite figures/personalities involved in various current events. It wasn't my best journalism, plus whenever I thought I had eluded the old desegregation/racial dysfunction bugaboo of reporting, my editors would suggest I go back to helping Sarita with her coverage of such news. This "subject nomad-ing" as I called it, probably also played a role in my non-journalism life at the time. My dating was all over the place—a black bank teller here, a white private school director there, the younger sister of a Frenchman girl who I'd previously dated, a white primary school teacher, a white former acquaintance from LSUS who stood me up, a black TV reporter who couldn't give proper directions to save her life, two clerical workers (one white, one black), and a black college PR administrator, to name just a few—and my social life had become aimless. I often wondered how people who did a lot of dating could keep up with all the different personalities, quirks, and oddities; it just seemed never-ending! Life developed into something like a carousel that—while free to jump on it and ride—exacted a price in terms of poor self-esteem and bad judgment. Occasionally, for a little stability, I'd continue to see my old Almagest/LSUS crowd, most of whom had gotten journalism jobs and were developing their own lives. We'd go dancing and to the movies, but that became rarer as Randy, as I said earlier, got married soon after studying for a social work master's degree at LSU in Baton Rouge, where he and his wife Eileen decided to put down roots; our visits had been reduced to their visits to their parents over the major holidays. In addition to variety dating, my friends and family at Blessed Sacrament were beginning to look at me as their project in developing Catholic leadership: At different times, they persuaded me to take the reins of the choir, the yearly bazaar, *and* the parish's most dedicated and most dependable men's group—the Knights of

Peter Claver (our equivalent to the Knights of Columbus). In addition to my interests in the church's social justice outreach, I had plenty to keep me occupied on non-working days. And it felt good and contextually grounding to deal with "real" people whose primary interest was trying to enjoy their families and do right; if I got a little life advice or had a few laughs, that was OK, too. But I didn't lack introspection, attending various retreats and religious conferences to go with all the near-daily advice that Nancy—who'd I see often in the newsroom, working on her Neighbors stories and always giggling about a turn of a phrase she'd just written—offered. Looking back with greater wisdom, I realize that all the above, the highs and the lows, simply came with being in my 20s and growing up. Sometimes, to get out of my head, I'd also drive to Dallas—anxieties about Interstate 20 and all—to visit a transplanted Missouri friend and experience a little of the North Dallas, big-city life that I had missed since my last

Chicago visit. And I still visited Mamoo and Daddy, usually after work, to enjoy a home-cooked meal and occasionally take Mamoo to visit relatives somewhere or play football with Kojak, the nickname of my little buddy who lived next door to my folks and the voice of childish reason in some of my columns. That interaction—and all the rest of it—began to feel like a search for something, but *for what* I couldn't deduce.

Enjoying a carefree moment in front of the car in Allendale, early 1980s.

For instance, to try something different, I joined Sarita for yet another education project—this time about a nearby college, Northwestern State University, at a financial and leadership crossroads at nearly 100 years old. More freshmen dropping out, declining or inconsistent enrollment, and declining interest in favor of colleges closer to home were some of the problems we found. The school also had an unreasonably high utility bill and aging and increasingly expensive-to-repair infrastructure (thanks to the unusually large 916-acre size of the old campus). The enrollment drops resulted in less-than-maximum state funding; but while ledgers and numbers suggested the school was on fire, its administrators would keep trying to spin a rosier picture of things. The school still exists and had its highest enrollment in five years in fall 2024, with its dorm occupancy 99 percent; so much for collegiate doomsaying! And I kept trying to make my columns interesting, even going to great lengths to create a Shreveport song contest, debating the pros and cons of quiche-eating, and entertaining what it took "to be somebody" in Shreveport. I hoped no one would keep score on my lameness, particularly on how often I'd offer thinly veiled criticism of my birthplace. Still, it could have been worse: I could have still been on the Caddo schools beat instead of Sarita, describing the opening-day logistical nightmare that was the first day of desegregation-decreed operation. So, I still felt luck on my side, even if I didn't know which side I was on; I had to find my special place, whether the life of a Frenchman, black, or white person. Writing the column was getting old, and the reporters weren't getting any smarter: Witness our new city hall reporter who, in planning a story on the city's newest chief administrator, thought she would visit one of his prior job stops to gather background. She took a plane to Wichita, Kansas; the administrator's previous stop had been in Wichita Falls, Texas. We also had to fire a new police reporter; it turned out he couldn't spell.

I even tried one last crusade before making my decision. I (sort of) took on the Reagan administration, detailing the depressing and futile steps the federal government was insisting on from Social Security Disability Insurance recipients. Your government was stripping these poor (and you're probably *considerably* poor if you're one of these souls) people from their benefits because they were able to muster some scientific studies showing many recipients were not *totally and finally* disabled—meaning there was the possibility of physical improvement to the point that they could be able to work again. Essentially, this whole situation was forcing bureaucrats to pose as Ebenezer Scrooge based on obscure (read: paper-driven) medical findings. What a way to try to save a buck: The government—whose primary purpose is to serve and protect the public—instead was serving poor (and often illiterate), physically handicapped people with unreadable paperwork in the name of stripping them of their stipends so that public funding wouldn't be squandered. Every time I thought of an administrative judge deciding to rescind these folks' last hope for buying groceries or paying rent, it made me ill. I got the local congressman to admit that the whole process was inhumane, considering many recipients were unable to complete the byzantine forms involved; he even said a congressional committee was looking at possible solutions. Some good did come of it: Both Houses of Congress voted to allow recipients to keep their benefits *during* the appeals process—small consolation if you were one of the 48 percent who eventually would lose your appeal.

It wasn't the final straw, but it came close. As a reporter, at first you think you're making a difference, "comforting the afflicted and afflicting the comfortable" as the saying goes. But you realize that people either don't listen, or they don't want to change and, instead, find something else that confirms their original, wrong-headed views. Even when you get people to talk about something you reported or wrote, they often choose the wrong element or miss the point; this happened more than I cared to admit in my five years at The Journal. With my Watergate-prompted good intentions, I was going to "stick it to the man." But the more I stuck, the more I realized the man didn't care and wouldn't go away. Racism is a bitch, financial inequality is difficult to get people to confront, and trying to eradicate it without peoples' collaboration can get complex, protracted, and impossible at times. Being the Mizzou-bred "egghead" that I mentioned as my earlier identity just didn't cut it. I was not who I thought I was; thinking back to all the contentious meetings, all the political "he said this/they said something totally different", all the talk about social justice, and all our well-intentioned attempts to draw our readers into the 20th century, I came to the decision that "eggheading" wasn't working. After I left the schools beat, Sarita still was writing about the same sanctimonious rhetoric and dog-whistling that I chanced upon in my first month in 1978. I wasn't learning anything but old news, it seemed. Sure, using anonymous sourcing certainly helped, as did all the individual school visits, as did the attempts to understand the context that sources would bring to the information they had, but in 1983 I wasn't the same, wide-eyed youngster who'd gladly left a job stacking pest-ridden textbooks in an empty middle school classroom just days after college graduation. I'd seen this story before—the one with the victims, the victimizer, and the person just trying to protect their children, or their job, or their organizational status. All the demographers, people with initials after their names, pastors who tried to practice compassionate conservativism, politicians who never seemed quite satisfied, and businessmen who had one eye on test scores and one eye on their profit margins—they all tended to blend together, each with an ax to grind or an insight to provide that would solve the whole problem, if people would only listen.

That listening, however, often is too much to ask, particularly of the faceless public. I often recall those black people I used to see every day riding the city buses, wondering how they tolerated going into white neighborhoods, working for low wages, in jobs that no one else wanted. They persisted; life went on; they had their own houses and yards to maintain, their children to clothe and feed, their bills to pay, their churches to support. That kind of attitude—persisting, pressing on, surviving—is only one way to live, and people on society's lower rungs often have no choice but to continue and endure. But those with choices, whether via mobility, education, or birthright, have more varied pathways before them. The problem, too, is that "having to" hang on or persevere can be habit- and rut-forming, and can lead to an internal staleness of a sort, where you feel as if you're standing still, or if life has other plans for you but you're too busy holding onto whatever it is—your belief system, your comfort zone, your physical or mental plateau—that you pass on or miss the opportunity. That's also the problem with the status quo—it's insidious, which makes it dangerous. And that's how I felt after five years on my second go-round in Shreveport. Maybe I was impatient, but my growth as a manager was being stifled, and I had run out of topics to write about that would deliver me from the humdrum doldrums I was feeling. There had to be a better way of knowing how to manage and I believed I could find it—all I needed was a little prompting. To that end, I caught the teaching bug after my one-semester stint at LSUS. I was hooked on seeing young journalists "stick it to the man" and find their voices, as I had. I also took advantage of a state program that would provide three years' funding toward graduate study in exchange for agreeing to thereafter return to Louisiana as a minority member of a state college's faculty. I jumped at the chance and was fortunate to be one of the grant program's recipients. I had to do so; it meant growth, and I didn't mind being classified as a minority or black or whatever in the process.

And I'd be remiss if I didn't say what role that race—in my reporting, in the newsroom, and in my private life—played in my decision to return to graduate school, this time in Austin, Texas. When May 1976 approached—the last time I had made another decision about my future, I only had to choose a newspaper where I would enjoy working. But I didn't go into that situation blind, having worked there as an intern some three times, during which I showed growth and skills—with which I was delighted and feeling vindicated, even when I started remembering all the things I disliked about Shreveport, creating doubts. But I approached it as a new beginning, as "a genuine human being," fully me. A new, more subtle George was going to emerge. And St. Louis investigative reporter George Curry was right: I had to be twice as good as everyone else, doubling the number of stories I did in the previous years during the year leading up to the School Board's agreement with the Justice Department. Code-switching surprisingly wasn't an issue; my sources appreciated my honesty and lack of hidden agenda. I truly tried to be open with them, racist or not. I made truth my first loyalty, especially after I got to know the regulars on the beat. I did so to do a good job, and, if I'm honest, to settle the unsettling questions of my mind regarding my racial identity. I became the occupation, which took no sides except pursuit of the truth.

Still, continually searching for the truth was part of who I was, which started to become a greater priority as the three years on that beat progressed, culminating in that come-to-Jesus moment the night I finished my Buckeye 3 adventure. Trying to be a solid citizen presented difficulties, as I experienced failures and ethical challenges. I thought back to my lying about attending that late night School Board meeting. I learned from that, but it didn't help the source in the story about the coerced buying of testimonial tickets to help retire the state education superintendent's re-election campaign debt: It led to a good, decent young lady losing her job—not my finest moment. And what about my duping the University of Florida demographer into a brief interview at the airport? Nothing gained in that episode by Caddo school students. Again, a failure on my part, trying to show my cleverness.

But returning to Shreveport from Mizzou also helped me bring a lot of confidence into social situations, as I used a multicultural approach. Of course, there were a couple weirdos in the group of ladies I dated, but no odd behavior stemming from anything racial—that I knew of, anyway. Every one of the young ladies had her own, individual, and unique circumstances on which I won't elaborate on here. I was lucky to have good, older friends in Shreveport who I could trust with helping me analyze my approaches to dating, and they helped tremendously. But honestly, I still had concerns about the Shreveport setting's impact, as opposed to what I had experienced with dating in Columbia. Shreveport being Shreveport, there weren't a whole lot of black women—aside from teachers and others in education—who I thought had the sophistication and what I'll call the "level-headedness" or emotional maturity to match what I thought I was seeking. If that sounds vague, fair enough, but it's hard to be descriptive when you have such a small sample size (because you have a job for which you're basically "on call" most days and nights); the numbers were even smaller for Frenchman or Creole women, who lacked the educational training, or—because it was Shreveport—had already self-identified as black, as they felt Shreveporters left them no other option as to who they were or how they could behave. Obviously, there's nothing wrong with identifying as black, but I assumed that their doing so was a form of self-denial, if that makes sense. I felt, as Mamoo had instilled in me, that you should be who you are, no matter what other people say. I knew that certain people considered me black first, and I wasn't trying to disavow anyone of that conclusion because it didn't affect my behavior, nor was it my fault that they made faulty assumptions, and because usually my interaction with that person was not centered on the topic of race nor influenced by it. But when I socialized with people, I expected them to bring self-honesty to the setting. Finally, when dating white young ladies, I had to consider how they handled the disapproving aspects of Shreveport's dominant race toward interracial dating: Could they handle the overt stares? Could they stare back? How would they handle "the redneck factor" of running into jerks who went out of their way to become obstacles (often in restaurants where they felt they had the "right" to do so)? How influential was religion (i.e., conservative doctrines) in their lives (especially if they were raised Baptist)? Were they opposed to outspoken or decidedly politically public females (e.g., Jane Fonda or Geraldine Ferraro)? How might they endure having to deal with confrontation, erroneous-but-well-meaning assumptions, or just plain seemingly harmless old ladies/men who might have been raised thinking that saying the "n-word" (or any of the southern variations thereof) was acceptable? How did they approach the subject of race? Could I envision them as the mother of a biracial child? I sometimes amazed myself at all the concerns that I had on this aspect of dating, but I'm sure all the young ladies I escorted probably had some similar mental list that they secretly applied. I wasn't the most stringent in applying these "qualifications" with everyone I dated. Sometimes I just wanted to have fun. But I'd be lying if I'd say these questions didn't often cross my mind, even if subtly so. I should also add that I strongly benefitted from listening to (or picking up a vibe from) all the young women I knew in The Journal newsroom—fine ladies, all, and not afraid to mince words when it came to discussing the male animal. They often demonstrated honesty, candor, humor, tact, intelligence, and just plain assertiveness that I admired.

Deciding to move to Austin, meanwhile, felt very natural, especially since I had graduate experience and I had some visits to Texas under my belt. And this time I was leaving Shreveport with considerably more wealth than in the previous time, providing much more confidence. Of course, I had to explain to Mamoo why I had to leave Shreveport *again*, telling her that there was a good chance of my return because of the state's *quid pro quo* requiring I teach somewhere in Louisiana—it could even be Shreveport! Leaving The Journal was probably harder, since I'd spent so much of the previous five years (seven, if you count the internships) there and had developed so many friendships across the entire paper (I think top editor Stanley seemed hurt the most, saying half-jokingly, that he knew I was "a quitter", but which I somewhat expected from him because of the high value he placed on loyalty) and the community. Still, Mamoo and my cousins helped me pack and even drove the 330 miles to Central Texas with me, as I started one more, fruitful, adventure. I also packed an additional five years of knowledge, and a curiosity about my chosen profession that I knew the academics at the University of Texas would help me sift through and determine the key factors. Despite getting burned out on the process of journalism, I knew that I had enough love of learning to keep me busy in Austin, plus I looked forward to living in a new town, in a new state that I thought would serve me well. Austin was beginning to change its own identity from a sleepy, good old boy, state capital to a hip, progressive, tolerance-loving, technological hub attracting Bubbas and chip-makers and making them into forward thinkers. The smooth highways of Texas beckoned more than the slumping Louisiana economy, providing a springboard for me to find my permanent identity and—it would turn out—much more in the grand scheme of things. I also wanted a new way to look at journalism and, honestly, a new way to look at myself. Shreveport in my rearview mirror was bittersweet; you never really want to leave a place that for many years you've known as "home". But my journey hadn't yet ended, and the search for my river needed one more push, one more bit of "oomph" to see how far I would have to go. In six hours, I'd be in South Austin.

Mrs. Graham, the key influencer in my undergraduate studies, in her element, dispensing wisdom to LSUS students.

Prof. Joye Patterson, my mentor at the University of Missouri.

6

Becoming A Class Act

Starting a new life in Texas was a thrilling return to academia, which I had grown to appreciate and love from my years at LSUS and Mizzou. Sure, I'd meet new people and learn new things, but Texas also had turned into a booming land of opportunity for anyone from Louisiana, still in the throes of an economic downturn in the oil and gas industries and quickly on its way to becoming a predominantly tourism-oriented spot. I'd had a couple of first cousins make the move to Dallas and Houston, both of which I'd traveled to with Randy and our Almagest gang several times, plus I'd frequently visited a friend in Dallas. And Austin was known for the University of Texas, the state's aim to make it into "Silicon Hills", the Hill Country to the west, San Antonio to the south, local music, the constant, moderate-80s climate, and its open, laid-back atmosphere—like no place else in Texas.

I settled in quickly, connecting with the daughter of a Journal colleague, meeting and making friends with a couple who had just moved from Philadelphia, re-connecting with a priest from my Jesuit days at the nearby Catholic Church, and using my reporting instincts to learn the locale of everything fun, necessary, and interesting. My first day alone I visited my first HEB (*the* dominant Texas grocer) and saw a woman in a yellow, multi-flowered bikini pushing a shopping cart down the meat aisle. "Yeah, baby," I thought to myself. "This is *it!*" A 29-year-old couldn't have asked for more: My apartment was in a mostly student section of the city, a mile off the interstate, 10 minutes from campus and 20 via the student bus system, which ran adjacent to the apartments. The graduate advisor was an agreeable, jovial, roundish man in a cabana shirt; demi-god to students and faculty alike, Wayne's approachable temperament, brilliant mind, and calm touch in solving what most thought were unsolvable issues was a blessing. Being the former dean of the entire communication college also helped.

Two major events happened while I was in Austin for those four years—first, I earned my Ph.D. My area of study centered on media management, specifically reporter and editor behavior. My time at The Journal had left a lasting impression; without going into too much detail, I largely spent most of my time in the library—these still were pre-internet days. I had fun searching for books and journal articles, taking notes where necessary, spending glorious hours perusing the various databases—hard and soft—that held the keys to so much material. That also meant spending at least an hour or two a day at the photocopier with the stuff the library wouldn't let you take home. It was wonderful—like being a reporter but only having to deal with documents, not people. The rest of the time involved reading, writing, attending classes, and writing some more. This entire process was expected to lead to presenting research papers around the ideas that all that information supposedly yielded. These papers were given at conference sites around the country, or, even better, the world. What a life, right? Of course, you're meanwhile expected to develop mentoring relationships with your professors or even those in other departments with an interest in your specific topic(s) of study. If you played your administrative cards correctly, took the required and necessary electives, wrote enough papers, traveled to varied conferences, occasionally published said papers in relevant journals, and networked with the right professors, you'd be prepared to take a job in academia. At Texas, you were expected to eventually work at a research-oriented school, such as Texas. At least, that was the ideal. Of course, not everyone in my classes did that, plus you also had master's students who simply wanted a journalism job or thought they might later pursue a doctorate. The whole process usually lasted from three to five years—and because you were at UT—you'd meet some wonderful, intelligent (some even genius-level) people (many from other countries) who'd often become your lifelong friends and had fascinating stories and awesome research ideas to share. Everyone was in search of The Next Big Idea in journalism and always wanted your feedback on their work. How could you not like it?

Well, for starters, it's often lonely work. Your topic, by the very nature of it being *your* idea, often had its unique properties, which meant you were the sole person in the school (or world) pursuing it. So, you often wound up researching in areas where few people had tread, meaning you were one of the few experts who could adequately explain it. As an example, my eventual dissertation topic dealt with how editors treated new technologies once introduced to the organization. Hard as it is to believe, there's usually a general body (or two) of applicable research, but somewhat more general, or indirect. The key is to find as much information as you can that deals with your topic, read it, and interpret or summarize how it fits into what you will propose to do. As you might expect, this can get detailed and cumbersome, and you'll occasionally need a friend or two or a mentor to help you wade through it. And you must be thorough—don't miss any relevant information, that can prove embarrassing—and have a head for multiple levels of analysis (not to mention deciding on the right method of investigation) to help you to make some helpful conclusions about the whole topic. Then, you try to publish it all—another prolonged process. And, in the loneliness department, remember that everyone else is doing the same thing, and usually alone; only the lucky or the extremely smart candidates find a partner or like-minded person to help with the process (again, either the exceptionally shrewd or the terribly lazy will piggyback onto, or delve into, a professor's own work; you can either be the envy of your peers or lose their respect this way).

It wasn't too long into the program—about 18 months, or so— that I realized that this was a steep hill to climb alone, which brought me to the second major event that happened, although it occurred first. Socially, up to that point, I had continued my haphazard attempts at dating, but not with much success: I'd either date someone who later would find someone else, or I'd "love bomb" the young lady into hiding by my overly infatuated attempts at courting. I was batting zero, as well, with the women I had met at or through the Austin Catholic church I frequented; they were too pious for my tastes. And these were all white women, mind you, as Austin has barely—and probably won't ever—had or have adequate numbers of young, degreed, black women from which to choose, and certainly no Frenchman community to mention. I did have visits from former Shreveport young ladies who had been living in Texas, but nothing that led to anything serious. Except for the UT graduate students, none of the ladies showed much interest, much less knowledge, in media management (no surprise there).

Then there was Kathy, Randy's sister-in-law back in Shreveport. We became very friendly over the years during Randy and Eileen's holiday visits, watching TV, playing Trivial Pursuit, going to the movies and out dancing with them. Kathy had red hair, was slightly tall, and laughed at most of my jokes when I visited her and her mother. She and I were maid of honor and best man, respectively, at Randy and Eileen's wedding in 1979. I used to tease her about her Tab soft drink habit, and she would spin these wild stories about the kids she taught at a local Catholic school, to the point that I went to meet them on their field trip to a skating rink. I'd sent her a couple of funny letters—pretending to be the governor of Louisiana or her favorite singer, Lionel Richie—my first year in Texas and, to my surprise, she got in the spirit and responded in kind. My first year at UT, I worked up the courage to ask her out when I visited on Spring Break. She was easy to talk with and we always had interesting conversations about current events and things going on in town. She shocked me that spring by sending a bouquet of flowers to me in Austin on my birthday. When spring semester 1985 ended, I returned to Shreveport for a couple weeks and we started dating more seriously to the point that, late one night, after we'd been dating several consecutive nights, we were kissing in the living room. For some reason I never could fathom, something made me stop abruptly and ask her if she would marry me. No bells or whistles went off in my head and I didn't know where the idea originated or why I had said it, but it just felt like the thing to do, surprising myself in the process. She said "yes". I didn't see it coming. For about a week afterward, I walked around in a state of shock, my mouth often agape: Not only was I going to be married, but to a white girl. Later that summer, Kathy moved in with me to Austin.

Things were never the same thereafter: They were better. I was never alone again. I had someone with whom I could discuss everything I'd ever experienced, which, while at UT, meant the world. It caused me to have only two jobs: to take care of Kathy and to get my degree and get on with life. Essentially, I could concentrate. But the story didn't end there, of course. Kathy and I had much to learn about each other, despite our friendship of six years. And marrying an Irish Catholic white woman implied also learning to navigate the class and cultural differences we each brought into the marriage. For example, how would my Frenchman parents react to having a white woman accompanying their handsome son everywhere he went? What would my Blessed Sacrament friends, relatives, and acquaintances say when they met Kathy? Why was I even worried about such things? In other words, you want the people you love to learn to love each other (and they did), but first reactions and inexperience in that situation can make for foot-in-mouth blunders or hesitance, much less the reticence you might feel in thinking you cannot be yourself in the presence of people of a different background or upbringing. I had no such concerns with my more sophisticated (we didn't have the term "woke" yet) UT friends, who openly welcomed Kathy into our group. But Shreveport and Cane River were another matter altogether, and one I would continually find challenging in our first years of marriage, and even somewhat later, on occasion.

Still, time seemed to fly by after we got married that June. Kathy soon became pregnant with Ryan Francis (the name means "little French king"), our first child, which—beside starting me on a

35-year span regarding adequate finances—meant I would have to sharpen my career-planning skills. I had to think about what kind of academic job I might like, as well as the best place to raise a biracial child. There also were the expectations of my UT mentors, who wanted to see me transition into an elite, research-oriented university. But there was the tiny obstacle of my stipend agreement with the state of Louisiana, meaning that—at least for three years—we would have to return. Being a prospective minority academic resulted literally in having the pick of the cream of what "crop" that Louisiana had to offer. But the pull of grandparents, the community support, and the built-in familiarity that we would have in Shreveport proved too great; we chose LSUS instead, to my mentors' disappointment (they thought LSU-Baton Rouge the only, logical choice as it was the only state-supported research-focused organization). In "returning to the scene of the crime", I came again to a place where I knew I was sorely wanted—to the point that they matched Baton Rouge's offer. Journal Publisher Dr. Beaird did the matching, creating a fellowship that supplied my (at the time) large salary, including a supplemental offer to continue to write a weekly column and become an occasional editorial writer, in addition to my teaching and advising duties.

Aside from the potential worry that Shreveport would pose, our time in Austin was near-idyllic. The moderate climate allowed for various tours and activities with UT friends. Soon after Ryan was born, the three of us moved into a bigger apartment in the same complex and Kathy and I worked: she was an elementary school teacher as I worked on my dissertation, for which I'd also received a national grant for traveling to Texas newspapers. Meanwhile, life with Kathy was all I'd hoped. It didn't feel as if I'd married someone white: She had always been a friend, and continued to be so, occasionally advising me on my studies, more often listening to all that went through my mind. I talked about my fears, my friends, The Journal, about my family, our Chicago days, and Shreveport lives, being a Frenchman, Pete's death, my stature and work at Blessed Sacrament—all of it. I left nothing out, and—to my amazement—she patiently listened and always would comment or say things I would expect a friend to say, even more so than my buddy Randy. Nothing seemed to surprise her or require too much explaining. She knew when I wasn't feeling well, sensed when my anxiety got the best of me, made me feel better—actually, that was something we both did: picking up the other when the other was down. On top of that, she and Ryan (and Emily, two years later) seemed to make everything all right. I never met a person who complemented my personality to such an extent. What's more, she listened to all my stories about being a Frenchman, my battles with my identity, the culture of the Cane River people, their shortcomings and strong points—all seemingly without judgment or commentary on what I thought was the strangeness of it all, as if she knew it was coming. She did share that her mom, Mamaw (Ryan's way of saying "Grandma"), had expressed reservations about her marrying a black man, but that Kathy quickly and confidently said she wanted to marry me and assured her that she knew what she was doing. Kathy made me feel as if I was an open book, which she'd pick up from time to time when she wanted to be informed, entertained, mystified, or amazed. She became a true friend, who showed me that there are a few people in the world—black, white, Frenchman, no matter—who were more similar to me than I could have imagined, who had the unique talent to listen, learn, and still love. I've met only a few people like her.

And, of course, falling in love with her caused me to wonder if diverse marriages were the key to understanding someone from another race. Is love—or what we think of as love—the answer to accepting someone wholly as they are, no matter how differently they act or seem to behave? You might argue, "Duh! Isn't that what love is supposed to be, genius?" It seems so obvious, but it belies the fact that I knew Kathy for the better part of five-plus years before I became romantically interested in her. So, what changed? We likely both did, but in what way? Was it because of my many disappointing dates with other girls, in which I got a sense of what I *didn't like* in a mate? If so, where did the magic suddenly come from? Or was it the familiarity created by the no-pressure, conversational atmosphere of all those visits I'd paid over the years whenever Randy and Eileen were in town? I didn't want to over-analyze a good thing, but it did set me to thinking—in a small way—as to what largely contributed to my sudden discovery of happiness. I never intended to include race or color as a factor, and, indeed, I've never seen Kathy as white first; that seems not only wrong but downright stupid—her personality, values, and looks always felt like the natural attractions. Plus, my search for my identity never entered my mind as dependent on the race of another person. You'd be correct if you'd view my babbling here as the ramblings of a confused man. Hey! Maybe that's it—being a man truly isn't the best way to go about objectively viewing the world, not if personal growth is your goal. My knowledge of world history, combined with personal experience, surely makes the case that women are more realistic and aware of how life works or should work. In any event, I accepted that life was teaching me *something*, even if I wasn't sure what. My last two years in Austin were, to that point at least, my happiest ever.

So, you probably can imagine what it might have been like for us to return to Shreveport two years later. Yes, we were both excited to start a normal life back in our hometown, looking forward to letting Ryan get to know, love, and spend quality time with his grandparents, and wondering how Shreveporters would react to seeing an interracial couple. We stayed at Mamaw's house in the Highland neighborhood while we scouted apartments. Ryan quickly took to Mamaw and her playfulness with him, and especially to Darlene, the lady to whom she rented a room. He charmed my parents, as well, and taught them what it was going to be like to childproof their home; Mamoo wasn't too keen on modern child-raising methods, always grumbling disapproval of things we'd say were non-negotiable, like Daddy's placement of the lawn mower in the same closet as the water heater. At 14 months old, no one could resist Ryan's curly hair, fair skin, brightly colored jumpers, and pudgy, constantly moving manner; but it was his surprisingly large vocabulary that wowed everyone; Kathy always read to him. It was great to have a little boy puttering about, especially on visits to the mall toy store, where I rediscovered my inner wonder, watching him put his hands on everything in the store (other shoppers thought his name was "Ryan-no!"), seeing what colors and shapes got most of his attention, and both of us falling in love in with the tiny, little diecast cars. After a month or so, we found a second-floor apartment near LSUS that was as far south from our parents—a whole eight or nine miles—but as close to the university—a three-minute drive—as we could get, in a more recently developed subdivision. Kathy made friends with some of the other mothers in the complex and I got my first real taste in full-time academia, settling in on the third floor of the same building where I had cut my journalistic teeth, attending meetings with some of the people who had personally taught me how to think. Heady times, yes, but it still felt familiar in many ways. I was the advisor to The Almagest, had three courses to teach, and was wrapping up the revisions on my dissertation. My classes were a mixture of moderately large (about 35 students) and extremely small (fewer than 10), and I spent many days preparing lectures and activities, while grading papers in the afternoon and at night. The newspaper students were eager and full of energy, while the rest reflected the same old LSUS mantra—let's hurry up and get this over with because I've got a job to go to. The students' attitudes—and emphasis on grades and grading—were an adjustment from UT, but not unexpected, and the afternoons provided a great working atmosphere because of the utter, deserted silence after 1 p.m. most days. I'd type—LSUS still hadn't fully entered the computer age—what I thought were solid, Socratically interesting and dynamic lessons, only to be reminded a couple days later that execution and planning weren't the same thing when it came to actual lectures. I also had to remember the students were products of Louisiana education, with which I was quite familiar; many of my rhetorical questions would draw only blank, quiet stares. They had to be lead into being curious. Meanwhile, weekly returning to The Journal to write a column was like fitting on an old glove, with some new faces thrown in but with a different feel, knowing that I'd only be there a couple hours and that I no longer would always have to use my reporting skills to produce a decent thought, that their expectations of a professor would often run toward the more cerebral and political. All these changes—Ryan, the new job, the column-writing, the family-man role, the dissertation, and then Emily—combined into one, huge challenge for a newly wedded couple, as well.

Getting into a routine, for Ryan's sake at first, proved tricky because academia wasn't always a 9-to-5 proposition. Part of this was by design because my years at The Journal taught me to hate schedules and deadlines. But part of it also was that the university had its own customs and rhythms: Being a faculty member came with its own set of expectations, specifically becoming a part of an academic "family" that had to meet often to hash out everything from course schedules, to curriculum changes, to classroom equipment, to the inevitable "task force to study (fill in the blank)". Then there were speakers to hear, guest-lecturing to plan, luncheon get-togethers, and new-professor orientations. Add in the endless one-on-ones of networking, getting to know colleagues, and informal meetings with students and administrators, and I discovered that classes weren't the biggest responsibility. In fact, I looked forward to them because you got a chance to discuss ideas—what you'd think would be the primary focus at a place of higher learning. Afterward, I'd try to get home at a reasonable hour to play with Ryan, cuddle with Emily, and give Kathy another adult to converse with, but there also were the inevitable disagreements—about everything from money to child-rearing to how to deal with grandparent expectancies. Of course, I got the lion's share of the benefits from these discussions, usually in parenting skills and the ins and outs of trying to be right all the time—an impossible task, if there ever was one, but one that I had to eventually learn to let go. Besides, I had a special purpose in getting home, wanting to provide what I missed as a child, the presence of a dad. I wasn't sure how to deliver it, but I did my best to be there, even for boring stuff. If that meant playing the female villain from a Superman cartoon, or walking to the next-door Dairy Queen to get an ice cream bar and to let the old ladies ooh and ahh over Ryan, or letting him ride his tricycle at LSUS and "squash" June bugs on the sidewalk, then so be it. I was enchanted with his joy, his sense of adventure, his non-stop talking, as well as his wonder at his picking "tree flowers" and "boolabongs", as he would call the apartment complex's many buttercups that were "presents" for Kathy. There were so many things to do, so many new things to explore, so many ways that I never knew that would constitute bonding with a child—each uniquely suited to what people at the time would call "quality time" but which I merely saw as a good time.

PROF-ING AIN'T EASY

As the kids and I grew up, though, the early days proved a little harder on me. I loved working with my colleagues, who were firm when they needed to be but mostly gentle in teaching me the art of teaching. When I first started, I simply believed that teaching was sharing knowledge that I'd already learned. That included sharing whatever I thought or believed on any topic—Mistake No. 1: I gave my reporting class a book to read—Woodward and Bernstein's epic account of their takedown of the Nixon administration, which wasn't only a chronology of their process but a lesson in dirty politics, about which I thought students would be highly interested. When the time came to take the book exam, their scores suggested no one had read the book. This was my first lesson about real people: They don't always do what they should. When I returned the tests, I suggested that not reading the book implied that they shouldn't even be studying journalism, that they should change their majors. Bad, bad George, or so raged my department chair, who told me I had no such business or right to do as I did. I'm sure my jaw was on the floor when he added that my act was the ultimate sign of disrespect for the students. He was so angry that I quickly agreed with him, not knowing what I had done wrong. My action seemed perfectly logical at the time; but academia had its own rules, or so I discovered. This time, it seemed, I had to learn that the customer was always right, and you can't transplant the newsroom to the classroom when you're working with students, who are works in progress. Harshness should always be tempered, which I learned again after a faculty meeting—Mistake No. 2: One day, the dean of the liberal arts college—my chairman's boss—scheduled a faculty meeting in my second or third month to discuss God-knows-what-I-can't-recall. But whatever it was, it was heatedly debated. I don't remember what prompted me to add my two cents' worth, but I did, thinking nothing of it. But full Prof. Jack London—his research specialty, not his name—took it upon himself to chide me, saying something to this effect: "Well, if you'd been reading the most recent The Chronicle of Higher Education, you would know…blah, blah, blah, and…you wouldn't feel that way." If my face could turn red, it would have been crimson; I was embarrassed, but I also was angry that a colleague would make a spectacle of dressing down another colleague in the middle of a meeting. So, I bade my time for a few minutes, and after the meeting, I stormed to my office, livid to the point of blinding rage. If I couldn't do it to students, why could a professor do it to another professor? I knew that Jack had an office on the floor below, so I quickly walked to the stairwell and saw him and the chief academic officer (provost) having a huddled conversation in the middle landing. I strode over there, visibly shaking, I said, "Jack, I like you and I know you're a real smart guy," and, in shaking my index finger at him, added, "But if you pull something like that again, I'll kick your ass." Then I turned around, and climbed the stairs to my floor, leaving him with his mouth agape and stuttering something about, "What? I can't believe you would…" I left before he could spurt the rest and before the provost could try to hide his sheepish smile. After my anger ebbed, I knew I had to tell my chair what had happened before "Jack" would. He, a big grin on his face, guffawed a couple of times, also smiling when he reminded me of the university's expectation of collegiality among faculty members. He suggested I go quickly to the dean's office and dutifully tell her as well. "And George," he said on my way out, "don't worry about it." The dean wasn't smiling, but she did tell me—off the record of course—that Jack had always been "a bit of a bully…and, if I'm honest…he's had it coming for a long while." She added that there would be a letter of reprimand in my file about the matter. But as far as she was concerned, the matter would be closed after I apologized to Jack. The next day I did so, shaking his hand and admitting that—being new to academia, I "misinterpreted" his intent. He accepted my apology and that was my second lesson about real people: They can do some of the most asinine things. Jack and I forever after studiously avoided each other. I remained undeterred, however, continuing to do my job in a fashion that emulated the better teachers I had observed in lectures over the previous 15 years. Although, as I mentioned earlier, I'd hit a few dead or hollow spots in my classes over the first few months, I thought things—apart from my two mistakes—were going well. That was when my students informed me of Mistake No. 3: Not knowing my place in the hierarchy of things. At the end of the first year, in an evaluative meeting with my department chair, I had a chance to discuss my teaching technique. My student evaluations weren't great, but they weren't that bad, either. Still, there seemed to be a running theme of a kind: complaints of my arrogance. Floored, I couldn't figure what that meant—I'd never heard anyone say that about me before. I knew that people describe as arrogant those who they believe to have a big ego or a sense of conceit. No doubt, I was proud of my academic achievements, but I didn't recall any bragging that I might have done in classes; I was mystified. But then it hit me: Indeed, as a bad journalist might, too much of my class commentary might have centered on insisting on correct or ethically proper behavior—of my journalists-in-training; I would warn of negative consequences of improper or altered acts while doing a journalist's job. In short, I was haunted by the ghost of my old Journal city editor Bill, the one to whom I'd lied about skipping out on a School Board meeting. In essence, I was teaching my students to "do right" instead of showing them or explaining *how*—at least that was what I preferred to tell myself. The alternative would have been to see them as pseudo-racists who thought only white professors could teach, that only white people—and especially white men—have the necessary credibility to be considered an authority figure—which would have been more difficult to broach and literally would have colored my view of most of the student body. I consciously chose to do better at teaching methods instead of morals, and censored myself when I thought I might be getting "preachy".

Still, there were other things to learn about being in this new profession in Louisiana. One day in September of my second LSUS year, I heard the news that a black man had been killed by one of two white women involved in a botched drug buy occurring in a convenience store parking lot in the predominantly black Shreveport neighborhood of Cedar Grove. This was a month after another black man was shot in a post-midnight scuffle at an all-night diner. The September shooting attracted a crowd of angry onlookers and devolved into a full-blown riot that lasted several nights and days. My reporting and research instincts still were too strong at that time and I decided to lean on my UT training and to conduct a study of the coverage of the riot, using the long-standing, defining concepts of news and the notion of competing newspaper organizations—The Times and The Journal—as an investigative context. Some editor at The Times disputed the results, calling and asking my department chair to withdraw or censor the study, which he declined, to my relief. But this showed me that race still was a very sore subject to many local people in the area. A short time later avowed racist David Duke came to campus to give a public speech in his 1988 presidential campaign, serving as a very visible reminder about race and testing my allegiance to the principal of free speech. Still later, I received an anonymous letter at home deriding my progressive views on race in my Journal columns. It included a thinly veiled threat that I was being watched, so I put myself on high vigilance regarding racial matters. Then it really it home as we were leaving the neighborhood McDonald's restaurant and—at a crosswalk not more than a couple blocks away—witnessed these people, standing on a corner, in varying stages of dress as they waited for traffic to provide an opening to cross the road. They—men and women—stood out like a sore thumb: one or two wore a white top, exposing a dress on one and pants on the other; two others wore floor-length white robes; one carried a pointy-topped, canonical white hat as he crossed the street.

I stopped our blue Nissan, somewhat abruptly, as Kathy's and my jaws opened as we watched the all-white parade through the windshield. Kathy unconsciously reached her arm toward the back seat to Ryan and Emily, as if in defensive mode. "Oh my God," I said. "Look! They're klansmen!" We both agreed later that day that we couldn't raise our children in such an atmosphere and that we wouldn't be in Shreveport longer than the three years' service the state had required. The rest of my tenure at LSUS proved non-eventful, as I devoted as much time as possible to writing my columns, teaching my courses, and looking for potential jobs elsewhere.

One area that I wish had been better involved dealing with my relatives and friends I had made in Shreveport prior to going to Austin. It seemed as if acquiring a doctorate put me in some sort of "social hell" that I'm sure could only be appreciated and understood by people such as my Chicago cousin Daughter's husband/deacon Doc, who was treated by every Frenchman I knew as the epitome of the top of the proverbial social status food chain, i.e., revered beyond belief and beyond words. Doc, as I said in the first chapter, was the stereotype of the "good Catholic" who observed every holy day and daily attended Mass—as evidenced by his seven children, their nice home, his managerial job, his penchant for formality (he wore a tie every day, and if you were a Frenchman, he never called you by your nickname, only by your proper given name), his quiet demeanor, his conservative dress, and his constant absence "to take care of some church stuff," as Mamoo would say. Even his choice of TV shows (Lawrence Welk over Jackie Gleason every Saturday) suggested a level of status. I'm not sure I ever saw anyone but Daughter truly have a real conversation with Doc; he was the demi-god of my Frenchman world—usually a teetotaler with rosary beads in his pocket and nothing but goodness in his heart for everyone. It wasn't until we arrived back in Shreveport that I learned to appreciate his position/dilemma. I thought bringing a wife and child back to my old, Louisiana stomping grounds would be nothing if not a great reunion featuring laughs and much backslapping. Wrong again: People treated me with a lot more reverence than they did when I was just a fellow worshipper or everyday reporter. Nobody seems to know what you talk about with someone with a Ph.D., or they believe you only talk to other Ph.D.s. They look at you as if you're a "brainiac" or some stranger from a foreign land, that you've transcended mortal being and are living on a higher plane, like some kind of Buddha maybe. In any event, whenever I happened to be in the company of any non-LSUS or non-Journal person, conversation toward me became very tight-lipped, very trite, never deep or detailed. Hardly anyone would ask me about my teaching, or what I did at Texas, or my columns. It was always, "Hey! How are you doing? Everything all right with the family? That's good, good." Then crickets, or discussions about the weather. I knew it was incumbent on me to get the conversation going, but honestly, I already knew a lot about them, their jobs, and their families, so I often was at a loss on where to go from there, as well. They don't prepare you for that in graduate school or if you're a Frenchman or black—the apparent class disconnect that emerges when you've graduated from working class to upper middle class, from shopping at Wal-Mart to shopping at Macy's, from watching Gunsmoke reruns to watching Downton Abbey or Masterpiece. The hardest part comes when you're visiting your former, most immediate family, and you realize that *you* now have to supply the questions and the subject matter that constitute the greater part of the conversation. You really are the grownup now! I once devoured an entire book about academics in this situation to try to figure the best way forward, only to discover there's always going to be some awkward silence, which almost always makes you feel like a stranger in your own home. And if you're an introvert to begin with, forget it; you're lost. I was fine if I could write how I felt and my opinions on family and world matters. But to sit down, coffee or drink in hand, and "chew the fat" or b.s. with some wordy relative or friend who took all day to get to his or her point, that was something I always left to Mamoo while I would find my way to the encyclopedia or magazine lying on the coffee table. Or going to a wake or a funeral alone wouldn't be the same without Mamoo doing her regular "verbal ice-breaking", extending condolences as only she could. Visiting Nanny's house without my (now grown) cousins around to interact with just wasn't the same. Seeing McCoy's wife Maria in the grocery store just didn't have the spark it did when I was a lonesome bachelor, dropping by their house for some laughter and some mothering. A primary academic caveat had taken hold: Thinking wasn't the same as talking, and vice versa; a difficult life lesson, especially so soon after your "adult" life starts to take shape. Sometimes you really *can't* go home, even when you're there. Class can be a bitch, but for the rest of our Shreveport stay, we did our best to keep things as normal as possible in matters of race. When Emily came along, we never made a big deal of her slightly different (from Ryan's) skin color, a pale shade of coffee with cream in it. But her fine, curly hair, sassy attitude, and love for raisins and the Disney/ Seven Dwarfs song "Heigh Ho!" showed she was going to have her own unique persona no matter what we did, and Ryan never noticed their slightly different hues. It may have been naïve and unrealistic, but we didn't want them to even have any racially sensitive bones in their little bodies. So, something as abrupt and unexpected as that bold, robed strut across the street that day on the way from McDonald's made us resolve to make our search for a new home the central focus in the last year of my LSUS contract. The choice came down to UT and Kent State, with the latter winning mainly because it was as far north as we could get and the faculty seemed like a better fit, plus the Ohio school's balanced emphasis on teaching and research, unlike UT, was highly appealing. LSUS crafted a substantial counteroffer, but no amount of extra pay could remove from our minds the vision of those white sheets strolling in broad daylight in one of Shreveport's supposedly more progressive neighborhoods.

Our Ohio stay, however, wasn't all that pleasant. Prior to being hired, I had gone to the journalism educators' summer convention in 1988 to interview at a minority job fair, hoping I might find some enlightened journalism school administrators who need to diversify their faculties. I ran into Judy, the director at Kent State, recently appointed and eager to show she could recruit with the best schools out there as she herself was a product of a large, prestigious East

Coast doctoral program. We hit it off well; she impressed me with her knowledge of what was going on in research and in the field of media management, and had mentioned some minority mentoring opportunities might be developing if a federal grant proposal that she had just submitted would receive approval for 1990. Kent State's former director was a UT grad who had pioneered one of the first decision-making software games for his doctorate and who I had met when I was a UT student. Later in the year, I visited Kent during one of its worst winter storms, but I was enchanted by all the snow, Judy's calm and confident demeanor, the nice give-and-take conversation from the faculty and the thought of being wooed, wined and dined again felt great, as was the job offer—so great that I didn't give poor UT another look, especially since their search and their attempt to take me as an "opportunity (minority) hire" ran into a few administrative obstacles and they couldn't match Kent's offer at the time. Once we got there, I should have seen that life was throwing signs at me suggesting I made a mistake. First, we arrived to find our mover had connected our Nissan's rear axle to the back of the moving truck, leaving it in gear and destroying the axle in the process and leaving it not worth repair. So, we had to immediately rent a car for a week or so before we were fully settled in; then we quickly got up to speed on the car offerings in Kent enough to arrange to hurriedly buy a new Toyota. I couldn't sue the mover because he was Ree's son, Joe. The next day, I made my first trip to the J School at Taylor Hall, and discovered it was where the poor students had been killed in the May 4, 1970, infamous clash between Vietnam War protestors and the Ohio National Guard. I can't remember: Either they told me about this historic fact on my recruiting visit and I forgot, or the snow covered so much that there was nothing to see. Regardless, they showed me to my office, and I noted that, while it was spacious and roomy, it had some loud, buzzy electrical equipment and several pipes running up, down, and along the walls. It turned out to be a former utility room, which was all they could offer until they completed the ongoing renovation of some future faculty spaces in the building's rear. I took a deep breath, hesitant but still sure that I'd get used to it and things would be OK, even though the room had a second door that opened onto an auditorium where large classes and meetings were often held. Things progressed well that fall, I'd had good introductory one-on-ones with most of the print faculty. Kathy's journey, however, was a bit rougher, as she noted the difficulty in making friends because these weren't the southerners she'd been used to all her life. It took time to get people to open up and, while I had my work colleagues to be my instant friends, she had no one—no family and she was a stay-at-home mom with two kids. Later that fall, she also noticed a sunset-driven feeling of mild depression setting into her mood. My first semester, on the other hand, was uneventful enough as I learned where everything was and connected names to faces. We endured our first winter, the kids braving the Ohio cold that permeated our living room because our sight-unseen first apartment had large, tall, sliding glass doors, upstairs and downstairs, to the point that we had to buy heavy curtains and put quilts up at night in the kids' bedroom. Not surprisingly, Ryan got sick Christmas day. In spring, my reporting class, my first-ever night course, took on real-world reporting atmosphere for the student paper that January as the U.S. started large-scale bombing of Iraq. I was proud of the dedication and effort of those kids that night, certain that I wouldn't have gotten the same effort from LSUS students. But it also marked the unofficial start of the recession of the early 1990s, with an oil-price crisis, fall of the Soviet empire, a savings and loan emergency, and other earth-shaking world events. The trickle-down effect resulted in Judy taking a similar job in Virginia, leaving me without the hoped-for take-action mentor I had envisioned when she hired me. There were other work factors, too. The recession eliminated long-distance calls, copying machines, and hoped-for raises, while causing consternation, anger, and angst of different forms in our abandoned faculty. For example, Joe, the software guru whom I'd befriended as a graduate student, turned surly, quarrelsome, and critical at times at faculty meetings in his diminished role in school affairs, especially since he viewed me as usurping what he thought was his media management course. And for the first time I had a shouting match in my office with a student, who wanted to argue every question on a recent test to bump up his grade. When he discovered that I had logical reasons for every one of his arguments, he began to slowly shout his reasons, which made me shout after I realized that he was too invested in trying to bully me into changing my mind—to the point that the whole incident appeared futile. After this went on for a couple minutes, I just loudly told him to leave my office. As time went on, students seemed to become more volatile. It might have had something to do with me teaching six different courses over the span of four semesters, or maybe it was the recession. Either way, I felt stretched thin. On top of that, our nerves were on edge as the town had a murder and an attempted murder on or near campus between our first December there and the following February, with the situation ending as police chased and killed a suspect—resulting in low safety marks in our mind for a town with slightly fewer than 30,000 people and causing extra caution on our part in the evenings.

Later that summer, another bit of unease developed with the implementation of the grant proposal that Judy had mentioned earlier put in the inexperienced hands of me and Evonne, the black broadcasting prof hired at the same time as me. On paper, the "institute", as we called it, seemed to be a perfect vehicle for increasing Kent State's minority journalism major population. The idea was to recruit a dozen-plus minority students from across the country who had, or were approaching, graduation. The grant would bring them to Kent for two weeks' journalism training, counseling, and mentoring in journalism and related fields, with the hope they would consider enrolling for their master's in journalism. We would hold training sessions, then provide transportation to on-the-job training as well in Cleveland/Akron area journalism outlets, with the idea of having them put together a publication with content from their activities, either in Kent itself, or off-campus. Perfect, no? We either underestimated their abilities or didn't carefully enough consider the potential pitfalls. Of course, the usual rivalries, jealousies, and mean-spirited teasing occurred. But some students ran out of money (which we also supplied in part), one young lady had a pregnancy termination, unprofessional conduct occurred in the performance of journalism (in-house and in other venues), there were outright arguments, and near-physical conflicts within and outside the group. I don't want to give the impression that they all were misfits; just *some*. But that was all in the first summer of the program; the second installment was better, but the journalistic output was inferior to the prior year as we accepted non-social studies majors. Because of the short time window and a jam-packed schedule, I couldn't offer much mentoring; I never got a chance to talk to any of the students about their prospects for continuing their collegiate education; the logistics and personalities kept us on our toes. The whole two years felt like a blur, but also constituted a missed opportunity, in that Northeast Ohio in general had many things going for it culturally—parks, zoos, leisure prospects, potential for lasting friendships, superior schools. Despite the unease with Joe, I liked all my colleagues. Our best opportunity for a good discussion of race occurred when an Akron Beacon Journal reporter interviewed Kathy and I about our reactions to controversy surrounding the then-recently released Spike Lee romantic dramatic film Jungle Fever, about the ups and downs of a fictional interracial couple. It was great getting to talk about something we were living, but the subsequent article discussed *only that topic*, making me think some readers might come away with the feeling that we were a one-dimensional couple with no other concerns or outlooks. Add the relative lack of sunshine (only about 160 days in Northeast Ohio vs. 230 in Central Texas), Kent's 1990 minority percentage (less than 12 percent), and the long summer drives to visit the Louisiana grandparents, then maybe you can see how our return to Austin made great sense to us. Overall, while we fled to Kent because of our fear of experiencing racial repercussions in Louisiana, Ohio was, racially speaking, peaceful. Perhaps it was the overwhelming whiteness of the area, to the point that whites didn't feel threatened by the presence of minorities—sort of "out of sight, out of mind". On the other hand, the absence of racial tension was replaced by economic uncertainty underscored by the many work-related consequences of the recession.

In contrast, Austin again seemed like a breath of fresh air, offering relief and an opportunity for the growth of our family. Texas was coming out of the recession, led by Austin's investment in technology and the University of Texas' stability. Not only did UT offer as much money as Kent did, Texas had no state income tax, plus prices were not as inflated as in Ohio. UT had abundant money for research, a diverse student populace, and smaller course loads. Austin had a nationally known tolerance for difference ("Keep Austin weird" is the unofficial civic motto), and experienced mild winters. UT, with enough top-notch graduate students to encourage and assist in research, seemed advantageous to my career, despite having to re-start the tenure clock. Moreover, UT still had several people I knew during my graduate years who would or could serve as mentors and guides to the holy tenure grail. There were tradeoffs, obviously: No job was perfect. For example, by that time, I'd accepted as fact that this third, consecutive academic job appointment was solidifying my role and classification as a minority, specifically a black male, although I never verbally declared myself as such. Ever since my Blessed Sacrament days in Shreveport, the predominant ideology/view from my peers and the community—as in the case at The Journal—was that I was a minority voice and, as such, a black employee. Still, no one ever directly spoke to the point or reference my race in conversations, pre-, during, or post-employment; it was assumed, and I didn't discourage it. I chose instead to "go along to get along" and offer my Frenchman credentials upon request only. I identified as black, since that's how everyone viewed me. Facilitating this: Every government agency in those days had affirmative-style hiring practices aimed at increasing its diversity, especially universities because minorities in academia were vastly underrepresented. So, it often became advantageous to be black. Blackness was what I had become most familiar with then, especially as it became the default identity (partly because of many black-Frenchman marital unions and prevailing job opportunities) for Frenchmen—from California to Maine to Florida and everywhere in-between. I'd mostly accommodate this convention, especially since my application for my first Louisiana driver's license: I had to provide my birth certificate, which said my race was "colored". So, I became accustomed to being placed on influential university committees that I otherwise wouldn't qualify for, as each group was increasing its diversity and, thus, saying it was increasing its racial or "community" input. And I played the game, doing what I perceived as my virtuous duty (since I had received so much in return), while boosting my networking capacity.

Committee work, as I learned over time, involved another tradeoff, or "game", of the UT job: winners vs. losers. University life, as it exists in most settings, often gets determined in these committees, which execute the bulk of academic policy and procedures—from curriculum decisions to admission rules. As you advance up the scale of a university, more desirable committees come with more power which—with the ascent of managers in academia—otherwise there is little for professors to attain. The upshot is that these committees often feature contentious arguments and fights between two dominant sub-groups representing some political view; the politics are much more precise and job- or cause-centered (think: dominant ways of teaching or doing research) than the usual conservative-vs.-liberal fights. The result: Committee members constantly want you to vote one way (their's) and not another (their opponents), putting you in uncomfortable positions that you'd never think would exist. A not uncommon example: When hiring minority teachers, do we pay them what they're worth in the professional market, or do we pay them a lower salary that would square with their academic experience? Imagine that you're a racial minority, recently hired and placed on this committee with older, veteran minority group members, and you benefitted from market competition in your salary dealings, but the group—in the case of a promising, young, minority applicant—declines to follow that example because it would mean they'd be paid less than the prospective employee. Do you do the right thing, and vote in favor of market-based salaries, or follow the group, many of whom will remember your vote and who secretly resent your salary? You get the drift. Now, imagine sitting on a faculty search committee, trying to justify why one job candidate stands out more, while secretly knowing that a powerful colleague on the committee prefers another candidate who happened to be his mentee, a graduate of his alma mater, and—it so happens—with whom he often has one-on-one mentoring sessions or, worse, has co-authored several research papers. You'd think that your colleague would declare a conflict of interest, but that rarely happens in the power-hungry halls of some colleges; in fact, many such colleagues would publicly say that—as intellectuals—they are trained to remain neutral and to judge candidates on their merits (or some other similar hogwash). Of course, over time, you may learn to accept that some people will differ on different issues, or that most people's memories are too short to harbor a grudge over one vote. Still, some people's memories can be extremely long—especially in academia, where people often work into their 70s (or later)—and they can have pet peeves or can be manipulative, despite what they say. You're better served by either skipping meetings altogether or accumulating enough power to enable you to withstand ideological assaults of these kinds; or have the potential to do greater damage to a foe at some later, more strategic point. Either way, such battles can become mentally straining and, if you're not careful, they can distract you from why you became an academic in the first place.

There were many other mental skirmishes, of course, but luckily most of the time I could concentrate on what mattered most: my family, of course, but also my desire to help students become the best journalists they could, and to become well-known in my research field. Happily, I had many paths I could take to do so, formal and informal. Formally, I was the minority liaison for several years, essentially working to make minority students fit more comfortably in the J School. Off the books, I took pains to try to guide minority students to their fullest potential. For years, I advised formal groups, such as the campus chapter of the National Association of Black Journalists. That meant helping them connect with professional mentors, writing recommendation letters, and creating assistantships to involve them in research or journalism work. I would speak and advise at meetings, serve as main advisor to their projects, participate in varying capacities in their organized events. What's more, I would organize events and educational workshops for teachers in predominantly minority high school student bodies. I'll be the first to admit, not everything went smoothly. For example, I doubt the black students at the Accounting Career Awareness Program Summer Residency Camp enjoyed my presentation on communication skills, but, hey, I'd try anything once. One-on-one conversations likely took prominence in such activities—asking kids about themselves, their dream occupations, their experiences, and aiding them to connect to someone who would help them in the way they felt most useful. These efforts came in addition to the numerous talks, discussions, and events that I lead that contained a minority component, issue, or worries—from talking to white government officials to understanding how media stereotype minorities. Of course, UT students usually were the top 10 percent of Texas' public schools system, meaning they were usually middle and upper-middle class kids. Many were the first in their families to go to college or were following in a parent's footsteps or simply wanted to make good money by using the skills they could develop in our College of Communication and across campus. As a result, they often were easy to engage, intellectually curious, politically savvy, aware of society's traps, and eager to succeed where, in many cases, their parents and siblings had not. Advising them was a dream come true because in many cases I was able to make a small difference in how they advanced through UT and, subsequently, in life. I stay in touch with many of them to this day.

Of course, there were highs, heartaches, and setbacks along the way. There was Dré, a Ft. Worth kid and Army veteran who wrote for several publications but ran into various, let's say predisposed and intolerable editors, who made life hell for him at times, and mistook his questioning manner for arrogance or insubordination; eight years after graduation, at age 36, he died of brain cancer. And there was Janessa, the Houston senior who was a dormitory resident assistant, who went on to master's and doctoral degrees and studied how to improve rules and customs shaping the growth and career path of black female academics. Those are extreme examples, however. Genesis, when I met him, was a difficult student who'd skip out of class at inopportune times (such as when we'd work on skills exercises) and who had a devil of a time trying to pass some assignments; he eventually became an admissions counselor and organizer at UT. Edith was another student who initially struggled but went on to create and own a successful private tutoring service. Shini was a reporter for the campus newspaper who, at first, was a shy, quasi-inquisitive person who hadn't really given much thought to badgering people for information; she learned that her fears and discomfort were just reflections of lack of experience, and that she held the key to how far she could go. Last time I looked, she was an assistant attorney general in a state in the Midwest. Of course, there were the not-so-successful students, whose knowledge or abilities would come up short a bit, or whose goals exceeded their grasps. But I tried to help each student who came through my office door to the best of my ability; many times, it wasn't the journalism that was deficient. Often, students would lack the resources or the contacts that would enable them to advance; many black students especially were unprepared when it came to gaining practical experiences besides those activities that came via official coursework. Many white students can afford to take an unpaid internship or two—and, unfortunately, that is the norm in the notoriously frugal news industry. But black students, often hamstrung by multiple loans or already committed to part-time jobs that help pay school bills, cannot or don't have the time for unpaid jobs because they couldn't afford *not* to work. Thus, they often had fewer professional contacts and mentors familiar enough to the students to help them get their feet inside the internship doors. Even in student club settings, when resources may not have been an issue, lack of planning, scheduling, and administrative skills on a black student leader's part often cripples the organization's abilities to get much done. These deficiencies create a strain on an advisor's capabilities, as well. Such difficulties also showed themselves at the doctoral level. For example, my advisee Amara had a full-time administrative job at the nearby historically black college, so getting her to concentrate on her various dissertation elements and their related deadlines was like pulling teeth. In addition, she always had logical or reasonable excuses that couldn't really be challenged because of a prior medical issue. It took her twice as long to finish her degree than most of the students who entered the program the same time she did.

After my experiences at LSUS and Mizzou, I didn't expect all roses, however. I knew and had already experienced many of the pitfalls of advising minority students. No professor whoever had extensive counseling experience expected to get rich from doing so. Prevailing structures—in which the last- or recently hired assistant professors usually were the first line of advising, e.g.—often revealed to you that your spot in the pecking order was at the bottom; this was especially true for professors of color. Your colleagues *expected* you to help engage or even to lead the fight against the challenge of dwindling or minimal minority enrollment, a fact of life for most public university journalism programs. Sometimes, the expectations are great, as in "*you* chair the committee" or "*you* do the research on what we need to do" or "*you* present the report" or "*you* lead the discussion"—all of which fell in my lap my first year. It was as if they felt that I was some "magic Negro" who would lead the department to the Promised Land of Full Integration or, what's more, that this was a *black faculty only* issue to tackle, no white faculty members needed or allowed. And when I finally presented the report—fashioned by me alone, as no white faculty ever consistently attended any committee meetings— we had no discussion of the report's contents. Nothing. Crickets. Not even from the other minority faculty. Just "Thanks, George. The next item on our agenda is…" What a sham; it was almost as if the faculty was saying, "Well, now that we've got that on the record and done, it's time to go onto something else." This was my first major disappointment with the UT journalism faculty. There was no mechanism for accountability in practical issues that mattered. The overriding truth of faculty life is that time is money, and time should be spent on what gets you money. And the most money usually comes to those who are the most creative, bring in the most research dollars, publish the most research or gather the most attention to themselves. It is damn hard to direct dollars elsewhere; it can be done, but it takes time.

And the money in a research university usually flows to the business, law, and science fields.

Still, I don't want to beat a dead horse or give the wrong impression. This didn't mean the faculty was made up of heartless elites; quite the contrary. They were some of the smartest, finest people I'd ever met and most cared deeply about students. But the university structure could make them come across as an uncaring, cold, highly paid, three-degreed group of individuals whose major interest involved getting a leg up on the department ladder, either through salary or rank or prestige or all three. Throw in the fact that all faculty members usually succeed via their critical thinking skills, then it's no wonder that any proposed change gets questioned to death about its possible drawbacks. It's akin to, when you're out shopping or walking into a business or any shop, when you start to leave and reach the door, you see a homeless person begging for money. You want to give that person something, but all you've got are credit cards or small change, so you walk by them, saying, "Sorry, you caught me at a bad time," or something to that effect. You feel bad, although you know you're a good person because of all your charitable contributions. Still, you say to yourself, "I don't have a choice; maybe next time." That's what happens to faculty members who aren't moved to action: They've often got to move on and "feed my family by doing my job". And then they totally forget about the homeless guy. Truthfully, it's more complicated, but in the end, when nothing gets done except venting and speeches, it feels like one giant morass of ineptitude and foot-dragging. By the way, we didn't get a diversity action plan until 20 years later, when it was mandated by our accrediting agency.

After such behavior, it's not hard to imagine that as a person of color, I had my doubts about academia's abilities to get anything done except what it had always done: teaching and research. Everything else seemed beyond the grasp of these highly educated, hard-working, driven-to-succeed characters, despite their best efforts, brainstorming, or whatever approach they might take. This made it easy for each of us to hunker down in our offices and simply "do our own thing", but it also made me question whether academia was ever going to be a place where a black or brown person could get anything of any significance done. All the administrators were white, meaning their networking and mentoring strengths rested with other whites, particularly white males. After my first two years or so, I often went solo for lunch as my mentors knew I was a self-starter who would come to them, not vice-versa. The fact that I had two prior jobs in academia probably worked to my disadvantage in the networking department, giving people the false impression that I didn't need any more mentoring; plus, I've always felt that socializing came easier with females, rather than with males. And I think the tenured, high-ranking white men on the faculty, unaccustomed to working with minorities, kept their distance because of lack of confidence or some weird expectations or assumptions about men of color. Either way, I had no way of knowing this at the time because I couldn't analyze what wasn't there. Also, I discovered white men had an "out of sight, out of mind" mentality toward many things, e.g., when one white male department chair forgot to read, sign, and pass to higher-ups a grant application of mine, thus missing the deadline and making the application moot. Though the "absent-minded professor" myth has a ring of truth, I doubt he would have forgotten an application from a closer associate or if I had been a product of his alma mater. But this wasn't just a white male thing: I also had a white female colleague who agreed to collaborate with me on a research project "completely drop the ball" on her end of the preparations, only to not tell me until I called her from another city where I had just arrived to conduct interviews for the project. I realized people make mistakes all the time, but I wondered whether there was something about me that compounded such failings. Oddly enough, this forgetfulness or lack of caring or commitment never occurred when they wanted to pass on a telephone call or inquiry from someone wanting a minority view on some critical issue; of course, it was never phrased as such, but we both knew that the point of the call was to "pass it off to the expert".

I had a bit of a respite from some of this atmosphere for about six years, when we made a black woman our department chair. Because of Lorraine's academic inexperience at that point, she appointed me as her associate chair after she arrived and we became fast friends, united in our fight against the faculty's stubborn ways. This was a double-edged sword because, while it felt great to finally be empowered somewhat to get things done, I also learned from her—as her confidante—how petty and ill-equipped some faculty members could be in the face of potential change and challenges. We often put our heads together on problems ranging from professional ethics to combative personalities to inability to think to political pet peeves to out-and-out professional jealousies. I got a close-up look at the nuanced dance she had to take when dealing with senior faculty, as well as the toughest part of the job—being the bearer of bad news: whether a cancelled course, student complaints, unsuccessful grant attempts, unwanted assignments, added courses, or, a simple "no" to a request. I also got to see and hear some of the nastiest reactions to some of her decisions, which I attributed to simple anger instead of what first went through my head—that the reaction would have been much different if the decision had been made by a white male. Since she often tried to institute many reforms, I also blamed many faculty reactions to fear of change.

REDISCOVERING MY SALTY RIVER

All this conflict, this butting of heads between people who are all supposed to be on the same political page, can be misleading if you don't look at it with a grain of salt, however. Lee, the beleaguered Caddo school superintendent often would say, "Hindsight is 20-20," amid criticism of his staff's faulty attempts to devise an acceptable desegregation plan. But his defensive retort also applies to how we look at the past, seeing things we could or should have done differently, given the circumstances we encountered. Thinking about my years at UT in retrospect, however, makes it easy to assign blame for the challenging times that made me contemplate whether advanced, progressive racial thinking and reform were something that I wanted to actively pursue. A bitter person might relish such retroactive analysis, but every person is different, often affiliated with many groups that supply them with several, varying viewpoints that impact their behaviors in diverse ways at variable times. I went through Jesuit, grew up in Shreveport, and often used the prism of race to observe people most of my life, so I should be somewhat bitter. But now—in retirement—I'm more confident that UT helped me discover some things about race and my identity that I never dreamed I'd find and to conduct my life in ways that surprised me and defied racial expectations and stereotypes.

For example, when I took the job at UT, as an alum I wanted in the worst way to blend in. During my graduate stay there, I had so much fun, made wonderful contacts who nurtured me and Kathy, and I learned a tremendous amount about what was expected of a scholar. I felt I owed it to the school to continue that tradition and confirm my mentors' faith in me. I was hired to help train undergraduates and simultaneously make a name for myself and the school in the field of media management. So, I carefully avoided putting too much emphasis on minority issues within media management; it would have constituted "low-hanging fruit" and would supply ammunition for potential enemies—who didn't highly value identity-based research—come tenure decision-time. The standard mainstream criticism of minority-oriented scholars is that their specialty usually falls within other, non-communication-based fields, rather than establishing a name in the principal areas of communication or journalism-related theory. It's akin to a newly hired scholar from Iraq only wanting to concentrate of media issues facing Iraqis—usually of a discriminatory nature—instead of using communication-based hypotheses. By choosing management *in media*, I was choosing an already-established line of academic research or inquiry. I did not entirely refuse to research minority issues, but the media remained my area of stress. What's more, I never refused any of the many race- or minority-driven committees and other assignments that I was asked to serve. The list was extensive: job searches, graduate minority liaison, graduate minority recruitment, minority high school recruitment, serving on "minority affairs" panels, speaking to visiting international journalists about diversity issues, chairing dissertation and master's theses on minority concerns, and creating a lecture series featuring black professionals. That doesn't include minority-related activities for which I volunteered—a separate, longer list. Finally, "blending in" also meant taking up the mantle of the journalism department when it came to the small-but-influential group of community newspapers across the state—ranging from attending conventions, participating in fundraising campaigns, coordinating our reporting program with newspaper coverage needs, and organizing and teaching the first online instructional program for small-paper journalists. I also made several trips around Texas to visit small papers, judged their contests, and often met with their officials. So, not only was I the "minority guy", but also part of the "good ol' boys Texas newspapers cabal," for lack of a better name—including attending weekend card games and participating in weekly football-season gambling pools.

Still, intermingling with the faculty and their causes and becoming "one of us" only partly covered my UT mission, which was multi-faceted, particularly when it came to teaching, which I loved. There's nothing better than seeing students' faces light up with wonder or curiosity at something you said or explained in the classroom setting. Despite sometimes low student ratings because of my refusal to lower standards, I tried to meet and anticipate each student where he/she was emotionally, culturally, preparation-wise, intellectually, in person or online. But from my days at Mizzou, I knew that Texas' prestige did not match the state's size when it came to journalism; Pulitzer Prizes were in short supply and the most politically savvy publication was a magazine (Texas Monthly), not a newspaper (although The Daily Texan counted more than two dozen alums as Pulitzer winners). I had visions of rectifying that when I started teaching at UT, but my reach was limited because I often was assigned to beginning writing courses. So, in trying to leverage the hand dealt to me, I attempted to help our majors see that you could do more with journalism than just rewrite press releases, cover press conferences, protests, and meetings, or report simply what people said. Course by course, I would show them how to do as I did in Shreveport—anticipate what would happen before it happened. That would transform into covering a meeting's most important agenda item *in advance* of the meeting or taking a particularly relevant aspect of a beat and *researching the hell out of it* to fully inform readers of its importance and impact, while other journalists just looked for something new. In other words, I believed the students should learn to *manipulate the coverage* rather than let it manipulate *them*. Such a journalistic approach uses proactive behavior instead of being reactive, and tries to wrest the agenda *away* from the politicians and *place it into the public's hands*—something any White House press corps could stand to learn, instead of running blindly behind the president's or Congress' agendas. That way, journalists aren't always worried about what I call "false objectivity"—what they usually call "getting both sides of a story"—when, in truth, every story has multiple sides. Reshaping this basic attitude toward news was a tall order at Texas, since many of my colleagues often began their lectures with a rundown or quiz about what was in that day's Daily Texan—regardless of whether it was exemplary journalism, which it usually was not because it was generally being written by students who'd hadn't taken a journalism course yet and who were following the dictates of other students, not mature, seasoned journalism teachers. This Daily Texan club-mentality—because many staffers worked 50- and 60-hour weeks there—was difficult to dislodge, given that some colleagues were Texan products and often sat on the paper's advisory board, reinforcing the "false objectivity" culture. At first, I capitulated and joined that board, thinking that working from within might make it easier to lay the groundwork for changing the paper's reporters' views on news values. But I encountered a strong Texan newsroom culture that included deriding the journalism department while laughing at non-Texan students' uncertain attempts at professionalism and praising its own sophomoric attempts at keeping pace with the University administration's shrewd and heavily veiled plans. So, I did not win many friends there as I took different tactics at changing the dominant journalistic narrative that our majors observed on a daily basis. One example involved providing workshops for Texan editors on how to properly manage their over-supply of student journalists. And when that didn't work, I'd send my better students to Texan offices to offer their good stories; the work would get accepted, but things were too hectic, haphazard and chaotic at the Texan for any consistent impact. For the better part of two years, I even became the very active advisor to The Austin Student, an alternative weekly started by a disgruntled Texan ad director; the under-staffed paper tried to cover everyday student interests—such as sex-life advice, academic cheating, cheap restaurants, dealing with parents, and studying habits—that didn't revolve around UT's administration. When I was associate director, we started our own semesterly course lab publication, The Texas Journalist, centered around elections and other critical issues, and gave each student a chance to contribute. These were small efforts, to be sure, but we were determined to give our students a taste of the professional process as practiced by real journalists, not students eating pizza in a basement, the home of Texan offices.

My long-term, most consistent efforts occurred in my reporting courses, however, where I put the full breadth of my reporting knowledge into effect—enacting such tools as source number, diversity, and credibility requirements; context and background elements; story timing, reader appeal, compelling quotes, and, of course, concise writing. These were tools we knew Texan reporters were not consistently including under the guidance of other students and, ultimately, I knew that they likely would ultimately cost me in my course evaluations; I was known among students as one of the toughest, if not *the* toughest grader in the journalism department, mainly because my students' grades didn't reflect the university's continuing, upward trend of grade inflation. "Easy A" was UT's middle name, as the same "customer is right" attitude took over the institution's official attitude toward grading and teacher evaluations by students. It didn't matter that study after study has shown such evaluations tend to go higher if students' grades are higher, making grading meaningless and pretending that students knew best what information they needed to learn—a slap in the face to the teaching profession and process. Let's not even discuss the bias students have toward any professor who's not a white man or a woman. As long as I stuck to these standards (which I did for most of the courses in my 25 UT years of employment), my evaluations were lower compared to those of my colleagues. This also gave some credence to the typical UT professor's belief that well-told "war" stories from their past, dynamic and colorful presentations, great guest speakers, and a light grading touch—not actual knowledge—lighted the easier path toward sailing through the promotion process to full professorship. Am I bitter? No, I taught my way, knowing that I taught something of value to my students; my own instincts and journalistic integrity—my knowledge that this was what the true journalism profession expected—trumped my popularity. Also, my determination to spend most nights with Kathy, Ryan, and Emily, as opposed to working on UT concerns, had to eclipse everything else. Family had become my main concern, especially after learning while at The Journal that there was more to life than work and perfectionism.

So, as a final, stabilizing element to the three-legged stool that became my UT mission, I became a dedicated servant of the various organizations with crucial roles in reforming the profession (**Reader warning:** The rest of this paragraph (and the other mission details) may come off to some as so much boasting, but nothing is further from the truth. Instead, I'm trying to show my depth of commitment to this duty). At first, I sort of fell into caring about a project that another colleague started and asked me to join. My work as associate chair of the department started with this project, which got underway long before Lorraine arrived, when the previous chair, Steve, asked for help with a workshop borne from a large, extensive grant he had secured from the then-named American Society of Newspaper Editors (ASNE). The work meant creating a curriculum for 30 or so high school journalism teachers, who would visit UT for two summer weeks to earn continuing education credit for brushing up on current journalism skills, as one of four similar workshops across the country. The idea capitalized on research showing collegiate journalism majors often learned early basics in high school; the thinking was that if we could find teachers who needed reinvigorating or updating their skills set *and*—as a bonus—if we could especially prioritize those teachers of substantial numbers of minority kids—we could establish a sustainable school-to-college pipeline of students, and, even better, enhance the university's reputation as a quality journalism center.

The first year went so well that Steve effectively turned over the entire project to me, starting a 15-year run that had many benefits, obviously. First, the workshop provided a chance to display our faculty's particular teaching skills and platform for sharing their research, especially in the areas of technology, diversity, and ethics. Second, after two weeks of an all-expenses paid, fine hotel in a city that featured lots of diversions, teachers went home refreshed, happy, and full of ideas and plans for their upcoming school year. Third, it provided extra funding for multitalented graduate students with a head for planning, logistics management, and practical journalism skills to share and teach. Fourth, it solidified university outreach to varying aspects of the community: hotel industry, teacher associations, restaurant industry, and summer stipends for participating faculty. Most importantly, however, I learned so much about the nuances and hardships of scholastic teaching, plus the worrisome state of that profession, that I encouraged our faculty to participate in teachers' annual conventions, student contests, workshops and online courses to strengthen our allies in Texas classrooms—resulting in appreciation awards for our department—and in outreach to local minority journalism students. Those efforts extended to several presentations to our collegiate journalism colleagues as well. The notion of "service" doesn't get much lip service or result in much action in academia, other than direct memberships on various panels and committee.

So, the ASNE institute didn't only serve high school students and their teachers, it served the university in myriad ways. Its crowning achievement, however, was in all the resulting professional contacts that our faculty made, most importantly representation on the panel determining the state of Texas high school journalism teaching certification standards. Another area of service dear to my heart was the

Texas black press, a group of small, weekly publications that primarily circulated in the state's large cities. At varying times, I did consumer advertising research for that group in its ad strategy preparations, individually consulted with several black publishers on matters specific to their newspapers, gave convention speeches about the status and future of the black press, provided internship candidates, assigned students to conduct reporting, and coordinated an AT&T technology funding grant program, among other activities.

As to how this mission helped me discover some things about race and my identity, in my dreams I supposed that identity simply was something that you obviously were. As time passed, however, and my identity seemed more elusive than ever, I realized that I was going to have to wait and work at it. My mission—while on its face seems to simply mimic the ideal academic job plan—was more than simply a plan. Initially I saw identity, in my Shreveport-based approach, as something that was race-based, because that was all I knew until then; the LSUS and Kent academic jobs seemed clouded—I don't want to say "tainted"—with the specter of race, as I was obviously integrating those faculties and working to increase their diversity. But I returned to Austin knowing that I was going to be applying what I'd learned at UT when I was earning my doctorate. For my fledgling family's sake, I wanted to make UT my destination job, so I knew I couldn't repeat any prior mistakes and, instead, needed a plan. Thus, the mission, and its consequences, which were many. For example, blending in meant becoming a scholar with a particular specialty possessed by no other faculty member. I didn't realize it at first, but choosing this research specialty constituted and formed a distinct role for me in the group, to the extent that part of my *identity* that my colleagues would use when the subject of management might arise. Not to overdo the obvious, but I was laying the groundwork of, at first, a resume'—which then became, through habit, a part of my identity, emphasis on "part". And the other blending roles that I amassed—resourceful, expert on black issues, friend to the small newspaper business, take your pick—amounted to a large part of what I did, but more importantly, who I was. The more roles, the more complexity my identity began to accrue. Again, these terms didn't enter my consciousness until much later; I was too busy simply doing what I thought I had to do—persisting, just like those bus riders back in Shreveport, only the setting and the intent were different. This kind of persistence could become so mundane at times, however, especially when it was the fourth or fifth time teaching a course, or when I had to go through the motions of the technical writing that academic publishing mostly follows. Or this persistence can be an actual problem in that—by serving on so many minority-related groups—you risk becoming pigeonholed as the "model minority" whose job was to "represent" his/her race to their white colleagues (who, coincidentally, simultaneously didn't want to see you do any research in that area).

Naturally, this identity-building process applied to other parts of my mission plan. In teaching, for instance, when after the normal six-year waiting period in 1998, the college dean promoted me to associate professor, she said I should concentrate on one thing—besides developing a top-notch research reputation. She wanted me to help transport the journalism department into a unit that would become known in the profession as a solid center for journalism throughout the state and the nation. She was fearful that its reputation at that moment wasn't placing it in the top tier of U.S. journalism schools. I was more than agreeable but I also was stunned in that I didn't know she felt that way about the department and that she was genuinely concerned—contrary to the vibes I was getting from my faculty colleagues. In short, in her mind, she wanted me to become what we called "a two-way player", someone with a solid foot in research *and* teaching. But she didn't use that word, trying her best to suggest not just uplifting the teaching reputation, but the public view of the school as an institution, and not something I had witnessed, much less thought of, up to that point. Armed with that charge, I felt empowered to make things happen and to try to bring the department closer to the dean's vision. To me, her directive meant sharpening or polishing my journalism practitioner bona fides in Texas. It was going to take time, as I just taught my courses and had done nothing much above that at the time. Then we started working on grants to make this happen; first, we worked on the black press advertising, then the ASNE Institute, and started to develop stronger connections to Texas high school journalism advocates. We did more press interviews on journalistic events, trends and the industry future in Texas and the country, while simultaneously starting a 20-year, grant-resulting love affair with the Dow Jones News Fund and bringing prestigious, top-tier editing interns to campus for two-week summer workshops. All that activity led to invitations to give "how we did it" presentations to national and state educators and culminated in a nationwide search that helped us recruit Lorraine as chair. The dean didn't stay long enough to see her wish granted but we continued to add to the department's new-found luster and growth in the early 2000s. So, the teaching part of the mission, while identifying me as the "hard-ass" teacher of basic skills, also provided me with the roles as "outreach dude", the alt-Texan advisor, and the online course guy, the quotable j-news prof, the news contests coordinator, and so on (on top of shoring up the skills of non-Texan students). The upshot was that Steve, Lorraine, and I put the department on a trajectory that would get it instantly recognized or cited in state and national journalism discussions at every level.

These roles also added to the identity of yours truly, of course, and I'm convinced they persuaded the new dean to grant me a semester's stipend to travel abroad and study Swedish newspaper management styles. This occurred thanks to a four-month invitation to visit and research from a leading Swedish business school, leading to Kathy, Emily, and Ryan to accompany me, and furthering their and my education. Add "international scholar" to that identity assemblage, and as my resources and repertoire expanded, I started to view the world differently. No surprise there, of course, as I was able to travel to Ireland, Norway, Finland, Denmark and France during my stay at the business school, and added two more solo follow-up trips to Sweden, naturally gaining an appreciation for the Scandinavian love for seafood and the outdoors, as well as their value of *lagom*, a version of the Golden Mean but quantifying it as "just enough" or "just right". I also got an appreciation for those peoples' insistence that they were a diverse populace. For example, while Finns aren't necessarily Scandinavians, many of them hate the Russians. And Scandinavians aren't considered Nordics by some, but the Danes can be Nords or Scandinavians—or either. Meanwhile, every non-Swede believes the Swedes are smug and have a superiority complex. More importantly, I discovered identity is more a state of mind and not always absolute, regardless of who's speaking. It's all part of that great mishmash of human interpretation—something that's simultaneously supportive and opposing of the notion of any, singular identity, much less the identities of black, white, or Frenchman. To say you are 100 percent one or 100 percent the other is not only folly, but in this current age of DNA testing, ridiculous.

And, continuing the critique of my UT mission, the notion of service is perhaps the most noble—albeit one of the less-devotedly followed—of all the quests I tried to match. There's no way to look humble while breaking it down to its core elements, so there's not much use in me trying. I'll simply ask you to briefly recall, when I said in the first chapter, that arguments almost constantly ensue when the word "creole" is mentioned or introduced, although self-proclaimed Frenchmen usually agree that they are neither black nor white. You can take that proclamation two ways: As truth, or truthfully—if the examples of the last page or two can be believed—as likely inaccurate, or at best, confounding. How can you be black *and* white and not be either? Say *what*? Recall that I never got a straight explanation in my childhood, resigning myself to the role of "smart kid", which became my primary role or identity for a large chunk of my life. My "Frenchmanhood" really became mixed with my role as a member of the larger, Frenchman family in Chicago, which constituted my whole world for a while. And within that role, my specialized role was that of cousin, brother, son, nephew, or a variation thereof. I tried to "branch out" to varying other roles, e.g., boyfriend, good neighbor, playmate, classmate, and "good Catholic boy" or altar boy. Then I discovered the will of others to impose an identity upon you, such as the n-word or black and, briefly at times, victim. It wasn't until I realized I had some say in the matter that I became "a pretty good baseball player", Cub fan, a "spin-the-bottler" (good times), music-lover, party- and wake-goer, and mosquito-hater. The point here is, evidently, you can have many identities—even when you're looking for the right one.

And that's the story that encapsulates the last part of the UT mission: Maybe it's because of my background as an education reporter, but I felt extremely comfortable in the job of teaching teachers, regardless of how far removed I was because of all the planning and logistics involved with all the facets of making them feel comfortable so they could concentrate on why they were in Austin. At the end of each workshop, inevitably we would receive heartfelt thanks from one or two participants, to which I'd always say something to the effect of, "No, thank *you*, for providing us the opportunity to serve you, because what you do is so important." And I meant it; listening to my reporting sources, day in and day out, complaining about uninformed politicians and apathetic parents, I couldn't help thinking that nothing was more important than helping teachers as they help society plot its future and guide young people, many of whom barely see or interact with a nurturing adult in an average day. After hearing from so many teachers about how tough it is to do a good job in the environment surrounding their specific schools, I've come to believe that the effort that they exhibit is near-miraculous, and their take-home salaries aren't practically enough compensation—particularly with all the distractions today of social media and smartphones. So that yearly two-week summer event for teachers that we at UT conducted couldn't come close to an adequate "thank you", in my mind; I always thought we could have done more, thus the genesis of our online course and our participation in their yearly conventions. But I didn't think of this part of the mission as an identity-building aspect. Rather, it became another extension of my first dean's vision of making our journalism department known—not just for what we did, but for the fact that we cared about who we served. Too many people in this world dutifully work at their job without much ado or without most people taking notice. That wasn't going to happen on my watch with the ASNE grant experiment. If we increased minority interest in journalism, fine, but teachers—and their colleagues and principals—were going to know that UT was a unique place to be and engage.

I viewed our additional work with the black press as an olive branch of sorts to a similar group of people: Black press publishers often are people who aren't looking to become rich; many have second jobs, others are using retirement funds to run their publication, while still others are continuing the family's tradition of giving back to the black community. In any event, their operations would be considered storefront, or "mom and pop" ventures that stem from their desire to make life better for the black middle, working class—folks with steady but only slightly stable incomes who are living paycheck to paycheck and trying to create a home and a community for their children. As a result, few usually have formal journalism or advertising training and are getting killed, competitively speaking, by other media for people's attention spans. That makes for an unsteady stream of revenue and a desperate need for professional advice—not something they've traditionally come to expect from the lily-white, behemoth state universities that historically treated black communities as if they barely existed. So, again, our outreach—whether formal or informal, depending on the request—was far more a labor of love and an opportunity to network with a different section of the journalism universe. I saw how a Dallas publisher, for example, was training her headstrong young son in the ins and outs of advertising salesmanship but with only occasional success as she also faced disloyalty from a key editor. And there was the Houston publisher who had extensive business know-how but had no great inkling of what the internet and social media would mean for her product. Building those relationships took considerable time, communication, and a bunch of small, mini-successes before we could establish trust and go on to more serious staffing and financial issues. So, in the process and quite by accident, I gathered additional personas to add to my identity: public servant was the most important, with being a friend to scholastic journalism and the black press a close second.

But, as I've noted, it's not by doing alone that we come into our identity. Recall how, in Chapter One, that because "Cane River" was our name for the Northwest Louisiana community of our Catholic Creole ancestors living around the Cane River, this book was about how I was searching for "the river", my place in life—who I was. Now recall how I mentioned my trips in and around Scandinavia as being instrumental in how I did my job. But, more than that, all the places that my job and my life afforded me the chance to visit—those places also left indelible blots on who I think I am. I won't bother you with a travelogue, but instead I have some general observations. I'd be remiss if I didn't say that churches played a strong role in my makeup—not simply as places of worship, but of solace, peace, meditation, rote comfort (thank you to the rosary, Second Vatican Council and the Book of Common Prayer), let alone some wonderful, irremovable images: the smell of incense and communion wine, the taste of "new-age" communion (just like banana nut bread without the nuts), the celebrant's shiny, colorful vestments, the altar candles, the yearly ashes on my forehead, the parishioners in all their finery on Christmas Eve Mass, to just list a few. Each, despite my advancing skepticism, provided a way to get back homeward, to think of motherly, blessed assurance. And if I couldn't be solemn, soulful Church George, then I'd remember the Circle in the Square nightclub and other venues, where I could "get down" and express the joy I felt from all kinds of music—from disco to slow-dance country—and the freedom to be College George, learning all kinds of stuff about women, friendship, Algebra, history, writing, psychology, and whatever else caught my fancy in my quest to learn how to express myself about whatever crossed my mind at the time. Of course, I'd be remiss if I didn't mention Classroom George, who—not to be confused with College George—can mansplain like crazy, but who delights in telling Dad jokes that reveal something subtle, or who can correct the governor on the cause of Texas' cold-weather electric grid misery. He can tell a newspaper editor why he'll never be able to control a college journalism department or can tell a colleague when his intended actions are illegal or out of line. All were and are made possible because settings elicit the craziest things from other humans, regardless of whether they make sense, screw with people's sense of self-importance, make people doubt your belief in your identity, or whether they're inappropriate, awaiting their moment to escape. And this list is incomplete without Committee George, often mistakenly labeled "Cursing George", who occasionally drops into common epithets—none of which will be named here—when frustrated by incompetent broadcast journalists, or non-listeners of any kind. This George also dislikes people whose attention spans dissolve to their smartphones instead of listening to others or paying attention to traffic lights. And God help the sportscasters who—when introducing an athlete or a sports team—often add a pause and then say, "He…" or "Well, they…" Cursing George also has been called, "Precision George" or "Time-Saving George". So, such places, and the resulting "Georges" that they nurtured, have left a deep-seated mark.

In finding out who George is, I'd be negligent to ignore the stories, happenings, and narratives, however. For me, death, oddly enough, at times seemed to loom larger than life itself. The voids that came with the passing of some of the most important people I've known—my cousin Meter, Daddy's sisters Nanny and Tuntie, Nanny's husband Uncle Braz, Mamoo's brother George, and others, on up to Mamoo and Daddy themselves, to name just a few—have caused me to not only ponder the afterlife but also to recognize their own identities still live on in me and my family. For example, Mamoo's death caused me to remember more vividly what it meant to do good, especially in the face of obstacles, to the point that I would think sometimes, "Whoa! Where did *that attitude* come from?" It could also make me impatient with those who dragged their feet. Or, I would wonder sometimes if my frequent, type-A behavior was really me or me emulating my Aunt Tuntie, who overcame extremely unfavorable odds in creating—to great public acknowledgement—Louisiana's "Bicentennial (Creole MaMan) Doll" and becoming an outspoken advocate of Cane River culture in the '70s and '80s. Did my drive to document the Caddo school desegregation saga reflect my curiosity and doggedness, or was I simply broadening the local movement established by my cousin Dr.

Joe Sarpy, who was instrumental in facilitating the Shreveport visits and necessary logistics of Dr. Martin Luther King and others back in the '60s? Such "whose footsteps are these?" moments not only obviously provided needed perspective but also jarring, chilling mindsets that come only when you're writing a memoir, as if to say, "You are not *just* who you are, you are part of something else." My begrudging (some would say "grouchy") manner when my kids' friends would vis-it past the welcoming point and usurp my evening with my family—I sound like Uncle Braz but I know I'm just being a good dad, right? This attitude can be highly personal, as when I wonder whether 25 years of Type II diabetes was set in motion by being a Frenchman who loves Louisiana cooking or, because of the Louisiana penchant to *laissez les bon temps roulez* (aka, "let the good times roll"), just like when, as a young lad, I used to wonder when I'd become an alcoholic like most of the men I knew.

A mid-1970s photo of Tuntie (aka Lair Sylvie LaCour) with her award-winning Bicentennial doll, Creole Maman.

Of course, not all iden-tity-revealing experiences have historical roots. There's the opportune event that begets something greater. For instance, what would have happened if I hadn't had that lousy Fall '73 semester at LSUS? Would I have met Randy? If not, would I not have met my future sister-in-law Eileen, who introduced me to my wife, the mother of my children? If that's too far-fetched, I still get spooky shudders thinking, "What if Mrs. Graham hadn't made that call on my behalf to Mr. Brooks at Mizzou?" And if you're not into serendipity all that much, ask yourself if the book you're reading now would have been here if I hadn't retired and tired of the UT grind when I did and then wandered aimlessly for six years afterward? I shudder to know I still have friends from my UT grad student group who still run on the academic treadmill, poor things. And what about inopportune events—the things we'd like to be able to go back in time and prevent or alter—like when my bike was stolen? I wonder if I'd feel more secure around strangers or would I have become more trusting when others ask me to share something. More to the point, if I had not been forced by my parents to return to Shreveport, would my attitude toward racial issues have been more like that of a black individual or a white person, or about the same? That's a tough one for me, because I can't do anything about Shreveport—it is what it is, and my view of its shortcomings are forever etched in my brain and in my approach to anyone or anything having to do with that city. If I could turn back time, I'd have been more open and accepting of Daddy and less closed-off, but 11-year-old me resented everything about going back to Louisiana. And then there are the narratives that we hold most closely to our breast: the smart, bookish, wiry kid who'd rather read an encyclopedia than go play outside with his cousins; the pro football-watching teenager who grew up to accept and embrace his father's theory that referees couldn't be trusted, especially if the other team was the Cowboys or the Packers; the reporter who believed that anyone with a North Louisiana twang or East Texas accent was not to be trusted and probably had a set of white robes hanging somewhere hidden in the garage.

Finally, I believe it easiest to pin identity leanings onto the people we know and love—no surprise there, as that likely has been the most dominant, overriding theme of this memoir, this search for "the river", if you will. Our parents, of course, are central to making this case, and I would argue that Mamoo, Daddy, and Kathy and my kids top my list. I'm sure you'd agree, as you only know what you've read on these pages. But we also meet more people than just our parents and immediate family members; I've tried to introduce the more significant ones, although there are dozens who barely rate a mention but who've been no less instrumental: all my teachers, doctors, religious clergy, and other professionals along the way—there's no doubt about them, as their jobs and vocations uniquely place them in positions of influence. And I was lucky to have made their acquaintances. Still, they know who they are, as I've tried my best to thank them for their contributions through the years. I think it more important, though, to call attention to the less noticeable among them, such as the homeless, who—when I saw the extent of this national problem a decade ago in places such Dallas, Chicago, San Francisco and other large cities—by their mere presence remind me of how lucky I am. There are also the untold millions of clerical, retail, and bureaucracy workers who, when called upon, do their jobs quickly and efficiently and usually with a smile. Then there's the acquaintances who we encounter in our daily routines, in offices, churches, businesses, and many more places than I can name here. At the expense of sounding like an Academy Award acceptance speech, we tend to be so busy with life that we usually ignore such people, but they serve every day. My favorites in this group tended to be the life's veterans, those "old heads" with several years' experience and know-how to the point of unflappability—like that multi-year grandmother who showed me around the Caddo Schools headquarters. Or the workshop coordinator, who retired but was working still to set aside money for her grandkids' college fund. Or the bubbly, optimistic housewife who took time out of her laundry day to listen to my problems with dating, deities, and dreads. Or the man who, though his hands were calloused, had a gentle enough touch to teach a young boy how to work. They constitute the little, occasional gifts that help shape our everyday experiences—and, eventually, our identities—by taking time for us, for me. I don't know where I'd be without them.

A FINAL WORD

So, after the better part of 70 years, I have finally discovered who I was and where the community and identity of Cane River ran in my life. Drawing on a stream of influencers, a spring of examples and role models, a creek of learning, and a glacier of life-giving experiences, I've decided that the word that best describes my ethnicity is "biracial" because, well, that's what I am: According to my DNA test, my ancestry is two-thirds European and one-third African. So, if I wanted, I could identify as both. But being raised Frenchman in Louisiana and mostly having black people for neighbors during the first half of my life, I strongly *identify with* African-Americans. Except for brief moments in their lives, Frenchmen in the southern United States are immediately lumped in with the black populace—not pink enough to be white, not brown or black enough to be pure African, but just enough of each pigment to save white people the trouble of trying to figure it out. It's a hard truth for those Frenchmen who aren't southerners to acknowledge or accept, because everyone just wants to be who they are.

Still, determining anyone's identity can take a lifetime, which is the essence of the story in which I place myself. I'm not exactly proud of any code-switching or indecision prior to making this choice, but I accept it as coming with modern territory that is the discussion of race in a country that calls itself—with differing degrees of pride sometimes—a "melting pot". That whole analogy begs the question: If we're all melting in this pot, can you really distinguish between any of us? For Americans, we tend to suspend belief in what we are, although sometimes in the quiet dark recesses of our own hearts, we know what the answer to that simple inquiry is. Sometimes, however, we just cannot bring ourselves to face the naked truth: None of us is born special, despite what history books tell us. In the beginning, we're just another human being, aspiring to the false, vain notion that we are *different from the rest.*

By reading this memoir, you now know that I went to great lengths to find my different self. Agreeing to the notion of "Frenchman" was enough to set me off on the path for "the river", acquiring years of schooling, perhaps thinking I'd find my definitive identity in all that data that is education, all those words—written and spoken by others. What I didn't recognize early on was that the answer wasn't just one thing, one classification. It took years of schooling to understand that everyone would say I was something different, and they all would have what sounded like a logical explanation for how they felt. What I failed to see at the time was that just analyzing these inputs individually wasn't going to suffice; there were feelings, experiences, and various communities that I had to engage, allowing me to grab more than one answer, one piece of a quilt, and add it to the next and to the next, and finally put the whole mosaic together at some point. This same process may not work for other Frenchmen or other ethnic people; they'll have to find the way that feels most appropriate to their lives. I'm just lucky to have lived long enough to have mine smack me right in the face.

For example, in Chicago, my school days and my transplanted Frenchman relatives combined to make me secure to a certain extent. Despite the best efforts of some idiots, I became a Chicago Frenchman, returning every so often to recharge that identity or finding a renewal station in the folks at Blessed Sacrament in Shreveport. Then the wider world creeped under my security blanket, blessing me with a strong academician's curiosity while cursing me to continue to live the segregation that so many Frenchmen had experienced earlier than me: learning how to navigate and keep their sanity. I acquired a dark sense of humor at Jesuit while learning that my place wasn't really going anywhere, at least not until I learned to do something about it. Deflated and slightly jaded upon graduation, I crossed my fingers and hoped LSUS studies could promise something better. My hopes proved a little higher than my reach, again because the things I learned—from dating, from studying, and from journalism—didn't quite exactly gel into a solid message that I could wholeheartedly grasp with conviction. Dancing every weekend and learning to write with empathy helped, showing me that everyone experienced and enjoyed *some* of the same things; but that only took me so far. I still felt hemmed in by social convention, by whom others saw me as, by my own capacity to create something (or was it someone?) capable of captivating or getting attention or grabbing a spotlight that would help me more closely examine the part of myself that needed development. I didn't know it then, but everything that happens in life is part of a process that has a beginning and an end.

During my studies at LSUS, I learned the beginnings of friendship, laughter, studying, and those things and subjects on which I concentrated, but it was just the start, and none of what I knew was guaranteed to last or endure or set me on a firmer path. Fortunately, Mrs. Graham had glimmerings of that path and did her utmost to help me to also see it, although I couldn't have described it at the time. While I loved her for what she did, I had mixed feelings about having so many "angels" in my life: beginning with Mamoo, extending to my siblings, my cousins, my Blessed Sacrament mentors, and so on. On the one hand, I wouldn't trade them for anything; on the other hand, I'd wish I could make the important decisions alone. Knowing that I occasionally needed help, made me realize I had so much more to learn, and that I wasn't as "smart" as I perceived myself. Building an identity also seemed to require leaving part of my prior identity behind—again, the process of life, like a rocket ship spiraling higher into space, but not entirely whole—taking on a new shape that neither looks familiar nor feels comfortable. Damn it to hell! Smarts alone didn't quite shorten the distance to "the river".

A huggable moment with me and Mamoo (early 2000s).

But again, like bereaved people or riders exiting a bus, I had to persist. When I wrote earlier about heading to Mizzou, I mentioned my tough transition, and there were times that I seriously thought about going back to Louisiana—the dread of having to get *another* journalism degree; looking around and seeing all the people who were younger than me and reminding me I was starting over; and having to listen to all the advice from teaching assistants who were, again, younger than me. What made it feel worse was, for the first time, I was missing Mamoo: no homecooked meals, no unsolicited advice. She couldn't afford more than one long-distance call a week; I had to sit in the Tiger Towers lobby on Friday and Saturday nights, waiting for my turn on the payphone; many days spent rushing back to Tiger Towers, hoping for a letter from her or my friends; feeling alone while walking the campus. I hated it, but I was unable to think of anything better that I could do at the time; I was out of choices, away from home, accruing debt and didn't know a soul. At least the folks leaving the Shreveport bus stops had lives to return to. My life sucked for those first few weeks. Doing something with my life felt as if it were an overrated pastime. Who the hell does this? Not many Frenchmen, I thought. Persisting took more guts than I felt that I had, and I knew that learning my way around the J School would be hard. I tried not to dwell too much on it. If I was weak at persistence, I made up for it by creating a new community once I moved to the dormitory. I won't repeat those experiences here, except to say that they were lifesavers in helping me to feel less lonely and giving me courage to persist. As I became a true graduate student, more disciplined, more organized, more friendly, and more self-sufficient, I learned. For example, you *can* lose your blues by engaging in activities and pursuits—a strong, handy lesson to take with me to The Journal, especially since I wanted to challenge my old impressions of what Shreveport used to represent. If I was going to find my own version of "the river", I wanted to do more than simply persist on the way. As I wrote earlier, I wanted to be a crusading journalist, impacting things, righting wrongs, educating readers, and making the world a better place for people less fortunate, but with nuance.

As it turned out, such responsible reporting became the largest, single symbol of my life, permeating every relationship I had in Shreveport and opening many doors, to experiences new and old. The depth to which I lived and ate journalism can't be underestimated, so much so that I knew that, after three intense years, my heart longed for something more. "The river" of identity still seemed several miles away, so I switched to editing—which gave me more time to think about what to write and to think about my future. Frenchmanhood seemed to get submerged in the wave of professionalism I was learning to perpetuate to my own satisfaction: truth, objectivity, fairness, ethicality, conflict-free, affliction of the powerful, and more.

But striving for personal satisfaction while working as a somewhat confined editor made me feel as if I were stranded on a peninsula, surrounded on three sides by waters, each side symbolizing how I thought about them: I could either (a) follow those elements being carried in "the river", (b) actually achieve them, or (c) watch people botch them. As I said in the last chapter, I wanted to jump somewhere, anywhere, as long as I could be in the middle of the debate. Meanwhile, just saying I was a Frenchman did me no good, making it feel as if I were just treading water; on the other hand, being black made me feel as if I were fighting a rip current; finally, being white just showed me that I lacked endurance and stamina to finish what I'd started. Every way I went, "the river" seemed unreachable, as if I were in a canoe with a ping pong racket for a paddle. In other words, being me felt as if I lacked the wrong tools to reach "the river".

But let's backtrack a second: My search for it has been an exploration for identity, so "the river" becomes a symbol for the self. Thinking about what a river is and does, however, puts the search into perspective. Clearly, a river is a body of water, basically a vital source for life, just as an identity functions as a fundamental element of life's substance, meaning, and spirit. This "river", this body of water, however, also carries some traditional functions. First, it functions as a source of erosion, dissolution and the wearing away of the soil that holds or contains the water. Putting aside modern notions of climate change for a minute, we can imagine that a river erodes its banks and its bottom by pure force of the gravity and momentum the water gathers as it moves. So, too, does an identity: By definition, it forces each of us to change our life's course as we navigate that life. Identifying as a Frenchman made me look at things differently than when I had no identity, going wherever and whenever my parents and siblings could take me—physically and mentally. Each time I moved, I partially erased one identity gradually, as I took on another, newer one, akin to what we do when we're younger, moving from adolescence to teenagerhood to young adulthood. This constant progression helped me to learn to develop a flexible personality that, when called upon to meet a new one, I would be able to successfully adapt, especially in more volatile times.

Another river function involves transportation—of many things, from water to watercraft, and, in doing so, a river creates a journey. Returning to the context of an identity, such "water" moves you forward, toward new people, events, and places—like the ones I've written about in these few pages. Obviously, I didn't have the room to name all the people I've met, but I've tried to show a natural progression of events, key people, and the venues where they came together. But I also wanted to show them as the separate, unique narratives that I felt they were, with definitive impacts and consequences prompted me to continuously seek change and growth. So it was that my life's search took me from Chicago to Shreveport and Blessed Sacrament, then to Jesuit, followed by LSUS, Mizzou, back to The Journal in Shreveport, then Texas, back to LSUS, and ending again in Texas—the places differed, but the influence of the people made the places seem as if they could have been anywhere. The differing locales didn't dilute the fact that I kept moving, in my self-search. Mamoo once asked me, before I left for Austin the first time, "Why do you have to keep leaving?" I can't remember my answer, just that it was the clear choice. My "river" seemed one of constant movement, not so much swift, but certainly sure. Arriving for our second stay in Austin, the varying parts of life—the job and its mission, letting our children settle in and start their own lives without interruption, growing older with and closer to my rock, Kathy—seemed to have coalesced or aligned better than in any other place or situation.

In a sense, then, we've also arrived for the third and last river function, that of deposition: the down-river site where the silt, soil, and other objects have been deposited, to settle and then accumulate. That buildup creates stability, thus allowing me to write with more clarity than I could have otherwise. The memories come clearly into view, providing perspective that I could use and reassemble into a complete narrative, a gathering of past lessons, a compilation of parts that have, for the first time, made sense. As a result, I confidently see all the ebbs and flows of my "river"—how it gave, how it took away, how it deposited—creating the gradient or slope, ramp, whatever you want to call it, of the ups and downs of my life.

This "river" of life, as I like to call it, has been, well, vital for George Sylvie. Not only have I received "water" or information that required examination, thought, and deliberation, but also the nutrition or "food" that came in the form of my decisions, actions and reactions that needed to happen to continue the journey and reach the river's mouth, where I could finally see what shape all my life's deposits had created. The search is over; I'm no longer on that three-sided peninsula. I've finally found my "river", and it's where I belong, where I can fully be me. Cane River still lives in my heart, but it's not the only "river" out there to navigate and discover. I hope that your journey takes you where you need to be.